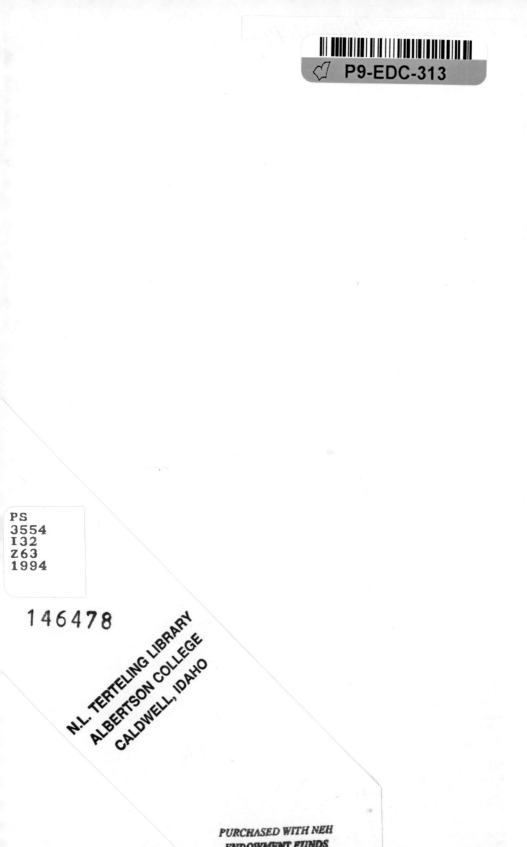

Critical Essays on
JAMES DICKEY

CRITICAL ESSAYS
ON
AMERICAN LITERATURE

James Nagel, General Editor
University of Georgia, Athens

Critical Essays on

JAMES DICKEY

edited by

ROBERT KIRSCHTEN

G. K. Hall & Co. / New York
Maxwell Macmillan Canada / Toronto
Maxwell Macmillan International / New York Oxford Singapore Sydney

For permission to quote from the copyrighted poetry of James Dickey, the editor and contributors are especially grateful to the following: Wesleyan University Press by Permission of the University Press of New England for *Eagle's Mile* copyright 1990 by James Dickey; To the Butterflies, The One, Circuit, Sleepers, Vessels, The Six, Nightbird, The Eagle's Mile, Eagles, The Little More, Weeds, The Olympian, Spring-Shock, The Three, Daughter; *Poems 1957–1967* copyright 1967 by James Dickey; The Jewel, The Performance, Trees and Cattle, False Youth: Two Seasons, For the Last Wolverine, May Day Sermon; *Buckdancer's Choice* copyright 1965 by James Dickey; The Firebombing, The Fiend, Slave Quarters; *Falling, May Day Sermon, and Other Poems* copyright 1982 by James Dickey; Falling, Reincarnation II, The Sheep Child, Encounter in the Cage Country, For the Last Wolverine; *Drowning With Others* copyright 1962 by James Dickey; The Heaven of Animals, The Lifeguard, Armor, Between Two Prisoners, A Screened Porch in the Country, Fog Envelops the Animals, The Owl King; *Helmets* copyright 1964 by James Dickey; Dusk of Horses, Winter Trout, Drinking from a Helmet, Approaching Prayer.

For permission to quote from the copyrighted prose of James Dickey, the editor and contributors are especially grateful to the following: Bantam Doubleday Dell Publishing Group, Inc. for "Deborah as Scion," from PUELLA by James Dickey, Copyright © 1982 by James Dickey. Used by permission of Doubleday, a division of Bantam Doubleday Dell Publishing Group, Inc.; "Turning Away," from THE EYE-BEATERS, BLOOD VICTORY, MADNESS, BUCKHEAD by James Dickey. Copyright © 1968, 1969, 1970 by James Dickey. Used by permission of Doubleday, a division of Bantam Doubleday Dell Publishing Group, Inc.; THE STRENGTH OF FIELDS by James Dickey. Copyright © 1979 by James Dickey. Used by permission of Doubleday, a division of Bantam Doubleday Dell Publishing Group, Inc.; THE ZODIAC by James Dickey. Copyright © 1976 by James Dickey. Used by permission of Doubleday, a division of Bantam Doubleday Dell Publishing Group, Inc. Excerpts from DELIVERANCE by James Dickey reprinted by permission of Houghton Mifflin Company. Copyright © 1970 by James Dickey. All rights reserved.

G. K. Hall & Co.
Macmillan Publishing Company
866 Third Avenue
New York, New York 10022

Maxwell Macmillan Canada, Inc.
1200 Eglinton Avenue East
Suite 200
Don Mills, Ontario M3C 3N1

Library of Congress Cataloging-in-Publication Data

Critical essays on James Dickey / edited by Robert Kirschten.
    p.   cm. — (Critical essays on American literature)
    Includes bibliographical references and index.
ISBN 0-8161-7311-7
    1. Dickey, James—Criticism and interpretation.   I. Kirchter, Robert.
1947–   .   II. Series.
PS3554.I32Z63 1994
811'.54—dc20   94-1767
                                                                  CIP

10   9   8   7   6   5   4   3   2   1

Printed in the United States of America

to the memory of
Elder Olson

Contents

♦

General Editor's Note

♦

This series seeks to anthologize the most important criticsm on a wide variety of topics and writers in American literature. Our readers will find in various volumes not only a generous selection of reprinted articles and reviews but original essays, bibliographies, manuscript sections, and other materials brought to public attention for the first time. This volume, *Critical Essays on James Dickey*, is the most comprehensive collection of essays ever published on one of the most important modern writers in the United States. It contains both a sizable gathering of early reviews and a broad selection of more modern scholarship. Among the authors of reprinted articles and reviews are James Dickey, Wendell Berry, Robert Bly, Carolyn Heilbrun, Marion Hodge, John Blair, and John Simon. In addition to a substantial introduction by Robert Kirschten, which offers a complete bibliographical survey of reviews and scholarship on Dickey, there are also five original essays commissioned specifically for publication in this volume. In these new studies Calhoun Winton provides a memoir of Dickey at Vanderbilt in the 1940s, Joyce M. Pair explores the role of totemism in "May Day Sermon," Douglas Keesey considers the macho persona in Dickey's verse, John Blair discusses Dickey's novel, *Deliverance* and *Alnilam*, and Gordon Van Ness treats the philosophic subtext of *The Eagle's Mile*. We are confident that this book will make a permanent and significant contribution to the study of American literature.

JAMES NAGEL
University of Georgia

Publisher's Note

◆

Producing a volume that contains both newly commissioned and reprinted material presents the publisher with the challenge of balancing the desire to achieve stylistic consistency with the need to preserve the integrity of works first published elsewhere. In the Critical Essays series, essays commissioned especially for a particular volume are edited to be consistent with G. K. Hall's house style; reprinted essays appear in the style in which they were first published, with only typographical errors corrected. Consequently, shifts in style from one essay to another are the result of our efforts to be faithful to each text as it was originally published.

Introduction

♦

ROBERT KIRSCHTEN

James Dickey has been a major presence in American literature for three decades. Dickey is the author of more than 17 books of poems, including *Buckdancer's Choice*, which won the National Book Award in 1966, and *Puella*, from which a selection of five poems won the distinguished Levinson Prize from *Poetry: A Magazine of Verse* in 1981. Dickey has written three novels, including the best-selling *Deliverance*, which won the Prix Medicis and became a celebrated Warner Brothers film for which Dickey wrote the screenplay and played the role of Sheriff Bullard. His second novel is a long epic of flight entitled *Alnilam*, and he recently published his third novel, *To the White Sea*, which like much of his work, is based on his combat experience in World War II. Dickey has also published two major collections of literary criticism, *Babel to Byzantium: Poetry and Poets Now* and *Night Hurdling*, as well as several books of commentary on his own literary experience including *Self-Interviews* and *Sorties*. In addition to two children's books, *Tucky the Hunter* (1978) for his grandson, and *Bronwen, the Traw and the Shape-Shifter* (1986), for his young daughter, he wrote the prose accompaniments to a series of watercolors in *Jericho: The South Beheld* and drawings in *God's Images: The Bible a New Vision*. In 1990, Dickey published *The Eagle's Mile*, his most recent and best single volume of poems, which is a richly textured culmination of topics and techniques that he has been developing since he began to write poetry in the mid-forties. His collected poems, entitled *The Whole Motion*, includes most of his lyric work in addition to previously uncollected material, and was published in 1992.

In addition to these awards, Dickey has also received the Poetry Society of America's Melville Cane Award, the Longview Foundation Award, the Vachel Lindsay Prize, an award from the National Institute of Arts and Letters, a Guggenheim Fellowship, the *New York Quarterly* Poetry Day Award, induction into the prestigious, 50-member American Academy and Institute of Arts and Letters, and most recently, the first Conch Republic Prize for

Literature. Twice-appointed consultant in Poetry for the Library of Congress (1966–68), Dickey read his poem "The Strength of Fields" at the inaugural celebration for President Jimmy Carter in 1977. In fall 1992 and through winter 1993, his 11-page poem, "May Day Sermon to the Women of Gilmer County, Georgia, by a Woman Preacher Leaving the Baptist Church," was performed in a one-woman show by actress Bridget Hanley and directed by John Gallogly at Theatre West in Los Angeles.

Like his education and discovery of poetry, Dickey's literary career began late, postponed for years by world war, as were the professional lives of many writers in his generation. Born 2 February 1923, in Atlanta, Georgia, Dickey attended North Fulton High School, where he played football and ran track. In 1942, he enrolled as a freshman at Clemson A&M College, where he briefly played football for Coach Frank Howard, then left before the end of his first semester, to enlist in the U. S. Army Air Corps. For nearly four years, Dickey served in the Pacific Theatre of the Second World War, where he flew on approximately 100 missions for the 418th Night Fighter Squadron. From Mindoro to Okinawa, Dickey was involved in reconnaissance and interception as well as firebombing raids over mainland Japan. As he testifies in his war poem "The Place of the Skull," Dickey discovered poetry in the long intervals between bombing runs when he read anything he could find. It was in these periods that he first read Shelley and Crane, among others, and thus came "to meet my holy masters in the Word."[1] After the war, Dickey graduated from Vanderbilt University, first with an A. B. then earning his M. A. in 1950. His writing career was further deferred when he was called to serve once again, this time in the Korean War. Upon returning home, he taught briefly then worked as an advertising copywriter in New York and Atlanta. During this period, while acting as account executive for such companies as Coca-Cola and Delta Airlines, he wrote poetry at night and published his first book of poems, *Into the Stone*, in 1960, when he was 37. With the help of a Guggenheim Fellowship, he abandoned the business world to travel and write in Italy where he worked on his second book, *Drowning with Others* (1962). This project enabled him to take a series of two-year teaching positions. Six years later, with the publication of *Poems 1957–1967*, he was appointed Carolina Professor of English and Writer-in-Residence at the University of South Carolina.

Critical reaction to James Dickey's work is diverse and contradictory, swinging from euphoric praise to condescension and personal attack. However, several critical patterns regarding Dickey's work emerge, beginning with a slowly growing ground of support which climaxed spectacularly with the appearance of *Poems 1957–1967* in the late 60s. With the publication of *Deliverance* (1970), his first novel, and two books of poems, *The Eye-Beaters, Blood, Victory, Madness, Buckhead and Mercy* (1970) and *The Zodiac* (1976) support began to fluctuate. With the appearance of *Puella* and *The Eagle's Mile*, as well as the novel *Alnilam*, a positive yet cautious evaluation developed for his work of the eighties; as may be expected, the criticism for the work of this period is still being formulated. Dickey criticism can be divided into the early, middle, and later periods, which correspond to the three central decades of his career.

THE EARLY PERIOD, 1960–1968.

Published with collections by poets Paris Leary and John Swan, James Dickey's first book of poems, *Into the Stone*, appeared in 1960 in John Hall Wheelock's series *Poets of Today VII*. Marked by a dreamy, melodic treatment of themes that continue to haunt Dickey's later poetry and novels—war, ritualistic exchange with nature and the family—*Into the Stone* contains some of his best lyrics, as well as a number of early, ambiguous works. "Sleeping Out at Easter," "The Vegetable King," and the much-anthologized war poem about the beheading of his comrade, Donald Armstrong—are as beautifully crafted and emotionally disciplined as the best poems in Dickey's more mature writing. Several critics found a combination of promise, ambiguity, and full-blown accomplishment in this first book. Writing in *Prarie Schooner* in 1961, Oliver Evans thought that *Into the Stone* exhibited the limitations of a first book in so far as some of the poems are "merely ingenious" and "deliberately complex." Yet, he also saw in the book signs of a considerable, yet undeveloped, power: "Those poems of Mr. Dickey which are wholly successful, like 'The Underground Stream' . . . display frankly the talent that is there—a talent, however, that as yet is not fully formed."[2] From an opposite point of view, Harold Bloom found the poet's talent fully developed in "The Other," Dickey's "guilt induced" poem about a brother who died before he was born. Bloom believed that " 'The Other' is almost the first of Dickey's poems, and in some ways he has never surpassed it, not because he has failed to develop, but because it is unsurpassable. The whole of Dickey is in it already, as the whole of Shelley is in *Alastor*, or the whole of Yeats is in *The Wanderings of Oisin*."[3] James Wright was even more enthusiastic in a review in *Poetry* in 1964, where he listed three "great gifts" which Dickey brings to his book: "an unpredictably joyous imagination," "a delicate sense of music," and "a courageous tenderness." Early on, Wright discovered these three central traits that mark the whole of Dickey's vision. From a technical point of view, Wright further found an "intelligent self-discipline" in the musical component of these lyrics and in their diction when he claims that he "cannot find a single phrase in Mr. Dickey's book which is not firm and clear." Wright ended with an affectionate endorsement: "Reader, for your own sake, go buy this book."[4]

Published in 1962, *Drowning with Others* is Dickey's second book of poems. Although it contains several lesser lyrics, this collection includes a considerable number of Dickey's major poems. Revealing a mature voice within fully developed forms, poems such as "The Heaven of Animals," "In the Tree

House at Night," "Hunting Civil War Relics at Nimblewill Creek," and the prize-winning "Dover: Believing in Kings" began to establish Dickey's reputation among major poets and critics. In 1963, in the *Sewanee Review*, Howard Nemerov was one of the first critics to identify several basic consti- tutents in Dickey's animistic world. Although suspicious about the poet's "willed mysticism," Nemerov nonetheless valued the poems' "noble simplic- ity" in which "[s]alvation is this: apprehending the continuousness of forms, the flowing of one energy through everything." Nemerov listed "some brilliant accomplishments" including "The Owl King," "Armor" and "The Summons," yet he also notes "There are . . . some that sound dead, or (what is effectively the same thing) that I do not much respond to, including some that I don't understand. Where his poems fail for me, it is most often because he rises, reconciles, transcends, a touch too easily, so that his conclusions fail of being altogether decisive. . . ."[5] In 1962, in the *Yale Review*, Thom Gunn likewise found strengths and weaknesses in *Drowning With Others*. Gunn values Dickey's "The Heaven of Animals" in which he finds a "muscular fantasy" which may be "described as the rhythm of the universe, in which death and violence are as important a part as their opposites." On the other hand, Gunn found two problems with this book: first, with the inherent limitations of Dickey's favorite meter, "anapestic tetrameter" which is "a limiting and monotonous meter at best." Second, Dickey's "distrust of conceptual language" results in a rapid "accumulation" of "images" that "tends to lack meaning."[6]

Dickey's third book of poems, *Helmets*, appeared in 1964. There are no weak poems in the collection; every one of the lyrics is stronger than each of those in Dickey's previous books. In addition, there are several outstanding poems, long and short, which as Harold Bloom has claimed, may be counted among "some three dozen or more poems in the first three volumes which . . . really have made for themselves a place in the canon of American poetry, and indeed the poetry of the English Language."[7] The strength of this collection was underscored by Richard Howard in *Alone with America* when he claimed that "*Helmets* . . . confirmed [Dickey] as the telluric maker Wallace Stevens had called for in prophesying that the great poems of heaven and hell have been written and the great poem of the earth remains to be written."[8] Two specific strengths of this book were indicated by Louis Martz and Dennis Donoghue. In the *Yale Review* in 1964, Martz commented that Dickey's "better poems are controlled hallucinations that work as parables."[9] In *The Hudson Review* in the same year, Donoghue stated that "James Dickey's new poems are moving beautifully" and that "[t]he human sound of these poems arranges and enthralls and enchants the acres, otherwise wild, and prepares hopeless things for miracle."[10] While favorable toward *Helmets*, William Meredith found some of the poems "taken by inept strategy," and further, the "poems and parts of poems that don't work are those where he is making heroic metaphors out of experience that doesn't come off on that scale." For example, Meredith felt that "Springer Mountain," Dickey's comic hunting poem about his imitating the movement of deer, "extended beyond the range of [its] own intensity."[11] In 1964, in *Poetry*, Wendell Berry also found a certain "over-straining of method" in "Springer Mountain" which he judges inferior to "The Dusk of Horses," but he finished his review more than favorably by claiming that "[t]here are poems here of such life that you don't believe they're possible until you read them the second time."[12] In addition to noting the volume's strength, Joyce Carol Oates also commented on a shift of focus and subject matter for Dickey, insofar as in *Helmets* he "begins to move out of the perfected world of eternal recurrence, no longer the awed, alert, but essentially passive observer, now ready to experience history" while his "subjects . . . are now shifting out of the hypnosis of love itself, beginning to elude his incantory powers: coming alive and separate."[13]

Dickey's next collection of poems, *Buckdancer's Choice*, appeared in 1965 and won considerable critical praise, including the National Book Award for Poetry in 1966. Not only is every poem uniformly excellent, but the book also contains several more candidates for canonization, "The Firebombing," "The Shark's Parlor," and "The Fiend," for example. Built out of Dickey's walls of words, each of these lyrics is dramatically energized by a different, suspenseful variation of the poet's compulsive mixtures of life and death, monstrosity and ecstasy, plus a primitive form of renewal which, like many shamanic cures, combines initiation with overwhelming social or natural evil. In *Commonweal*, in 1966, Charles Monaghan said that "*Buckdancer's Choice* is the finest volume of poetry to appear in the sixties."[14] In the *New York Times Book Review* of the same year, Joseph Bennett noted that "James Dickey's fourth volume, *Buckdancer's Choice*, establishes him as one of the most important younger poets of our time."[15] In his review of *Buckdancer's Choice*, published in the *Michigan Quarterly Review* in 1967, Radcliff Squires went farther and claimed that "In the short span of the last five years, James Dickey has brought off a one-man revolution in American poetry" and that "Mr. Lowell and Mr. Dickey are our most important living poets."[16] In the October issue of *Poetry* for 1966, Robert Huff claimed that " 'The Firebombing' is the best poem produced thus far out of the combat of World War II."[17] In the *Nation*, David Ignatow noted of the same poem that "One gasps in admiration at the daring word combinations which achieve the dream-like affect."[18] In the *Northwest Review*, William C. Strange details Dickey's strengths and weaknesses: "Dickey's verbal skills were always considerable; [here] they have grown more sure. In his earlier books the fluent movement of his verse was overwhelmed at times by a surge of anapests, and diction was marred by conventional insincerities. . . . Now, such cadences are modulated by carefully indicated pauses within the line . . . and his familiar elegaic and meditative vocabulary includes new tones. . . ."[19]

Buckdancer's Choice marks a watershed moment in and is one of the triumphs of Dickey's career. For, whatever the book's poetic merit, it appeared during the escalation of fighting in the Vietnam War. Two years later, 1968 was one of the most traumatic years in the history of the country, filled with political assasination, urban riot, the resignation of one president and the election of another who not only prolonged the war unnecessarily but would be forced from office in the Watergate scandal, and generational confrontation and conflict from which many American families and friendships never recovered. The entire country was polarized politically on a massive scale. In this atmosphere, you were either for the war or against it; there was no middle ground. In just such a polarized political situation, Robert Bly launched one of the most personal and vitriolic attacks against Dickey. This type of personal attack began to snowball in many literary and political circles to such an extent that, in 1984, Paul Rice claimed in a review of Dickey's extremely strong volume of critical essays and poetry entitled *Night Hurdling* that "[m]ore than any poet in America since Pound, James Dickey has been on the bloody end of *argument ad hominem.*"[20]

In spite of Bly's attack, Dickey's collection of his previous volumes in *Poems 1957–1967* met with considerable critical approval and confirmed for many his status as one of American's major contemporary poets. In *Saturday Review*, in 1967, Louis Untermeyer stated that *Poems 1957–1967* "is the poetry book of the year, and I have little doubt that it will prove to be the outstanding collection of one man's poems to appear in this decade."[21] Of American poetry in the sixties, James Tulip noted in *Poetry Australia* in 1968 that "[Robert] Lowell and Dickey have played a major role" and that "James Dickey has moved quickly and with considerable panache into the forefront of American letters. *Poems 1957–1967* represents his claim on greatness to the present point."[22] In *Poetry* for March 1968, Donald W. Baker observed that Dickey "continues to shape a suburban mythology" and that "poetic intelligence glows behind all Mr. Dickey's work, and he is a lucid pleasure to read."[23] In a *Wall Street Journal* review of this volume in 1967, Edmund Fuller thought that of books by poets writing since World War II who deal with "anguish or horror," "[t]he most exciting book is by James Dickey." Fuller went on to make a literary estimate of Dickey which was characteristic of its time, namely, that "[s]ome regard Dickey as the most fertile, powerful American poet currently practicing. However that may be, he is a master."[24]

Poems 1957–1967 also received less adulatory notices. In *Harper's* of 1967, Louis Simpson was not convinced by "Slave Quarters" which he found "like a bad movie. Sometimes Dickey seems to be writing in a panic. He seems to be faced with a choice: either to inflate and lose himself, like Thomas Wolfe, in volumes of pseudo-writing, or to tell the truth." However, Simpson went on to say that, "When he does the latter he is a magnificent poet."[25] Mixed, and sometimes more negative, were the opinions of Ralph J. Mills, Julian Symons, and Harry Morris. In *Triquarterly* for Winter 1968, Mills praised Dickey's poem "A Screen Porch in the Country": "the imaginative rendering of its implications [are] so extraordinary that the reader's habitual way of looking at things . . . is profoundly shaken." On the other hand, Mills also claimed that "Dickey's imaginative gift collapses at the moral level" in "The

Firebombing" because these "events and details are dramatized without ever arousing a commensurate moral—which is to say, human—awareness. . . . for the pain and terror of his victims are dwelt on . . . without sympathy." Stepping up his attack, Mills asserted that poems such as "The Fiend" and "Slave Quarters" "employ speakers whose chief desire is the fulfillment, through a warped masculine sexual power, of their own sick fantasies."[26] In the *New Stateman* in 1967, Symons found Dickey's long poems "practically unreadable in long stretches. His poems, filled with abstractions and cliches, often using only . . . visual punctuation . . . drift on and on."[27] Finally, in the *Sewanee Review*, Harry Morris noted of Dickey's verse that he found "the observation myopic, sometimes filmed completely over; form is adhered to but so meaninglessly or inexactly as to suggest casual concern only or incredibly inept management." Dickey was said to manifest "a total inability to achieve conciseness within a single poem" and "[p]recision in diction is of so little concern to the poet that in many cases even prepositions are employed awkwardly or improperly."[28]

THE CENTRAL PERIOD, 1970–1980

In 1970 Dickey published his first novel, *Deliverance*. Now translated into 25 languages, the novel was a best-seller when it appeared, yet soon attracted negative academic criticism. In the *Saturday Review*, Benjamin DeMott called *Deliverance* "entertaining, shoot-'em-up mindlessness." When Lewis Medlock, the action hero in the novel, has his hip broken and is replaced by "the hitherto cool narrator," DeMott argued that the "result is that in place of a novel, where qualities of character and understanding are set in full view, compared and assessed, the reader is offered an emptily rhetorical horse-opera played in canoes. . . . the experience as a whole is weightless, silly, soft."[29] Like DeMott, Warren Eyster in the *Sewanee Review* faulted Dickey's characterization, claiming that his characters were "interchangeable and indistinguishable." Eyster noted that Dickey's simplistic "vision of life cannot even exist when it is confined to the animal world, to the world of sub-humans, or to stock outdoor charac-ters."[30] From a political point of view, Frederic Jameson found the novel fascistic: ". . . an adventure story like Dickey's . . . causes you to posit the need for Leviathan, or the authoritarian state."[31] Carolyn Heilbrun found *Deliverance* to be sexist, saying, "Dickey's . . . achievement is one more version . . . of . . . the woman-despising American dream."[32] Later readings in a mythopoeic vein have reassessed the novel. Linda Wagner-Martin saw the novel as "a masculine initiation story . . . a kind of gothic, even bitter, *Adventures of Huckleberry Finn*." The message of the book is, in fact, redemptive, for Dickey's adventure gives the three surviving male characters "and perhaps Dickey himself, the kind of freedom from the stereotyped male image, and from the pride, that blinds so many would-be powerful men."[33] In a 1978 review in *Western American Literature*, Don Kunz pushed Wagner-Martin's point farther and contradicted Heilbrun by arguing that *Deliverance* deconstructs "the prison of gender" because the men in Dickey's novel "discover not so much how to be men as how it feels to be women abused by the kind of men they have dreamed of being." The novel reveals "the full horror of men who try to live by such a code."[34] Representative of this newer, mythic direction for reexamining *Deliverance* is Peggy Goodman Endel's article, "Dickey, Dante, and the Demonic: Reassessing *Deliverance*," which is collected in this volume.

With the publication in 1970 of an experimental book of lyrics with an equally experimental title, *The Eye-Beaters, Blood, Victory, Madness, Buckhead and Mercy*. Dickey's "central period" began with a critical reaction often as surrealistic as the poems in his collection. After praising *Poems 1957–1967*, Herbert Leibowitz noted the "balance of pure abandon and meticulous observation breaks apart in Dickey's latest volume," and, further, that a "stagy, unpleasant hysteria enters the poems."[35] An early, enthusiastic supporter of Dickey, Richard Howard warned the reader that "[t]he look of these poems on the page is disconcerting: forms are sundered, wrenched apart rather than wrought together; rhythms are an inference from the speaking voice rather than a condition of it. . . ." In conclusion, Howard lamented that "[t]he cost to [Dickey's] poetry is tremendous, for it has cost him the poems themselves— there are not poems here . . . only—only!—poetry."[36] In the same review of *Deliverance*, Benjamin Demott noted of this new book of poems that the "poet runs on unrestrainedly," giving "no shapely object to delight in, little refinement of feeling or subtlety of judgment, no intellectual distinction, no hint of wisdom. On the altar of projective power, in the name of Big Scenes, everything is sacrificed; Vibrancy is all."[37] Michael Mesic commented that: "James Dickey's poetry appeared like a tidal wave to flood the poetic landscape of the 'sixties, washing inland as far as it could, but then settled into one of the lowest depressions . . . producing one of our newest imaginative swamps."[38] While these critics failed to embrace *The Eye-Beaters* as a whole, other critics found merit in individual pieces. Joyce Carol Oates thought the title poem "The Eye-Beaters" to be "an extravagant, curious fantasy" and the later poems in the book to contain "a dramatic ferocity that goes beyond even the shimmering wall of words [Dickey] created for "Falling" and "May Day Sermon."[39] Calhoun and Hill discovered considerable value in "Mercy," Dickey's surreal, nighttime poem about Fay, a nurse. These critics maintained that the poem has a "masterful blending of the actual, the fantasy, the inner thoughts, and the outer dialogue, of the narrator . . . who rumbles at the boundaries of death and finds in his woman some ecstatic new life."[40]

Published in 1976, *The Zodiac* is Dickey's book-length poem based on a translation from the Dutch by Adriaan Barnouw of Hendrik Marman's long poem of the same title. *The Zodiac* encompasses an Easter weekend in the life of a drunken poet who seeks to discover his creative method and who comes home to die after years of traveling. Like the critical response to *The Eye-Beaters*, reviews were divergent. Dave Smith found Dickey's main character insufficiently motivated, and that the poem relied too heavily on sensation and too little on reflection. Smith noted that *The Zodiac* is "important as an impressive failure and as a transitional poem for Dickey. Its failure is partially caused by the absence of narrative and hence an absence of event which might generate the storm of emotional rhetoric and partly caused by the artificial organization of zodical panels which remain static and shed little if any of the Pythagorean aura on cosmological abstractions."[41] Simarly, Turner Cassity charges that "*Zodiac* is the most elaborate and most explicit example we have of the idea of poetry as the unconsidered utterance of the bardic genius aided in his unreason, if need be, by drink and drugs."[42] In the *New York Times*, Thomas Lask disliked Dickey's new style: "If 'Zodiac' doesn't persuade, it is not simply because of its clotted lines and convoluted ideas, but because . . . it is too strident. There are too many emphases, too many capitalized words, too many italics."[43]

On the other hand, in an earlier review in the *Times*, Robert Penn Warren called the poem "a major undertaking and, I should hazard, achievement." Warren also thought that Dickey's diction was especially strong: "I can think of no poem since Hart Crane's 'The Bridge' that is so stylistically ambitious and has aimed to stir such depths of emotion." However, Warren also discovered some problems in the work: ". . . this poem has certain limitations and defects . . . for instance, the structural principle of progression for the first seven or eight sections is not always clear."[44] In *Contemporary Poetry*, Christopher Morris took a different view from these critics, that was basically linguistic and extremely insightful. Morris claimed that *The Zodiac* is "the culmination of the themes of [Dickey's] earlier work," one of which is "the destruction of the old image by the new, the weaker by the stronger" which is "for Dickey the poet's sole, but mandatory obligation." According to this reading, the poem dramatizes "the physical violence of creation" whereby "Dickey justifies the introduction of new images into previously-accepted designs by implying the arbitrariness of all such modes of apprehending the universe."[45] In complete contradiction to the reviews of Cassity and Lask, Stanley Burnshaw in *Agenda* was overwhelmingly enthusiastic about the poem. Like Warren, Burnshaw found its diction filled with "the dazzling ranges and riches of thought that flail at the world-wearied man who is drunk with his search as with aquavit." Marked by "raw vitalism," "convincing speech" and "unflagging intensity," "*The Zodiac*," Burnshaw goes on to say, "sets a new height in this writer's achievement. It is surely the most disturbingly remarkable book length poem in decades."[46] One of the best recent readings of *The Zodiac* is Romy Heylen's, included in this collection, in which she focuses on the poem as an act of interpretation, writing, and thus a translation of not only of Marsmen but of Dickey into himself.

In 1979 Dickey published *The Strength of Fields*. He read the title poem at the inaugral celebration of President Jimmy Carter in 1977. Divided into two sections, the book contains a body of 11 lyrics—almost all very strong— plus 15 translated poems which are analogous to "imitations" in Robert Lowell's sense of the word. Dickey calls these versions "improvisations from the unenglish," which are "freeflight" expansions of translations of poems by Eugenio Montale, Georg Heym, Pierre Reverdy, and Octavio Paz, among others. In the *New York Times Book Review*, Paul Zweig was especially enthusiastic about this volume: "The poems in James Dickey's new book . . . are like richly modulated hollers; a sort of rough, American-style bel canto advertising its freedom from the constraints of ordinary language." On the other hand, in the *Western Humanities Review*, Robert Peters criticized most of the book, except for the "improvisations," as "a deterioration of [Dickey's] work" with poems spoiled by "an easy metaphysics" and "Momentosity."[47] Other judgments were at odds with each other. Dave Smith commended "Root-Light, or the Lawyer's Daughter" as "an epiphany of passion's beginning," while praising "False Youth: Autumn: Clothes of the Age" and "Exchanges." However, Smith found "pronounced disasters" in "For the Running of the New York City Marathon" and "For the Death of Lombardi."[48] In *Understanding James Dickey*, Ronald Baughman thought the translations "noteworthy" but believes that "the works in the first section are more significant." Unlike Dickey's war poems about death and destruction, Baughman finds one of the central strengths in this volume to be the "quietly contemplative and accepting voice" which "illustrates the extent to which the healing process has helped the poet gain acceptance of himself and his new life."[49] Of Dickey's translations, Lawrence Lieberman thinks them "radical and innovatory" because they "break new ground in the art of transcribing the poetry of foreign tongues ('unEnglish') into his native tongue. As Dickey moves across the sound barrier between the inscrutable *other* language and his own, we sense a wizardry of infinitesmal shifts and adjustments not unlike the atomic transmutations of one metal slowly alchemizing into another."[50]

THE LATER PERIOD, 1980–1992

In 1982, Dickey's new book of poems, *Puella*, was dedicated to his second wife: "Deborah" to "her girlhood, male-imagined." Consisting of 18 tautly constructed poems, delineating different aspects of an energized Deborah "crackling with vitality" and presented in a style reminiscent of Gerard Manley Hopkins, *Puella* met with many positive responses. William Harmon thinks that *Puella* is Dickey's "best work since *Buckdancer's Choice*" and that it marks a major change in his method in so far as it "differs substantially from most of Dickey's earlier work." Further, while the titles of the poems are "vivid," they also possess "uncommon eloquence"; the Deborah of these lyrics is "heraldic, totemic, mythic, atavistic, primal."[51] James Applewhite noted that "in *Puella* the powerful Dickey of old is still at work, and that he has succeeded in adding at least a handful of these new poems to the central canon. . . . At least, 'Deborah Burning a Doll Made of House-Wood,' 'Deborah, Moon, Mirror, Right Hand Rising,' 'Veer-Voices: Two Sisters under Crows,' 'Ray-Flowers,' and the first section of 'Deborah as Scion' will join the other great central Dickey poems we remember and reread."[52] Monroe Spears perceived a shift in *Puella* from the "cosmic vision" of *The Zodiac* to the "domestic. The poet is not tamed but gentled as he lovingly describes what Hopkins calls the *mundus muliebris*, the woman's world inhabited by the daughter-wife figure whose girlhood he relives." Using a political perspective, Spears went on to say that "the book is Dickey's reply to the radical feminists, for Deborah in it is both herself and Dickey's ideal modern woman, enacting her archetypal feminine role in full mythic resonance, but not enslaved or swallowed up by it."[53] Susan Ludvigson echoes this political notion when she observes that in *Puella* Dickey "does what many of us are trying to do—in poems and in living: to put ourselves . . . entirely into the minds and heart and bodies of those unlike ourselves." Ludvigson then perceptively elaborates on Dickey's conception of difference. "To escape the limits of sex is to make possible a similar erasing of the boundaries of race, nationality, age—all those demarcations that separate us from each other."[54] Approaching the book from the notion of influence, Eugene Hollahan followed Harold Bloom by arguing a very suggestive "hueristic hypothesis," namely, that "the origin of *Puella* can usefully be traced to Dickey's forgotten encounter with the most important medium-length poem of the late-Victorian age, Gerard Manley Hopkins' *The Wreck of the Deutschland* (1876)." Hollahan's thesis in this inquiry was that Dickey's "anxiety of influence" was "in this instance an anxiety overcome and an influence happily and successfully embraced."[55]

Alnilam (1987) is Dickey's second novel, set in 1943 in at an Army Air Corps training base in North Carolina. His narrative runs 682 pages and tells the story of a blind man, Frank Cahill, whose son Joel, a pilot, dies in a plane crash at the base, after which Cahill, with his huge, guardian-dog Zack, goes in search of the reason for Joel's death. Told from both the narrator's point of view and from Cahill's blind barrage of sensations, the novel elicited mixed reactions from critics. In the *New York Times*, Robert Towers praised the book's "set pieces" from which "a richly detailed picture of a region and an era emerges . . . with the most loving exactitude." Towers also found "[a]nother of the novel's strengths . . . to be . . . the characterization of Cahill." However, Towers spoke for many critics when he noted "overwriting and windiness" in the book which is "handicapped by its inordinately slow pacing." It also lacks "a propelling action energetic enough to sustain its digressive and centrifugal aspects," for "[t]he mystery of Alnilam [the secret military cult at the air base] is too vague to engage us." On the other hand, in a review in *The Philadelphia Inquirer* in 1987, Ronald Baughman commented that the plot of *Alnilam* was not a function of external events but of the internal changes in Cahill himself. Baughman believed Cahill to be "a kind of Oedipus, a blind man seeking and discovering many truths," and thus, both the narrative method and the story reveal a sequence of confusions and clarifications which are "a kind of inner sight" for a blind man.[56] In the *Washington Post Book World* in 1987, John Calvin Batchelor, like Baughman, saw Frank Cahill as "a truth teller as well as seeker." Batchelor praises many other strengths in the novel, one of which is Dickey's unique gift for "evoking the tall-tale Southland, where language stalks with the ferocity of a hunter" and explores "the depravity of a world of boys at war."[57]

Dickey's *The Eagle's Mile*, which collects his major lyric work of the eighties, appeared in 1990, and may very well be Dickey's best single volume of poems. Like *The Strength of Fields*, this book is divided into two parts: first, an assembly of 26 original poems, some a half-page long, others sprawling over three and four pages; and second, a section of 11 "collaborations and rewrites" which extend Dickey's practice, begun in the seventies, of writing "imitations" based on the work of other poets. While some are stronger than others, the pieces in the first half of *The Eagle's Mile* are uniformly excellent. Not only beautifully crafted, they also cover a wide range of genres, ranging from exquisite meditations on motion and perception in "The Three" and "Meadow Bridge" to moving elegies such as "Tombstone" and "To Be Done in Winter" (for Truman Capote) and, finally, to two hilarious comic poems, entitled "The Olympian" (almost as long as an olympic marathon itself) and "Spring Shock." The collaborative pieces in the second half are also extremely strong. Perhaps, the two best are "Purgation / homage, Po Chu-yi" and "Farmers / a fragment / with Andre Frenaud," which both appeared earlier in *Night Hurdling*. While critical reactions to *The Eagle's Mile* are still coming in, Fred Chappell had high praise for it in 1990: ". . . this new volume contains strong, highly original work, strikingly different from the work that built Dickey's formidable reputation." Chappell called Dickey's new style "the high Bardic, the vatic, the transcendent—the Pindaric Grandiose, if you will." Speaking of the book's title poem, Chappell said of this poetic "magnitude" that "almost every page of *The Eagle's Mile* will offer passages of similar delight and awe." On the other hand, Chappell quibbled with elements of Dickey's diction; there are elements of "jarring slang," "disingenuous address," and recurrent signals "of loss of authority" because of overuse of the word "Yes!" with an exclamation point. Even so, Chappell concludes that "overall the book is a victory."[58]

Dickey's most recent book of poems is *The Whole Motion: Collected Poems, 1945–1992*. Like *The Eagle's Mile*, critical response to this 462-page volume is still forthcoming. In an early appraisal, however, poet Richard Tillinghast offered an overview which to some extent reflects the three-part division of early adulation, a middle period of mixed response, and enthusiasm for many parts of the later period. Tillinghast began his review with a just balance of the public image and the poet: "[b]y the mid-seventies Dickey had become so much of a legend that we tended to forget he was, before anything else, a superb and stunningly original poet." Of the early Dickey, Tillinghast wrote, "[i]t may be that Dickey's greatest work still lay ahead of him at this point, but I wonder if he ever again achieved the exquisite purity, the Botticelli-like sanctity, of the poems he wrote in the late-night isolation of the Atlanta suburbs." This critic went on to say about the middle Dickey that "I have never been as enthusiastic about Dickey's work from *Falling, May Day Sermon, and Other Poems* on [;] . . . [his] wall of words . . . seems to sacrifice some of the quieter, more subtle effects Dickey achieved in his early writings." Nonetheless, Tillinghast concluded his review by noting that a later piece such as "The Rain Guitar" "is as tight, as inspired, as jaunty as anything he has ever written."[59]

In addition to the reviews and articles mentioned previously and those indicated in the following section on collections of material about Dickey, a number of extended scholarly pieces that should be noted. In "We Never Can Really Tell Whether Nature Condemns Us or Loves Us," Richard Howard has written one of the early and central mythopoeic inquiries into Dickey's poetic "ritual universe" which Howard found characterized by "an imagery . . . of killing and of ecstasy" within "a circular movement, a conjugation of rituals . . . best expressed, in terms of action, by the gerundive form." Howard also noted the function of miracle, terror, and "eternal return" in Dickey's lyrics in addition to "an erotic mastery of metamorphosis" in "Falling" and "May Day Sermon." In its emphasis on myth, motion, and the dream, Howard's essay rightly located the basic impulses in Dickey's poetry and accurately pointed in a fruitful direction for further Dickey criticism.[60] Linda Mizejewski's "Shamanism toward Confessionalism: James Dickey, Poet" is an insightful, though critical, reading of *The Zodiac* in which she claimed that the poem lacks "the integrity of a justifiable character and a clear structure." According to Mizejewski, the lyric also needs a "credible animism" to take the speaker beyond the realm of mere cosmic assertion which runs the risks of a confessionalism that cannot "transcend [its] intense subjectivity."[61] In "Ezra Pound and James Dickey: A Correspondence and a Kinship," Lee Bartlett and Hugh Witemeyer have published an illuminating, often humorous, series of letters and postcards between Dickey and Pound which were written from 1955 to 1958 after Dickey visited Pound at St. Elizabeth's hospital in Washington, D. C. During this communication, Dickey, as a fledgling poet, viewed Pound as "an older dad who talked to you like . . . you would be talked to by your own crackpot father." To bear witness to this claim, at one point, Pound suggests that Dickey enroll in "a super Klu Klux Klan" which so unnerved Dickey that he suspended their correspondence for nine months. At the end of this article, the authors offers interesting conjectures on the influence of Pound on Dickey in light of Dickey's 1979 lecture at the University of Idaho, entitled "The Water-Bugs Mittens: Ezra Pound: What We Can Use."[62]

In addition to these articles, several other studies should be mentioned. H. L. Weatherby's "The Way of Exchange in James Dickey's Poetry" is one of the early seminal articles on Dickey. Weatherby pointed to the intermingling of traits and powers that Dickey receives by participating not only in the worlds of animals but also in exchanges between the living and the dead and other nationalities.[63] In addition to Joyce Pair's article, collected in this volume, Thomas O. Sloan's "The Open Poem is a Now Poem: Dickey's May Day Sermon," remains one of the two best readings of what may well be Dickey's best poem, "May Day Sermon to the Women of Gilmer County, Georgia, by a Woman Preacher Leaving the Baptist Church." Using a rhetorical analysis which centers on the kind of nonlinear time characteristic of oral language, Sloan developed a valuable conception of the poem's structure based on "listened" rather than "read" poetic form.[64] With "Whatever Happened to the Poet-Critic," Richard J. Calhoun has written one of the best articles on Dickey's criticism. Calhoun examined *Babel to Byzantium* and *The Suspect in Poetry*, and likened Dickey's critical efforts to those of poet-critics such as Eliot, Randsom, Tate, and Warren. In spite of Dickey's reputation as a poetry review "hatchet-man" for the *Sewanee Review*, Calhoun finds Dickey more generous than many other critics both in his estimation of specific poets and in his treatment of prevailing schools of critical theory.[65] "James Dickey's War Poetry: A Saved, Shaken Life" by Ronald Baughman is one of few treatments of the psychological effect of war on the personna in Dickey's war poems. Using a thesis taken from psycho-historian Robert Jay Lifton, Baughman explored Dickey's treatment of the guilt that a war veteran experiences for surviving while so many of his colleagues did not. According to this line of inquiry, Dickey must work his way from static to animating guilt through three stages: confrontation, reordering, and renewal, all of which can be found, for example, in Dickey's long war poem, "Drinking from a Helmet."[66] Finally, in "Traditionalist Criticism and the Poetry of James Dickey," Thomas Landess provided an overview of Dickey's poetry by acknowledging that his is not a poetry of "broad political and social patterns" but is, nonetheless, a "genuine poetry which affirms the ancient pieties."[67]

In addition to scholarly articles on Dickey's verse, a number of studies of *Deliverance* are also central to his bibliography. In "Love and Lust in James Dickey's *Deliverance*," Paul G. Italia focused on the themes of "struggle, copulation, and death" while arguing that the structure of the novel hinges on episodes of sexual abuse and repayment in which one crime compounds another.[68] In "The Harmony of Bestiality in James Dickey's *Deliverance*," Donald J. Greiner discussed one of Dickey's central topics in both his poetry and prose, namely, that behind the facade of apparent civilization lies a human impulse for killing that one finds in the harmonic balance of life and death in the world of beasts.[69] "Subversive Narrative Strategies in *Deliverance* and *Tucky the Hunter*," by Rosalie Murphy Baum, used a dialogical critical method to examine "the struggle for power" by seeing the novel as a quest which subverts "the male paradigm of the hunt." Ultimately, *Deliverance* liberates "the protagonist—from isolation, gender boundaries, and partial, inconsequential lives."[70] In "Myth and Meaning in James Dickey's *Deliverance*," Daniel L. Guillory, like Baum, saw the novel as a critique of "the self-insulating boredom that frustrates the search for human wholeness and creativity," yet also saw its mythic character as going beyond a heroic quest. For Guillory, *Deliverance* propels the narrator, Ed Gentry, out of his suburban malaise into a "basic clarification of human values."[71]

Ronald Schmitt saw *Deliverance* not only as quest myth but also asserted that "[f]ar from being a macho adventure novel, *Deliverance* calls into question the entire notion of heroism as it has been established through the centuries." Schmitt claimed that Dickey challenges us to write new myths that do not end in death and nightmares.[72] Charles E. Davis read the novel as a series of ironies both in the transformations of characters and in their conversations.[73] In "*Deliverance* as James Dickey's Re-vision of [Stephen] Crane's 'Open Boat,' " Grace McEntee offers an provocative reading of the novel as "a rethinking of Crane's philosophy of naturalism" by inventing characters such as Ed and Lewis who change their lives through "their heightened awareness of nature's indifferent forces and by the knowledge that they can circumvent some of nature's determinism through effort and self-determining modes of perception."[74] Henry J. Lindborg also believes that there is a creative element in the characters' struggle in *Deliverance*. Lindborg argues that the book is "a means of discovery" or "an exploration of the process of creation" for Ed Gentry whereby in retelling his tale he invents himself and thus "tap[s] the vital force of nature through art."[75] Finally, working from the perspectives both of the novel and Dickey's screenplay for the film *Deliverance*, Robert C. Covel offered a valuable comparative study in "James Dickey's *Deliverance*: Screenplay as intertext." While noting Dickey's delight and despair in the ways director John Boorman brought his novel to the screen, Covel compared the ideal version of the movie Dickey claimed he imagined with the actual version which altered "Dickey's story [and screenplay] from a psychological study of self-discovery and spiritual deliverance to an adventure story with mere overtones of psychological conflict." Covel argued that Boorman's change of Aristotle's hierarchy of dramatic parts by making spectacle, not plot, foremost.[76]

BOOKS, BIBLIOGRAPHIES, AND JOURNALS ON JAMES DICKEY

The Achievement of James Dickey: A Comprehensive Selection of His Poems with a Critical Introduction by Laurence Lieberman begins with an essay on Dickey entitled "The Deepening of Being," then reprints 24 poems from Dickey's first five books.[77] Though a slim volume at 84 pages, Lieberman's book offers the first introductory overview of Dickey's work. The introductory essay intelligently points to literary mysticism—whereby the poet awakens "the reader to the unexpected realization that a profound spiritual life lies hidden just below the surface of most routine experiences"—as one of Dickey's basic poetic stances. In addition to this early collection, Lieberman has done outstanding critical work on Dickey. Three of his essays, "James Dickey— The Deepening of Being," "Notes on James Dickey's Style," and "The Worldly Mystic," are crucial for an understanding of Dickey's work. From the beginning of Dickey's career, Lieberman has staunchly championed his poetry, even offering his support in print for the publication of "May Day Sermon" when the poem came under attack in 1967.

Eileen Glancy's 107-page *James Dickey: The Critic as Poet*, the first book-length bibliography on Dickey, covers material from 1951 to 1970.[78] It begins with a 33-page essay, which contrasts Dickey's basic themes with those of poetic contemporaries such as Thom Gunn and Galway Kinnell. The following section, "Works by James Dickey," includes "Books," "Sections of Books," "Poems" (including location of reprints), "Essays," "Short Stories," "Letters" and "Reviews." The contents of each division are listed chronologically by date of publication as is the second half of the bibliography, "Works About James Dickey," which includes "Books," "Periodical Essays," "Book Reviews" (listed by individual books), and finally, "Letters" (letters addressed to Dickey, often contesting his reviews). In addition to providing important early coverage of Dickey's work, the second half of Glancy's book presents a brief summary or representative quote from each entry to give the reader a sense of its contents.

James Dickey: The Expansive Imagination; A Collection of Critical Essays, edited by Richard J. Calhoun, is the first collection of essays on Dickey.[79] In addition to Peter Davison's comparison of Lowell to Dickey, this book contains H. L. Weatherby's seminal essay on "the way of exchange" in Dickey, two early pieces by Lieberman on style and poetic mysticism, and Thomas Sloan's impressive reading of "May Day Sermon." Calhoun's central analysis of Dickey's criticism, Robert Hill's appraisal of Dickey's comedy, and Paul Ramsey's work on Dickey's meter (one of the few critical essays dedicated to this important aspect of Dickey's verse) appear in this collection. This volume, especially valuable because it reveals critics' reactions to Dickey's work during his spectacular ascent in reputation in the 1960s, introduces several terms, such as "mysticism" and "romanticism," as keys to critical discussions about Dickey.

James Dickey: A Bibliography, 1947–1974, by Jim Elledge, is the foremost early bibliography on Dickey.[80] At 270 pages, Elledge's book is comprehensive and detailed, with a broad range of subdivisions falling under two main categories. Like Glancy, Elledge divides his bibliography into "Works by James Dickey" and "Works about James Dickey." Yet, unlike Glancy, there are nine separate headings under the first category, ranging from "Books and Pamphlets" to "Poetry" to "Films" and "Records." In addition, this section lists the locations of special collections of Dickey's papers and anthologies in which Dickey's work has been collected. The second category, "Works about James Dickey," ranges in scope from "Periodical Literature" to "Interviews," "Dissertations," "Scripts," and "Biographies." The first section on "Periodical Literature" is extremely broad, and runs to almost 100 pages. In both major sections, the book contains extensive notation about where each entry has been anthologized and excerpted. Further, Elledge's annotations on critical essays and articles summarize more fully than other bibliographies the central outlines of each piece. In addition to this volume, Elledge has also published "James Dickey: A Supplementary Bliography, 1975–1980, Parts I and II" in the *Bulletin of Bibliography*.[81] Elledge's bibliographic work is one of the most thorough and basic sources for the Dickey scholar, especially in its listing of periodical literature on Dickey.

James Dickey: Splintered Sunlight, Interview, Essays, and Bibliography, edited by Patricia De La Fuente, is a pamphlet of 80 pages, published in the Living Authors Series.[82] Consisting of five brief articles, an interview, and a checklist of scholarship from 1975 to 1978, this collection contains some interesting remarks by Dickey on "May Day Sermon" and warm, personal responses by students to Dickey's reading at Pan American University.

James Dickey by Richard J. Calhoun and Robert W. Hill, is a short, introductory survey to Dickey's work, which begins with a biographical sketch of the poet, covers the poetry chronologically, then deals with the fiction and literary criticism in its final chapters.[83] The chapters are organized by relevant topics such as "Guilt and Survival: The Emblem-Poems of War," and are then developed in paragraphs discussing each poem, which give an insightful overview of themes and techniques running throughout Dickey's career. If Calhoun and Hill feel that a poem fails, they say so and give substantial reasons. When they praise Dickey, they do so on equally solid grounds. Their readings are smart and precise. In the world of Dickey criticism, this book is an excellent place to begin for many reasons, not the least of which is its value in orienting the reader to a vast body of poetic material.

Since its appearance in 1984, *The James Dickey Newsletter*, founded and edited by Joyce Pair, has appeared bianually in the fall and spring.[84] This journal has not only published important original articles on Dickey's work, reviews of new books by or about Dickey, and informative personal appraisals of Dickey's teaching and poetic influences, but it also has provided a crucial continuing bibliography for Dickey scholars while serving as a unifying center for further work. The *Newsletter* has sponsored poetry workshop sessions on the poet at DeKalb College and at the South Atlantic Modern Language Association and has stirred critical debate on how best to approach Dickey's work. The *James Dickey Newsletter* insures that a high quality of commentary on Dickey is continually forthcoming. With her dedication to Dickey's work and insistence that the *Newsletter* serve both students and the critical community at large, Pair has widened the appeal of Dickey commentary and given it a venue.

Edited by Bruce Weigl and T. R. Hummer, *The Imagination as Glory* is an extremely serviceable collection of essays on Dickey.[85] The book begins with early reactions to Dickey by Nemerov and Robert Duncan, includes classic essays by Joyce Carol Oates and Lieberman, and ends with two statements by Dickey himself on the energizing power of the poetic imagination. From a chronological point of view, this collection picks up where Calhoun's leaves off by documenting critical reactions from the late sixties through the seventies and by finishing with Dave Smith's insightful essay on *The Zodiac* and *The Strength of Fields*. Pieces by Ralph Mills and Herbert Liebowitz begin to articulate the critical controversy. This book is necessary for the scholar's shelf because it provides an excellent collection of the second stage of Dickey criticism.

James Dickey: The Poet as Pitchman, by Neal Bowers, is an 86-page volume, almost a pamphlet.[86] While the book contains perceptive readings of the poems, its thesis is that Dickey has used his public readings to sell his poems. The book's premise is foregrounded in Bowers' statement that, aside from Dickey's poetic merit, "James Dickey will unquestionably be remembered as one who vigorously promoted himself and his work to gain whatever place he will eventually occupy among the poets of his time." Despite the author's protestations in the introduction, the pejorative term "pitchman" suggests yet another critic or poet unhappy with Dickey's celebrity status who has decided to assign himself the task of placing Dickey in the pantheon of postmodern poets. Whether or not this is so, I continue to wonder why this brief study was written except to mount a personal attack. Bowers has done brilliant work on Theodore Roethke. His study of Roethke's mysticism, *Theodore Roethke: The Journey from I to Otherwise*, is one of the best in the field. Instead of looking at Dickey as a self-promoter, Bowers may have more fruitfully paired Roethke with Dickey on a common topic such as literary mysticism. Bowers' considerable critical skills would have been better served by this kind of poetic inquiry.

Understanding James Dickey by Ronald Baughman is intended as a volume in "a series of guides or companions for students as well as . . . nonacademic readers."[87] This book provides another introductory overview to Dickey. Beginning with a description of Dickey's career, Baughman surveys Dickey's work chronologically, first the poetry, then *Deliverance*, concluding, as do Calhoun and Hill, with Dickey's own criticism. Baughman's readings are sure-handed and intelligent. For the student beginning to explore Dickey criticism, this book and the selection on Dickey in the Twayne Series are good places to start.

Edited by Harold Bloom in the series "Modern Critical Views," *James Dickey* is a collection of essays which begins with Bloom's own impressive reading of Dickey's early poem "The Other."[88] Oates' central essay is reprinted here as are Lieberman's and Ramsey's. Also included are an early piece by Richard Howard, the incisive essay on *Deliverance* by Linda Wagner-Martin, and a chapter from Bowers' book. James Applewhite's fine appraisal of *Puella* finishes off a volume which fills in several gaps in Dickey scholarship and presents key reviews such as Robert Penn Warren's on *The Zodiac*, in addition to Nelson Hathcock's perceptive reading of the relation between predator and prey in "The Heaven of Animals."

James Dickey and the Gentle Ecstasy of Earth: A Reading of the Poems, by Robert Kirschten, is a neo-Aristotelian inquiry into the major patterns of action and effects which characterize Dickey's poetic universe.[89] The book aims at generating a vocabulary to insure that the descriptions used to form general critical principles about Dickey's poetry are explicable in terms of the plot, character, narrative techniques, and diction which the poet employs to produce specific emotional ends. Divided into four hypotheses—mysticism, Neoplatonism, romanticism (the "gentle" elements), and primitivism (the "ecstatic" aspects)—the first half of the book moves inductively through readings of poems to what the Chicago Critics call poetic forms. What better critical document to use as a paradigm for inquiry than Aristotle's *Poetics*, for a poet whose work depends so much on narrative? This section is not an investigation into literary mysticism or romanticism as independent issues but, rather, into Dickey's specific uses of these topical and methodological traditions for his own ends. The second half of the book moves deductively from the general hypotheses through basic literary parts—representation, imagery, metaphor—then culminates in the application of the four hypotheses in a reading of Dickey's wonderful, comic, rite of passage, "The Shark's Parlor." This book is the first to argue that Dickey's poetry has been multicultural since its inception.

The Voiced Connections of James Dickey: Interviews and Conversations, edited by Ronald Baughman, is a rich collection of interviews given by Dickey over a period extending from 1965 to 1987.[90] Ranging from exegetical clues about Dickey's poetry based on his reading of anthropology and world poetry to descriptions of his daily working habits, this collection gives a fuller picture (based on personal testimony) of the man and the many changes he has gone through as an artist. Both serious and humorous, technical and anecdotal, Baughman's collection aids the Dickey scholar by presenting very varied commentary in a single volume, whether on Dickey's high estimation of Yeats, or his comic account of the problems of a New York taxi driver who just broke up with his mistress of sixteen years. This volume also includes statements by Dickey about his interest in Pythagorean mathematics and music, his enthusiasm for anthropological studies and world poetry, and full statements on his use of the poetic "split-line" in relation to punctuation, and his theory of how the mind experiences blocks of associative imagery in its perception of the poetic line.

James Dickey: A Descriptive Bibliography, by Matthew J. Bruccoli and Judith S. Baughman, aims to establish "the author's canon: to identify the first appearance in print of everything he wrote."[91] Bruccoli and Baughman have done a thorough job of cataloging and describing the vast number of Dickey's books, pamphlets, posters, and broadsides, published and unpublished, beginning with the appearance of *Into the Stone and Other Poems* in 1960, in the series *Poets of Today* and ending with an excerpt from *Bronwen, The Traw, and the Shape-Shifter*, published in 1986. Accompanied by photographs of dust jackets and title pages, the description of each entry includes a list of contents, typography and paper, binding, and the number of copies printed. This book is a virtual history of publication detail regarding Dickey. For instance, it is interesting to note that in 1980 Doubleday published 20,000 copies of *The Strength of Fields* in the second printing alone, a staggering run for a book of poetry, much less for a second printing. While the first section of this bibliography includes chronologically organized material published "wholly or substantially by James Dickey," the second consists of material by Dickey which appears in a publication written or edited by others. Bruccoli's and Baughman's first-rate, comprehensive book (423 pages) and Jim Elledge's compilation, are the two central bibliographies on Dickey.

Gordon Van Ness' *Outbelieving Existence: The Measured Motion of James Dickey*, is an excellent, scholarly overview of 30 years of Dickey criticism.[92] Van Ness has painstakingly collected and assembled critical reactions to Dickey's work which he groups by responses to individual books, in roughly chronological order. While, as Van Ness points out, systematic Dickey criticism really begins with the publication of *Buckdancer's Choice* and *Poems 1957–1967*, this book offers its own history of reaction to Dickey by citing commentary on his first book of poems (*Into the Stone*) and ending with observations about his critical works, such as *Babel to Byzantium* and *Nighthurdling*. By combining the poet's own statements about his work with plentiful direct quotation from a series of astute readers, both positive and negative, Van Ness provides a single, extremely valuable and detailed assessment of a writer who has generated a wide range of critical reaction. The bibliography in the back of this book is current and comprehensive.

Assessing the Savage Ideal: James Dickey and the Politics of Canon by Ernest Suarez is also a history of response to Dickey, yet of a different kind.[93] Based on a highly perceptive account of contemporary ideological and cultural changes occurring over the past decade, Suarez addresses the issue of Dickey's changing literary reputation by focusing on this specific problem: "How is it possible, within less than ten years, for a writer to go from being hailed as the most important poet of his time to being virtually ignored in assessments of post–World War II poetic history?" Arranged chronologically, Suarez' chapters answer this question by examining Dickey's relationship with Pound, Modernism, and the New Criticism, then the traumatic effect of the Vietnam War on Dickey's critical reception, and, finally, how contemporary critical modes such as the confessional allow no place for Dickey in the current poetic canon. Aided by accurate, intelligent readings of Dickey's politically controversial poems such as "The Firebombing" and "Slave Quarters," Surarez' book is the fullest analysis now available on the contours of Dickey's career and on the ways in which academic and historical fashions determine wide shifts in value, response, and the very nature of poetry.

THE PLAN OF CRITICAL ESSAYS ON JAMES DICKEY

The purpose of this book is to celebrate Dickey's achievement by collecting a representative overview of critical response to his work. This collection is, accordingly, divided into two sections. The first consists of a survey of initial reviews, beginning with James Wright's enthusiastic appraisal of Dickey's first book of verse, *Into the Stone*, in 1961, and ending with Fred Chappell's cautious yet enthusiastic response to *The Eagle's Mile* in 1991. In between, the range of reaction—positive and negative—to Dickey's poetry and prose constitutes a critical narrative which is controversial and in conflict with itself. This collection highlights the central areas of praise and contention regarding his work. Arranged chronologically, these pieces appear in an alternating sequence which enables a charge to be articulated then addressed by a competing position. For example, Robert Bly's "The Collapse of James Dickey" appears directly before Paul Carroll's "James Dickey as Critic" which vigorously defends Dickey against Bly's claims. This volume begins with favorable impressions by Wright and Wendell Berry but also includes both Frederic Jameson's and Carolyn Heilbrun's negative readings of *Deliverance*. Bly, Jameson, and Heilbrun bring together three central areas of political attack against Dickey: racial / Vietnam, social, and sexual. While I believe all three critics have severely distorted Dickey's literary work to suit their own political agendas, their charges should be put on the table so that the reader may make the final judgment. Before a political judgment is rendered on these negative allegations, it would help the reader to remember that Dr. Martin Luther King, Jr. used excerpts from Dickey's article defending the Civil Rights Movement in the South in the late fifties in his own speeches, that Dickey made suggestions for speeches and raised money for anti-war presidential candidate Eugene McCarthy during the Vietnam War, and that Dickey called for cultural diversity while supporting the presidential candidacy of progressive liberal Jimmy Carter in the mid-seventies.

The second section consists of full-length essays that extend from the 1940s to the present. Beginning with Calhoun Winton's affectionate memoir of his student days with Dickey at Vanderbilt University, the section ends with Dickey's recent essay on poetic imagery entitled "Lightenings or Visuals." Many of these essays address in a fuller manner than the sympathetic reviews those controversial issues raised by negative reviews and may also be read in conjunction with them. After reading Robert Bly on "The Firebombing" and Frederic Jameson on *Deliverance*, the reader may wish to read Ross Bennet's "'The Firebombing': A Reappraisal" and Peggy Goodman Endel's reassessment of *Deliverance*. After reading Carolyn Heilbrun on Dickey's machismo and masculinity, the student may wish to read Douglas Keesey's thoughtful response to these charges. Concerning the role of women in Dickey's work, Joyce Pair's " 'Dancing with God': Totemism in 'May Day Sermon' " and my own "Form and Genre in James Dickey's 'Falling': The Great Goddess Gives Birth to the Earth" make strong cases that, instead of his public reputation for macho poetry, Dickey's mythopoeic vision has been matriarchal and multi-cultural—even revolutionary feminist—for 25 years.

Notes

1. James Dickey, "The Place of the Skull," *The Whole Motion: Collected Poems 1945–1992* (Hanover, NH: Wesleyan Univ. Press, 1992), 7.

2. Oliver Evans, "University Influence on Poetry," *Prarie Schooner* 35 (Summer 1961): 180.

3. Harold Bloom, "Introduction," in Harold Bloom, ed., *Modern Critical Views: James Dickey* (New York: Chelsea House, 1987), 3.

4. James Wright, "A Shelf of New Poets," *Poetry* 99 (December 1961): 178–83.

5. Howard Nemerov, "Poems of Darkness and a Specialized Light," *Sewanee Review* 71 (Winter 1963): 99–104.

6. Thom Gunn, "Things, Voices, Minds," *Yale Review* 52 (October 1962): 129–38.

7. Harold Bloom, "James Dickey Symposium: A Celebration," in Ronald Baughman, *Dictionary of Literary Biography, Volume 7: James Dickey, Robert Frost, Marianne Moore*. Edited by Karen L. Rood. (Detroit: Gale Research, 1989), 97.

8. Richard Howard, "We Never Can Really Tell Whether Nature Condemns Us or Loves Us," in Bloom, *James Dickey*, 48.

9. Louis Martz, "Recent Poetry: The Elegiac Mode," *Yale Review* 54, 2 (December 1964): 289.

10. Dennis Donoghue, "The Good Old Complex Fate," *The Hudson Review* 17 (Summer 1964): 274–75.

11. William Meredith, "James Dickey's Poems," *Partisan Review* 32, 3 (Summer 1965): 456–57.

12. Wendell Berry, "James Dickey's New Book," *Poetry* 105 (November 1964): 130–31.

13. Joyce Carol Oates, "Out of Stone, Into Flesh," in Bloom, *James Dickey*, 84–85.

14. Charles Monagham, *Commonweal* 84 (15 April 1966): 120.

15. Joseph Bennett, "A Man with a Voice," *New York Times Book Review*, 6 February 1966, 10.

16. Radcliffe Squires, "James Dickey and Others," *Michigan Quarterly Review* 6 (October 1967): 296–98.

17. Robert Huff, "The Lamb, the Clocks, the Blue Light," *Poetry* 109 (October 1966): 47.

18. David Ignatow, "The Permanent Hell," *Nation* 202, 20 June 1966, 752.

19. William C. Strange, "To Dream, To Remember: James Dickey's *Buckdancer's Choice*," *Northwest Review* 7 (Fall–Winter, 1965–66): 42.

20. Paul Rice, *Georgia Review* 38 (Fall 1984): 647.

21. Louis Untermeyer, "A Way of Seeing and Saying," *Saturday Review* 50, 6 May 1967, 55.

22. James Tulip, "Robert Lowell and James Dickey," *Poetry Australia* 24 (October 1968): 39, 44.

23. Donald W. Baker, "The Poetry of James Dickey," *Poetry* 111 (March 1968): 400–01.

24. Edmund Fuller, "The Bookshelf: Poets of Affirmation," *Wall Street Journal*, 24 May 1967, 16.

25. Louis Simpson, "New Books of Poems," *Harper's Magazine* 235, August 1967, 90.

26. Ralph J. Mills, "The Poetry of James Dickey," *Triquarterly* 11 (Winter 1968): 232, 229, 240.

27. Julian Symons, "Moveable Feet," *New Stateman* 73, 16 June 1967, 849.

28. Harry Morris, "A Formal View of the Poetry of Dickey, Garrigue, and Simpson," *Sewanee Review* 77, 2 (Spring 1969): 319.

29. Benjamin DeMott, *"The 'More Life' School and James Dickey,"* Saturday Review 53, 28 March 1970, 25–26, 38.

30. Warren Eyster, "Two Regional Novels," *Sewanee Review* 79 (Summer 1971): 471.

31. Frederic Jameson, "The Great American Hunter, or Ideological Content in the Novel," *College English* 34 (November 1972): 180.

32. Carolyn Heilbrun, "The Masculine Wilderness of the American Novel," *Saturday Review* 29 January 1972, 41.

33. Linda Wagner-Martin, *"Deliverance: Initiation* and *Possibility,"* in Bloom, *James Dickey*, 112, 114.

34. Don Kunz, "Learning the Hard Way in James Dickey's *Deliverance*," *Western American Literature* 12 (February 1978): 290, 301.

35. Herbert Leibowitz, "The Moiling of Secret Forces: *The Eye-Beaters, Blood, Victory, Madness, Buckhead and Mercy*," in Bruce Weigl and T. R. Hummer, eds. *The Imagination as Glory: The Poetry of James Dickey*, (Urbana, Illinois: Univ. of Illinois Press, 1984), 130.

36. Richard Howard, "Resurrection for a Little While," *Nation* 210, 23 March 1970, 341–42.

37. DeMott, 38.

38. Michael Mesic, "A Note on James Dickey," in Robert Burns Shaw, ed., *American Poetry Since 1960* (Cheadle: Carcanet Press, 1973), 153.

39. Joyce Carol Oates, Weigl and Hummer, 99, 101.

40. Calhoun and Hill, 92–93.

41. Dave Smith, "The Strength of James Dickey," Weigl and Hummer, 155–56.

42. Turner Cassity, "Double Dutch," *Parnassus* 8, no. 2 (1980): 193.

43. Thomas Lask, "Serene and Star-Crazed," *New York Times*, 22 January 1977, 19.

44. Robert Penn Warren, "The Enunciation of Universality," Bloom, 103, 105.

45. Christopher Morris, "Dark Night of the Flesh: the Apotheosis of the Bestial in James Dickey's *The Zodiac*," *Contemporary Poetry* 4, no. 4 (1982): 31, 41.

46. Stanley Burnshaw, "James Dickey," *Agenda* 14–15 (Winter–Spring 1977): 122–24.

47. Robert Peters, "The Phenomenon of James Dickey, Currently," *Western Humanities Review* 34 (Spring 1980): 159–60.

48. Dave Smith, 158.

49. Ronald Baughman, *Understanding James Dickey* (Columbia: Univ. of South Carolina Press, 1985): 130, 129.

50. Laurence Lieberman, "Exchanges: Inventions in Two Voices," *Sewanee Review* 88 (Summer 1980):65.

51. William Harmon, "Herself as the Environment," *Carolina Quarterly* 35 (Fall 1982):91.

52. James Applewhite, "Reflections on *Puella*," in Bloom, 153–54.

53. Monroe Spears, *American Ambitions* (Baltimore: Johns Hopkins Press, 1987), 83, 85

54. Susan Ludvigson, "A Radical Departure for James Dickey," *Columbia* [South Carolina] *State*, 31 October 1982, G6.

55. Eugene Hollahan, "An Anxiety of Influence Overcome: Dickey's *Puella* and Hopkins' *The Wreck of the Deutschland*," *James Dickey Newsletter* 1.1 (Spring 1985), 2.

56. Ronald Baughman, "In Dickey's Latest, Blindness Opens a Man's Eyes to Life," *Philadelphia Inquirer*, 31 May 1987, S1, S8.

57. John Calvin Batchelor, "James Dickey's Odyssey of Death and Deception," *Washington Post Book World*, 24 May 1987, 1–2.

58. Fred Chappell, "Vatic Poesy," *State*, 9 December 1990, 5F.

59. Richard Tillinghast, "James Dickey: The Whole Motion," *The Southern Review* (Autumn 1992):972, 976, 979.

60. Richard Howard, 37–62.

61. Linda Mizejewski, "Shamanism toward Confessionalism: James Dickey, Poet," Weigl and Hummer, 140–41.

62. Lee Bartlett and Hugh Witemeyer, "Ezra Pound and James Dickey: A Correspondence and Kinship," *Paideuma* 11 (1982):81, 87.

63. H. L. Weatherby, "The Way of Exchange in James Dickey's Poetry," *Sewanee Review* 74, 3 (Summer 1966):669–80.

64. Thomas O. Sloan, "The Open Poem is a Now Poem: Dickey's May Day Sermon," in *Literature as Revolt and Revolt as Literature: Three Studies in the Rhetoric of Non-Oratorical Forms*. Proceedings of the South Annual University of Minnesota Spring Symposium in Speech Communication, 3 May 1969, 85–104.

65. Richard J. Calhoun, "Whatever Happened to the Poet-Critic?" *Southern Literary Journal* 1 (Autumn 1968):75–88.

66. Ronald Baughman, "James Dickey's War Poetry: A 'Saved, Shaken Life,'" *South Carolina Review* 15 (Spring 1983):38–48.

67. Thomas Landess, "Traditionalist Criticism and the Poetry of James Dickey," *Occasional Review* 3 (Summer 1975):5–26.

68. Paul G. Italia, "Love and Lust in James Dickey's *Deliverance*," *Modern Fiction Studies* 21 (Summer 1975):203–13.

69. Donald J. Greiner, "The Harmony of Bestiality in James Dickey's *Deliverance*," *South Carolina Review* 5 (December 1972):43–49.

70. Rosalie Murphy Brown, "Subversive Narrative Strategies in *Deliverance* and *Tucky the Hunter*," *James Dickey Newsletter* 9.2 (Spring 1993):2–11.

71. Daniel L. Guillory, "Myth and Meaning in James Dickey's *Deliverance*," *College Literature* 3 (1976):56–62.

72. Ronald Schmitt, "Transformations of the Hero in James Dickey's *Deliverance*," *James Dickey Newsletter* 8.1 (Fall 1991):9–16.

73. Charles E. Davis, "The Wilderness Revisited: Irony in James Dickey's *Deliverance*," *Studies in American Fiction* 4 (Autumn 1976):223–30.

74. Grace McEntee, "*Deliverance* as James Dickey's Re-vision of Crane's 'Open Boat,'" *James Dickey Newsletter* 7.2 (Spring 1991):2–11.

75. Henry J. Lindborg, "James Dickey's *Deliverance*: the Ritual of Art," *Southern Literary Journal* 6 (Spring 1974):83–90.

76. Robert C. Covel, "James Dickey's *Deliverance*: Screenplay as Intertext," *James Dickey Newsletter* 4.2 (Spring 1988):12–20.

77. Laurence Lieberman, *The Achievement of James Dickey: A Comprehensive Selection of His Poems with a Critical Introduction* (Glenview, Il.: Scott, Foresman, 1968).

78. Eileen Glancy, *James Dickey: The Critic as Poet* (Troy, NY: Whitson, 1971).

79. Richard J. Calhoun, ed., *James Dickey: The Expansive Imagination* (Deland, Fla.: Everett / Edwards, 1973).

80. Jim Elledge, *James Dickey: A Bibliography, 1947–1974* (Metuchen, NJ: Scarecrow, 1979).

81. Jim Elledge, "James Dickey: A Supplementary Bibliography, 1975–1980, Parts I and II," *Bulletin of Bibliography* 38:2–3, 92–100, 150–55.

82. Patricia De La Fuente, ed., *James Dickey: Splintered Sunlight, Interview, Essays, and Bibliography* (Edinburgh, TX: Pan American University, 1979).

83. Richard J. Calhoun and Robert W. Hill, *James Dickey* (Boston: Twayne, 1983).

84. Joyce M. Pair, *The James Dickey Newsletter* (Atlanta: DeKalb College).

85. Bruce Weigl and T. R. Hummer, eds., *The Imagination as Glory* (Urbana: University of Illinois Press, 1984).

86. Neal Bowers, *James Dickey: The Poet as Pitchman* (Columbia: University of Missouri Press, 1985).

87. Ronald Baughman, *Understanding James Dickey* (Columbia: University of South Carolina Press, 1985).

88. Harold Bloom, ed., *James Dickey* (New York: Chelsea House Publishers, 1987).

89. Robert Kirschten, *James Dickey and the Gentle Ecstasy of Earth: A Reading of the Poems* (Baton Rouge: Louisiana State University Press, 1988).

90. Ronald Baughman, ed., *The Voiced Connections of James Dickey: Interviews and Conversations* (Columbia: University of South Carolina Press, 1989).

91. Matthew J. Bruccoli and Judith S. Baughman, *James Dickey: A Descriptive Bibliography* (Pittsburgh: University of Pittsburgh Press, 1990).

92. Gordon Van Ness, *Outbelieving Existence: The Measured Motion of James Dickey* (Columbia, SC: Camden House, 1992).

93. Ernest Suarez, *Assessing the Savage Ideal: James Dickey and the Politics of Canon* (Columbia: University of Missouri Press, 1993).

REVIEWS

◆

[From "A Shelf of New Poets"
A review of *Into the Stone and Other Poems*
by James Dickey]

JAMES WRIGHT

"Reader, for your own sake, go buy this book"

In one of his brilliant and disturbing essays in the *Sewanee Review*, James Dickey writes the following about a poem which he admires: "It is only after the Inevitable has clamped us by the back of the neck that we go back and look carefully at the poem, and see that it is written in *terza rima*. And so, hushed and awed, we learn something about the power of poetic form, and the way in which it can both concentrate and release meaning, when meaning is present." It would be difficult to find a more lucid statement of the true relation between the form of a poem and the strange world of imaginative vision where the true form reveals itself. It would also be difficult to find a more lucid description of Mr. Dickey's own best poems, twenty-four of which appear in his first collection, *Into the Stone*. His long poem, *Dover: Believing in Kings*, is not included, no doubt because of its length. It is one of the few great poems written by an American during the past few years; it is fully equal, if not superior, to W. S. Graham's *The Nightfishing*, which in some ways it resembles. However, since Mr. Dickey's *Dover* is still resting in the darkness, like some beautiful and silent clipper ship poised for its launching, I will limit myself to some brief observations on the poems in *Into the Stone*.*

Mr. Dickey's poems invariably embody his confrontation of some of the most difficult and important experiences that a human being can have. The experiences are sometimes public and horribly shared, like war; or they are domestic and affectionately, painfully shared, like the love a man achieves and fulfills for brother and son and wife; and sometimes they are solitary, spiritual, frightening. To all of these experiences the poet brings three great gifts: an unpredictably joyous imagination, which is able to transfigure the most elemental facts of the universe and to embody the transfiguration in an

"A Shelf of New Poets," by James Wright, first appeared in *Poetry*, was copyrighted in 1964 by The Modern Poetry Association, and is reprinted by permission of the Editor of *Poetry*.
*Note: Mr. Dickey's poem, *Dover: Believing in Kings*, [appeared] in the August 1958 issue of *Poetry*. . . .

unforgettable phrase (the moon is a "huge ruined stone in the sky," the sunlight is a "great ragged angel," and, as the moonlight falls on grass, "a weightless frosted rain has taken place"); secondly, a delicate sense of music, which sometimes takes shape most beautifully in the skillful use and variation of refrains (as in the lines "Light falls, man falls; together. / Sun rises from earth alone"); and, finally, a humane quality which is very hard to characterize, but which I should call, inadequately, a kind of courageous tenderness. Of these three gifts, the first is accidental; the poet has been touched by the capricious gods, and there is nothing anyone can do about that. The second gift is a matter of accident, in part; but it is also a matter of intelligent self-discipline; it would be easy for a writer with such a delicate ear to lose himself and his vision in a euphonious haze, but I cannot find a single phrase in Mr. Dickey's book which is not firm and clear. However, it is the final gift, the courageous tenderness, which seems to me most important, which assures us that the many remarkable talents have not been lavished on a man for nothing. Perhaps what I mean has already been stated more clearly by Mr. Dickey himself, in the few sentences which I quoted earlier: poetic form "can both concentrate and release meaning, *when meaning is present.*"

And meaning is present in these poems. I do not have enough space to list the meanings; and, in any case, I would rather have the reader experience the joy of discovering them for himself. However, to illustrate, I might point to the poem entitled *The Performance*. Here Mr. Dickey commemorates a man whose nobility expressed itself through his skill in standing on his hands. And this very man, Donald Armstrong (there is no vague "Humanity" in Mr. Dickey's poems, there are only particular men and women and children, often named and always deeply felt in their solid physical being), was later beheaded by the Japanese. The poet imagines Armstrong giving his performance in the very face of his grotesque death. Armstrong is perhaps, among other things, an image of Dickey's own imagination and skill: in the very presence of realities which are mysteries—like one's own death—the poet, like the old friend from the war, responds to the fact of personal annihilation by suddenly transforming himself into actions that are nobly graceful and that are performed for their own everlasting sake.

Reader, for your own sake, go buy this book.

[From "James Dickey's New Book" A review of *Helmets* by James Dickey]

Wendell Berry

"There are poems here of such life that you don't believe they're possible until you read them for the second time . . ."

Going into this book is like going into an experience in your own life that you know will change your mind. You either go in willing to let it happen, or you stay out. There are a lot of good poems here. *The Dusk of Horses, Fence Wire, Cherrylog Road, The Scarred Girl, The Ice Skin, Drinking from a Helmet, and Bums, on Waking* aren't the only poems I thought moving and good, but they are the ones I keep the firmest, clearest memory of.

Thinking just of the poems I've named, I realize to what an extent sympathy is the burden of this book, how much there is of seeing into the life of beings other than the poet. The reader is moved imaginatively and sympathetically into the minds of horses at nightfall, of farmer and animals divided and held together by fences, of a young girl scarred in a wreck, of bums waking up in places they never intended to come to.

Drinking from a Helmet represents not the fact of sympathy, but the making of it. The poet moves from his own isolated experience of war into an almost mystical realization (and assumption) of the life of the dead soldier from whose helmet he drinks. A tense balance is held between the felt bigness of the war and the experience of the one young man.

Cherrylog Road is a funny, poignant, garrulous poem about making love in a junk yard. It surely owes a great deal to the country art of storytelling. It's a poem you want to read out loud to somebody else, and it's best and most enjoyable when you do.

But I think that Mr. Dickey is also capable of much less than his best. There are poems that seem to have been produced by the over-straining of method, ground out in accordance with what the poet has come to expect he'll do in a given situation. *Springer Mountain* will illustrate what I mean. The poem tells about a hunter who, on impulse, pulls off his clothes and starts

"James Dickey's New Book," by Wendell Berry, first appeared in *Poetry*, was copyrighted in 1964 by The Modern Poetry Association, and is reprinted by permission of the Editor of *Poetry*.

running after a deer. I can't help believing that the power of insight and feeling that is the *being* of a poem like *The Dusk of Horses* becomes *equipment* in *Springer Mountain*. The poet seems to be using capabilities developed elsewhere, and to be using them deliberately and mechanically. The hunter's gesture, or transport or whatever it is, seems to have been *made* to happen, and isn't seen with enough humor to mitigate its inherent silliness and clumsiness. After a good many readings I don't yet feel I know how it is meant or what it means. And more than that, I have no faith in it, no belief that anybody ever did any such thing. It's like watching a magician's act that, in spite of a certain brilliance, remains flatly incredible.

Usually involved in the weakness of the weaker poems is a dependence on a galloping monotonous line-rhythm (nine syllables, three or four stressed, five or six unstressed, the last unstressed) that can be both dulling and aggravating. The point isn't that this happens, but that it happens often. And when it happens it acts as a kind of fence, on the opposite sides of which the poem and the reader either give each other up or, worse, go on out of duty.

But I want to end by turning back to the goodness of the book. There are poems here of such life that you don't believe they're possible until you read them the second time, and I've got no bone to pick with them.

The Collapse of James Dickey
[A review of *Buckdancer's Choice*
by James Dickey]

ROBERT BLY

". . . a huge blubbery poet, pulling out southern language in long strings, like taffy, a toady to the government, supporting all movements toward Empire, a sort of Georgia cracker Kipling"

Buckdancer's Choice has received a lot of attention from reviewers, but curiously no one has talked about the content. I thought the content of the book repulsive. The subject of the poems is power, and the tone of the book is gloating—a gloating about power over others.

"Slave Quarters" is a perfect example. A true work of art is sometimes able to be a kind of atonement. It moves into deep and painful regions of the memory, to areas most people cannot visit without wincing, and so do not visit. No one needs works of art like that more than we do. All over the American brain, there are huge areas like cutover forests, lobes made sterile by collective cruelty toward a race, by one egotistical murder after the other to keep a people in poverty as one keeps cows . . . the psyche, faced with twentieth-century ideals, goes groggy with guilt. An art work can pierce that mass of guilts, gradually loosen it, help it to fall apart. But to do this, the work of art must carry real grief; it has to carry a masculine and adult sorrow. That is what Turgenev's, Chekhov's, and Tolstoy's work expressed when they talked about Russian serfdom. They told the truth both about the masters and about the serfs. Mr. Dickey's poem, "Slave Quarters," however, brings with it no grief: it gives the old romantic lying picture of the slaves and of the slaveowner. It is pure kitch, a *Saturday Evening Post* cover, retouched by the Marquis de Sade. Being sentimental, it does not help cure illness, but instead increases the illness. Far from expressing remorse, the poem conveys a childish longing for ultimate power, a desire to go back and simply commit the offences over again:

Originally published in *The Sixties* (Spring 1967): 70–79. Copyright © 1990 by Robert Bly from *American Poetry: Wildness and Domesticity* (New York: Harper & Row). Reprinted by permission of the publishers.

33

> I look across low walls
> Of slave quarters, and feel my imagining loins
> Tense with the madness of owners
> To take off the Master's white clothes
> And slide all the way into moonlight
> Two hundred years old with this moon.

The poet feels that the old South treated the Negro pretty much all right. He accepts, in fact, all the southern prejudices and, by adding artistic decoration to them, tries to make them charming. "Slave Quarters" pretends to be a poem about the moral issue of ownership, but instead lingers in the fantasies of ownership.

> A child who belongs in no world   my hair in that boy
> Turned black   my skin
> Darkened by half   his, lightened
> By that half exactly   the beasts of Africa reduced
> To cave shadows flickering on his brow.

The poem becomes ugly as he sniffs the Negro women, and prepares to do his great deed in the slave huts. He feels the same thrill from his power over dogs as over people:

> In the yard where my dogs would smell
> For once what I totally am
> Flaming up in their brains as the
>   Master

On the whole, I consider this poem one of the most repulsive poems in American literature. The tone is not of race prejudice, but of some incredible smugness beyond race prejudice, a serene conviction that Negroes are objects. It is not great life-enhancing poetry as the critics burbled, but bad tasteless slurping verse. The language is dead and without feeling.

>   and above
> A gull also crabs slowly,
> Tacks, jibes then turning the corner
> Of wind, receives himself like a brother
> As he glides down upon his reflection:

The language after all can be no better than the quality of the imagination, which in this poem is paralytic. The poet is sure the Negro women would have welcomed his rape, and when he envisions his half-Negro son grown up, the well-worn pictures pop up in the shooting gallery: a heavyweight champion, a waiter in "epauletted coats," a parking lot attendant, a construction worker, and so forth.

At the end the poet asks, thinking of his bastard Negro son, What would it be like, not to "acknowledge" a son, but to "own" him? This question is a gesture in the direction of the northern liberals, showing he knows it is wrong to own people. The only *feeling* in the line however is curiosity.

The tone of "Firebombing" is like the tone of "Slave Quarters." As objects of sadism, the Negro women have been replaced by the civilian population of Asia. We shudder when we realize we are talking about the psyche of the United States. In these matters, Dickey balances on his shoulders an absolutely middle-class head. He embraces the psychoses of the country and asks us to wait until he dresses them up a bit with breathless words: then all the liberals will see those psychoses are really "life-giving."

"Firebombing" makes no real criticism of the American habit of fire-bombing Asians. It starts off with some criticism of the pilot. We learn that the bomber pilot, twenty years after his fire raids on the Japanese, feels no remorse in his overstuffed kitchen, feels no guilt for having burned people to death, feels no anguish, feels nothing, and this is intended as a complaint. He has burned up families: "The others try to feel / For them. Some can, it is often said." The poem soon drops this complaint, however, and concentrates on the excitement of reliving the bombing.

> All leashes of dogs
> Break under the first bombs, around those
> In bed, or late in the public baths: around those
> Who inch forward on their hands
> Into medicinal waters.

We notice the same curious obsession with power over dogs and over cows:

> Singing and twisting
> All the handles in heaven kicking
> The small cattle off their feet
> In a red costly blast

and people: "With fire of mine like a cat / Holding onto another man's walls." Everything, dogs, cats, cows, people, are objects to use power on. If this were a poem scarifying the American conscience for the napalm raids, we would feel differently. But this poem has no real anguish. If the anguish were real, we would feel terrible remorse as we read, we would stop what we were doing, we would break the television set with an ax, we would throw ourselves on the ground sobbing. We feel no such thing. The poem emphasizes the picturesque quality of firebombing instead, the lordly and attractive isolation of the pilot, the spectacular colors unfolding beneath, the way the fire spreads. It reminds one of Count Ciano's lyrical descriptions of his bombs falling on the Ethiopians in 1938: "The bombs opened beneath like great red flowers, beautiful in the center, like roses." Mr. Dickey remarks that in the cockpit he is "deep in aesthetic contemplation." "He sails artistically over / The resort towns." Some kind of hideous indifference numbs us, after having already numbed the language: "The heads come up with a roar / Of Chicago fire." How cozy the whole thing seems to him is shown by:

> Dogs trembling beneath me for hundreds of
>   miles, on many
> Islands, sleep-smelling that ungodly mixture
> Of napalm and high-octane fuel,
> Good bourbon and GI juice.

The poet feels so little anguish, he provides charming little puns: "Where (my) lawn mower rests on its laurels." In its easy acceptance of brutality, the poem is deeply middle class. Dickey appears to be embarrassing the military establishment for its Japanese air raids, but he is actually performing a function for the establishment. He is teaching us that our way of dealing with military brutality is right: do it, later talk about it, and take two teaspoonfuls of remorse every seventh year. In short, if we read this poem right, we can go on living with napalm.

The third ugly poem is "The Fiend." "The Fiend" is a foggy, overwritten fantasy about another sort of power—this time the power the man who is utterly cold has over those who still feel human warmth and enthusiasm. It is about the power the Snow Queen has over the human children. The power is symbolized this time by a window peeper, who is sexually not quite all there. The poem begins with some good descriptions of window peeping, interiors of houses seen by a tree climber. The poem then tries to become "poetic" and talks about things Dickey used to make poetry out of—how the man interacts with the tree, how the tree itself perhaps is human too. The poem finally returns to its sadistic business at hand, the cold, excitable window peeper and the curious malignance he feels toward defenseless people, toward stenographers and working girls:

> and when she comes and takes down
> Her pants, he will casually follow her in like
>   a door-to-door salesman
> The godlike movement of trees stiffening
>   with him the light
> Of a hundred favored windows gone wrong
>   somewhere in his glasses
> Where his knocked-off Panama hat was in
>   his painfully vanishing hair.

The question is: why does the poem abruptly end there? My guess is that when the peeper went into the house, he cut the girl up with a knife. The knife is mentioned early in the poem. Of course speculations about what doesn't happen in a work of art are futile, like asking what Fortinbras did after Hamlet's death, but here the abrupt end calls for some explanation, and an escalation of sadism seems the only possibility. We realize reading it that something sadistic has entered wholeheartedly into Dickey's fantasy. The poem breaks off where it did, in my opinion, because Mr. Dickey realized that if he described the next scene he would lose his *New Yorker* audience. He didn't quite have the courage of his own sadism.

"Slave Quarters," "Firebombing," and "The Fiend," the three long pieces in the book, have a similar content and fail artistically for the same reasons. The language is inflated, the rhythms manufactured. All three are obsessed with power and driven by a childish longing for it, disguised only by the feeblest verbal veil. The humanistic mumblings at beginning or end hide the naked longing for power about as well as a Johnson white paper on foreign policy hides its own realities. The amazing thing is that none of the reviewers noticed what the poems were saying. Even reviewers as acute as David Ignatow, and as aware of American ambiguities, praised the pointless violence of these poems and accepted the poems' explanations of themselves at face value.

We can only lay this blindness to one thing: a brainwashing of readers by the New Critics. Their academic jabber about "personae" has taken root. Instead of thinking about the content, they instantly say, "Oh, that isn't Dickey in the 'Firebombing' poem! That is a persona!" This is supposed to solve everything. Yeats did use personae at times, a beggar, for example: yet as we read his beggar poems we are very conscious that Yeats is *not* the beggar. A great impersonal poem could be written on the old South and its slaves, shaped like "Slave Quarters." One could imagine an artist like Yeats in fact creating such a poem, yet all through the poem, we would be conscious that the poet was none of the characters, that he was outside of or beside the poem, his judgments made even more clear by their absence in the poem. But in "Slave Quarters" the umbilical cord has not been cut. Mr. Dickey is not standing outside the poem. On the contrary, the major characteristic of all these poems is their psychic blurriness. There are no personae. The New Critical ideas do not apply at all. Readers go on applying them anyway, in fear of the content they might have to face if they faced the poem as they face a human being.

Not all the poems in the book are as bad as these three, although all are touched by the same inflation. The best poem I think is "Sled Burial." "The Escape," about buying a grave lot, is also touching. Reading these two poems, some of the old affection I have always felt for Dickey's good poems returns. But even in the poems that are not sadistic, even in the "innocent" poems, a curious alienation takes place. James Dickey reminds you of some nineteenth-century flying enthusiast, whose deflated balloon is on the ground, and he is trying with tremendous wild power and large lungs to blow it up himself. In "The Shark's Parlor," he succeeds. As he puffs, the genial poem grows larger and larger. But then an unexpected thing happens: the balloon leaves without him. The poem floats away, we and the poet are left behind, standing in the same place we were before all the effort started. Fundamentally, "Shark's Parlor" has no meaning. Rilke thought that when the poem had meaning, it carried the author to a new place. Frost, too, said that a true poem, like a piece of ice on a hot stove, moves on the stream of its own melting, and by its end, the true poem is far away from its starting place. Thinking of Dickey's poems in this way, it is clear they are worked up. As someone said recently, Mr. Dickey takes his life and laminates poetry onto it.

When Mr. Dickey visits college campuses for readings, he makes clear his wholehearted support of the Vietnam War. This is his business, but we must note again the unity of the man and his work. Of course the pilot he describes feels no remorse. If the pilot he describes felt any remorse for the earlier firebombings, he would be against the firebombings now. As a poet and as a man, Mr. Dickey's attitudes are indistinguishable from standard middle-class attitudes. In an article about him, Mr. Dickey boasted that he had made $25,000 on poetry last year. Obviously his decision to make poetry a "career" like professional football or advertising is associated with the abrupt decline in the quality of his work. In any event, his decline from "A Mountain Tent" in *Drowning with Others* to "Slave Quarters" is catastrophic, enough to make you weep. One cannot help but feel that his depressing collapse represents some obscure defeat for the United States also. He began writing about 1950, writing honest criticism and sensitive poetry, and suddenly at the age of forty-three, we have a huge blubbery poet, pulling out southern language in long strings, like taffy, a toady to the government, supporting all movements toward Empire, a sort of Georgia cracker Kipling. Numerous American artists have collapsed over a period of years—John Dos Passos is an example—but in Dickey's case the process seems accelerated, as in a nightmare, or a movie someone is running too fast.

James Dickey as Critic
[A review of *Babel to Byzantium*
by James Dickey]

PAUL CARROLL

". . . I want to try and put into perspective a nasty attempt at poetic fratricide
in which James Dickey has been the target."

After I talk about this collection of book reviews and essays on modern poets—
which seems to me the sanest, most invigorating and most fun to read since
Randall Jarrell's *Poetry and the Age* (1953)—I want to try and put into
perspective a nasty attempt at poetic fratricide in which James Dickey has
been the target. Why I bother with such dirty literary linen is simple: I want
everybody to read and enjoy Mr. Dickey without the distraction encouraged
by the scuttlebutt resulting from the attempt at fratricide, which was manufactured, for the most part, by envy, it would seem. Not only has James Dickey
shown the unmistakable "blue sign of his god on the forehead," as St.-John
Perse describes the true poet, which holds the promise that we may have a
major poet in our midst (indeed, why his collected *Poems: 1957–67* failed to
win the 1968 Pulitzer Prize remains, to my mind, more baffling than the
intricacies displayed in most of the theories regarding John F. Kennedy's
assassination) but he also writes the kind of criticism I admire—namely, direct,
personal talk about this poet or that poem in his or its own skin, as it were.

What commends the prose in *Babel to Byzantium* is similar to what makes
the best of Mr. Dickey's poems memorable: the honesty and authority of the
insight, unburdened by literary fashion or even by the critic's previous judgment; and the originality and power of the imagination at work on material
that counts.

When I suggest that the insight is honest and has authority I mean that
it is the last thing from that type of tidy, judicious opinion one reads (only
during Lent, hopefully) in so many reviews and essays. One learns to trust
Dickey to say only what he feels. What he feels can compel you, in turn, to
reread a writer whom you may have dismissed as an adolescent infatuation or

Originally appeared as "James Dickey as Critic: *Babel to Byzantium*" in *Chicago Review* 20 (November 1968):
82–87. Reprinted by permission of *Chicago Review*.

to open yourself to one whom you've never read. Of Kenneth Patchen for instance, Dickey says: "It is wrong of us to wish Patchen would 'pull himself together.' He has never been together. He cannot write poems, as this present book (*When We Were Here Together*) heartlessly demonstrates. But his authentic and terrible hallucinations infrequently come to great good among the words which they must use. We should leave it at that," he concludes, "and take what we can from him." Or of John Logan and the lack of wider recognition his work merits but hasn't received: "His strange kind of innocence, walking in and out of his ecclesiastical and literary knowledgeableness, is not an easy thing to talk about, though anyone who reads Mr. Logan cannot fail to be excited and uplifted by it." Then the insight blazes: "(Logan) is far beyond the Idols of the Marketplace and works where the work itself is done out of regard for the world he lives in and the people he lives among because he is helplessly and joyously what he is."

Fluctuating quotations on the literary stock market obviously do not interest Dickey. He refuses to take on faith alone, for example, the veneration afforded Charles Olson and his poetics of "composition by field" by some of the poets associated with the old Black Mountain College and by some of the Beat poets, as well as by some of the younger poets, longing, it would seem, for apostolic succession. Examining Olson's theory and its practice in *The Maximus Poems*, Dickey finds both second-hand and not too interesting news. But he is not out to hatchet another poet, granting that Olson's mind "seems to me quite a capable one, and at all points working hard to say what it has been given it. That is enough, because it has to be." On the other hand, J. V. Cunningham, John Frederick Nims, Elder Olson, and Reed Whittemore are treated as poets and not as "minor voices from the '40s." Nims, for one, is often dismissed by fellow poets and critics as a virtuoso. Not by Dickey: "Mr. Nims has worked hard for a good many years to achieve his style of unremitting brilliance, and it behooves us to look closely at what he is doing"—which he does, with care and energy.

And the originality and power of the imagination seem without equal, in my opinion, among practicing critics. "Opening a book by Robert Penn Warren is like putting out the light of the sun," Dickey observes, "or like plunging into the labyrinth and feeling the thread break after the first corner is passed." His is an imagination which leaps beyond mere critical insight: "One will never come out the same Self as that in which one entered. When he is good, and often when he is bad, you had as soon read Warren as live." Truths such as this, arrived at only through the imagination, occur again and again throughout this book.

In addition, Dickey almost always exhibits that rare gift: he is able to transcend a fundamental antipathy to some poet's work—which he describes, however, clearly and forcefully—and to discover what he feels is genuine in the poems. After arguing that Robert Duncan, for instance, is "certainly one of the most unpityingly pretentious poets I have ever come across," he also praises Duncan's "ingenuousness," the originality of his intellect, and several "marvelous" Duncan poems. Richard Wilbur, James Merrill, Allen Ginsberg, and Gene Derwood are other poets whom Dickey dislikes. In each, however, he finds nuggets of genuine poetry.

In brief, these book reviews of some 65 American and British poets are free of that myopia, parochialism and occasional smugness or patronizing tone found in much criticism. Instead, Dickey's reviews are clearsighted, catholic in taste, and exuberantly respectful as only one poet can be towards the effort of one of his fellows. Best of all, Dickey ignores what he calls the critic's expected "System of Evaluation," which he is supposed to defend not only on its practical and local instances but in its broader theoretical and philosophical implications as well. On the contrary, Dickey explores only his immediate, existential experience of this poet or that poem. And he does so in clear, masculine prose. (His lack of a critical system is the only possible fault I can find in this book. As far as I'm concerned, however, such lack is a virtue.)

In addition to the book reviews, there are longer essays on Edward Arlington Robinson—a valuable discussion which I know will send me back to Robinson soon—and on Robert Frost—an analysis so accurate in defining both Frost's genius and his spiteful, egocentric personality that one feels like laughing and weeping at once. Then there are five good shorter essays on individual poems, ranging from Smart's "A Song of David" to Francis Thompson's "The Hound of Heaven" to Williams' "The Yachts." (An entire book on individual poems he loves would be a happy event, I think, from which everybody would benefit.)

Finally, three essays are grouped under the umbrella, "The Poet Turns on Himself." "Barnstorming for Poetry" delineates what it feels like for a middleaged man suddenly to find himself a literary lion overnight as he sings, staggers, and suffers from college to college during an exhausting, exhilarating reading tour. Every poet who has ever run such a curious gauntlet will read this piece with (what Melville called in a far different context, I'm afraid) "that shock of recognition." "Notes on the Decline of Outrage" should be read, and read carefully, by anyone who likes to think of James Dickey as a Georgia redneck. He isn't. What we come to know instead is a man, who was born white and raised in the Georgia of 40 years ago, trying to explore, as much in touch with his feelings as he can get, what it means *to him* to think about abandoning inherited, familial attitudes towards Negroes. What that man decides, as well as how he reaches the decision, will not satisfy those addicted to easy abstract slogans; but I suspect the essay will be admired by those who care more about individuals than abstractions or clichés or finding a mirror which will reflect their opinions and prejudices. I know I admire the essay almost as much as James Baldwin's masterpiece, "Down at the Cross: Letter from a Region in My Mind," and for the same reason: both offer one man, feeling and thinking with his own heart, memories, and brains.

Now, I'd like to turn to the attempt at poetic fratricide mentioned at the beginning of this review.

"The Hunting of the Dickey" has become a popular, if vulgar, sport among a growing number of poets and poetasters. A few weeks ago, for example, I heard one of the younger poets, who is bright and well-read, dismiss Dickey as being the David Ogilvy of American verse. When asked if he'd read such magnificent Dickey poems as "The Sleep Child," "Slave Quarters" or "The Heaven of the Animals," he admitted, rather sheepishly, he had not; even more depressing, the poet confessed that, due to bad-mouthing against Dickey he'd heard along the literary grapevine, he'd decided not to bother with the criticism collected in *Babel to Byzantium*.

Exactly what *are* Dickey's crimes or sins? I thought, after this melancholy encounter. Most of the charges I've heard poets make against Dickey seem to have been brought into melodramatic focus by Robert Bly in his well-read essay, "The Collapse of James Dickey" (*The Sixties*, Spring, 1967). In that piece, Mr. (I almost said Captain) Bly tries to secure Dickey to the yardarm and flog him because some of the poems in *Buckdancer's Choice* (National Book Award, 1966) exhibit "a gloating about power over others." According to Bly, this gloating manifests itself most clearly in such poems as "Slave Quarters"— that almost classic work depicting the sensibility of a contemporary white Southerner enmeshed in the cunning bondage of memory and fantasy of what an antebellum plantation owner might have felt—and in "Firebombing"— a long, often tedious poem which, with considerable honesty and power, embodies an attempt by a middleaged suburbanite to relive in memory the excitement and youthful virility felt when he was a bomber pilot flying missions over Japan during World War II. Both are poems of "memory and desire": haunting, masculine, poignant. Clearly the first is not the apologia pro rednecks Mr. Bly discovers, nor is the latter a paean to "the American habit of firebombing Asians." But Bly shows little interest in reading them as poems: instead, he chooses to bully poems into being flagrantly "repulsive" examples of what he claims is their author's moral leprosy.

The Bly essay concludes, then, with a libel against Mr. Dickey. The poet is branded as "a sort of Georgia cracker Kipling," presumably because he earns an annual $25,000 from activities resulting from his being a poet, publishes some of his verse in *The New Yorker*, allegedly supports the Vietnam war, and reveals himself in general as "a toady to the government, supporting all movement toward Empire."

Frankly, the Bly essay appalled me. How could a critic with his sensibility and extremely wide reading, I wondered, allow his argument to be grounded on the silly assumption that since the Dickey poems espouse few of the virtues cherished by white Northern liberals, the poems were "repulsive" and their author an Establishment stooge and moral pariah? Mr. Bly's essay is so shrill and wrong-headed that it almost seems unnecessary to recall that Ezra Pound and T. S. Eliot despised equalitarian democracy and, by implication, most, if not all, liberal goals; or that Apollinaire adored the war on the Western Front; or that Dante firmly believed that unless one were a baptized believer in the One, Holy, Roman, Catholic, and Apostolic Church one was destined for eternal misery in either hell or limbo.

Here, then, are the crimes for which Mr. Dickey stands accused by Mr. Bly and other devotees of "The Hunting of the Dickey" clan. In his poems, he explores feelings and memories of one man existing in his own flesh and bone, instead of using poetry to elicit attention by mouthing this or that current liberal or Far Left attitude about the Negro revolution or the Vietnam conflict. In addition, he earns a decent living for his family by doing what he can do with consummate skill: write poetry, read it in public, and teach it in the classroom. In other words, his crimes or sins are the ancient ones: talent, independence of attitude, and recognition and reward. Worst of all, he is only 45. Ten years ago, he was unpublished and unknown. Today, he stands as the first of his generation to have published a collected poems and a volume of criticism on modern and contemporary poets. Success is, as Ambrose Bierce reminds us, "the one unpardonable sin against one's fellows."

(Regarding Mr. Dickey's views on Vietnam, I know only that when we talked about that wretched war one afternoon in September, 1967, the poet said that, after a lot of hard thought, he hadn't made up his mind as yet. In my opinion, our involvement in Vietnam is murder—barbarous, immoral, infectuous—and I told Dickey as much. But I also remembered that Camus refused to join the supporters of the Algerian rebels in 1957, stating that he hadn't made up his mind, thereby provoking vicious denunciations from intellectuals of the Left, including Sartre. Moreover, Dickey mentioned the possibility that he might become a speech writer for Senator Eugene McCarthy. What began as a casual acquaintanceship in 1966, when the poet assumed his responsibilities as poet to the Library of Congress, had matured into what Dickey implied was a closer relationship. At that time, he clearly was a McCarthy man; I don't know how he feels today, and it doesn't matter, of course, in so far as the irresponsible smear that he's a toady of the Pentagon and White House is concerned.)

I've spent time in describing this inept attempt at poetic fratricide by Mr. Bly—most of whose criticism and work as editor, translator and gadfly-at-large to the literary community, and whose exemplary public stands against the Vietnam war I admire without reservation—in order to say to him and to other members of "The Hunting of the Dickey" society, including that young poet: If you allow such popular but false images of James Dickey as "redneck" or "war-lover" or "careerist" to keep you from reading *Babel to Byzantium*, or from reading it with an unclouded eye, you'll be depriving yourself of criticism as it should be written. The man who wrote this book clearly loves and serves the god of poetry and the god's faithful disciples with (as the Baltimore Catechism prescribes with regard to another deity) his whole heart, and his whole soul, and whole mind, and whole strength.

From "The Difficulties of Being Major: The Poetry of Robert Lowell and James Dickey"

PETER DAVISON

"Of all American poets of fifty or under, there are only two who could yet be thought in the running to pass Mr. Auden's tests [for 'major poets']: Robert Lowell and James Dickey."

The common lament on our campuses is the dearth of "major poets," and the critics are scuttling to find one. If they cannot find him, surely they can invent him: study someone until he turns out to be major by simply dominating the course catalogues. The distinction between major and minor in poetry has not often been useful except when discriminating between a Homer, a Dante, a Shakespeare, a Goethe—and the others. Yet today critics pick over the contemporary and near-contemporary crops of poetry with all the concentration of cannery workers sorting and grading fruit.

W. H. Auden, in the introduction to his recent fascinating anthology *19th Century British Minor Poets*, sets down some suggestive rules in the matter:

> One cannot say that a major poet writes better poems than a minor; on the contrary the chances are that, in the course of his lifetime, the major poet will write more bad poems than the minor. . . . To qualify as major, a poet, it seems to me, must satisfy about three and a half of the following five conditions.
>
> 1. He must write a lot.
> 2. His poems must show a wide range in subject matter and treatment.
> 3. He must exhibit an unmistakable originality of vision and style.
> 4. He must be a master of verse technique.
> 5. In the case of all poets we distinguish between their juvenilia and their mature work, but [the major poet's] process of maturing continues until he dies. . . .

Before going a step further, note that Mr. Auden, not a native American, omits one criterion that most American poets would probably put at the head

Reprinted from *One of the Dangerous Trades* by Peter Davison. Copyright by the University of Michigan, 1991. Published by The University of Michigan Press. Used by permission.

44

of their list: The major poet tries harder, is more ambitious, more "serious." We think we must huff and puff in order to blow the house down.

Of all American poets of fifty or under, there are only two who could yet be thought in the running to pass Mr. Auden's tests: Robert Lowell and James Dickey. In most respects they are as different as American poets can be. Lowell is a son of New England; Dickey, of the South. Lowell comes from and makes much of one of America's great aristocratic families; Dickey writes as a Populist without politics. Lowell looks constantly to the civilized past—to Rome (both pagan Rome and Christian Rome), to the puritan ethic and the puritan neurosis, to the city (both in Europe and in America), to the dramatic aspects of poetry, to the sound of voices, to the tradition of Coleridge and Matthew Arnold and T. S. Eliot. Dickey, no less learned than Lowell, carries the literary past more lightly, but his poems explore our overgrown forest of archetypal scenes and situations; they deal with animals and hunting, with war and wounds, with drowning and flying; with domestic life rather than family history; with pantheism rather than Catholicism; with death and transfiguration rather than funerals; with transformations of shapes and states of being rather than with the damage wrought by time and society. In form, Lowell leans toward the elegy, the dramatic monologue, the verse play; Dickey toward the dithyramb, the narrative, the sermon. Lowell looks to the Atlantic Ocean and across it, Dickey to the great American wilderness and within the continent. . . .

James Dickey began publishing poetry in 1957; and in an explosive ten years his work has developed in remarkable ways technically and imaginatively, yet all his poetry has dealt with the same central concern. The world is not for him a classical structure of society based on a City governed by law, with a terrible ocean nibbling at its edges. For Dickey the world has depth and dimensions that can be explored only by a sensibility that penetrates deeper and deeper beneath the guises of reality in the hope of finding a unity at the center. His poetry is, in the words of his poem "Buckdancer's Choice," "the thousand variations of one song." Unlike Lowell, whose work had matured in technique before he was thirty, Dickey, starting from scratch at thirty-four, brought a fully inhabited imagination to his work, but he had to find his own technique, a rhetoric that would enable his ideas and sensations to move freely in verse. It took him almost ten years to reach his full powers.

How was he to express his mystical intentions in concrete images? At the outset his poems sought elemental strength similar to the simple, gentle, poignant language of Edwin Muir. Lines like these, opening "The Heaven of Animals,"

> Here they are. The soft eyes open.
> If they have lived in a wood
> It is a wood.

> If they have lived on plains
> It is grass rolling
> Under their feet forever . . .

bear a blood relation to the mysterious magnificence of Muir's "The Animals":

> They do not live in the world,
> Are not in time and space.
> From birth to death hurled
> No word do they have, not one
> To plant a foot upon,
> Were never in any place.

The similarity is more than stylistic. The older Scottish poet concerned himself with the same range of urgencies as Dickey: the "archaic companionship" of man and nature; the appearances of God in the world; the spirits of animals, trees, and water; the symbols of dream; the mysteries of flying and drowning in elements other than earth. Stylistically, Dickey's rhythms imitated Muir's in being unpretentious, conventional, deliberately unruffled; but there were more turbulent currents to trouble Dickey's underground river than Muir's still waters.

Dickey's work is a search, in a sense, for heaven on earth. He seeks order and resonance in the inchoate; ransacks through obsession, through trial and error, changes of costume and skin, through transformation of personality and the accidents of experience, to discover some sort of relation between the human and animal worlds, a bridge between the flesh and the spirit, and, more than these, a link between the living and the dead. One source of this concern, frequently reiterated in *Into the Stone* (1960) and *Drowning With Others* (1962), emerges in reference to his dead brother:

> I look in myself for the being
> I was in a life before life. . . .
> I cannot remember my brother;
> Before I was born he went from me
> Ablaze with the meaning of typhoid.

This brother is radiant with life in the poet's dreams and in his fantasies of companionship and resurrection. He is an alter ego which borrows the poet's body and connects the poet with the world outside.

But he is hardly the only medium. Dickey's atavistic vision is like an echo, taking on shapes that shift into one another imperceptibly, unpredictably, mystically, as in "Inside the River":

Break this.   Step down.
Follow your right
Foot nakedly in
To another body.
Put on the river
Like a floating coat,
A garment of motion,
Tremendous, immortal. . . .

Live like the dead
In their flying feeling.

Drowning and hunting are frequent images in the early poems. To drown is to become one with water, one with the dead. To drown in nature is to die on behalf of it, to enrich nature by losing yourself. Those who live are already the dying; only the dead therefore are spared the threat of extinction.

In his first two books Dickey had already established his poetic identity as a man restless within the confines of himself who must always be putting on other shapes (armor, helmets, hides, feathers, water) so as never to be only a single self, so as to become others, to rescue others ("The Lifeguard" is a particularly interesting poem on this theme). He remarks with amazement: "Someone lay with his body shaken / Free of the self. . . ." The ultimate way of becoming more than the self is to die. Dying unites us with others, with the animals, with the animal in ourselves; and the only way to understand the secret of death is to penetrate, to thrust, to cleave beyond the surfaces of nature to the ultimate kinship.

However, his technique was still at some distance behind his aspirations. He was handicapped as a poet by having come to his craft late, already knowing what he wanted to say, but not how to say it. Most of the poems in the first two books, as also in *Helmets* (1964), leave the reader with the feeling that the poem has begun at the wrong place, or ended too late, after the reader's attention has already been used up.

Yet there are vibrant exceptions, like "Fence Wire," "Cherrylog Road," "The Scarred Girl," and "Drinking from a Helmet." In the last, several of Dickey's obsessive themes join forces: during World War II the poet is in a line of soldiers waiting for water. He sees his face reflected in the water in a dead man's helmet: "I kept trembling forward through something / Just born of me." To see himself in another's helmet brings back once again Dickey's sense of substituting for his dead brother: "I knew / That I inherited one of the dead." The poem leads the poet backward in time, "into the wood / Until we were lost." Dickey had yet to discover a technique that would liberate him from his natural limitations—or else one that would take advantage of them. This poem, the last in *Helmets*, may have been a turning point. It brought him face to face with the memory of war, with the painfulness of the past remembered, and it embodied his theme in a narrative setting. He could no longer confine himself to sequences of images clustered around a central statement which was often weaker and less pungent than the images themselves, and sometimes even banal. He had to find a method which would enable him to move backward and forward in time as well as in space, and he had to escape from the tyranny of the dactylic drone.

With *Buckdancer's Choice* (1965) Dickey began to break free, and this volume brought him the National Book Award. He now opened up and exploited the possibilities of narrative—poetic narrative, not mere prose narrative in verse. Moreover, his liberation seemed to be accompanied by a liberation of violence, as though personal memories and poetic themes alike had long been suppressed. Now he began recovering for poetry his war experiences. Was it the memory of war, opened up almost twenty years afterward, that suggested new rhythms to him? Or was it the fighter pilot's memory of flying? Both themes, hereafter in his work, made their presence more keenly felt than before. More urgent, too, is the reality of the past side by side with the present. A new metric, a new emphasis on narrative, the exploration of new themes and the extension of old ones, a freer use of the dimension of time—these four elements distinguish Dickey's maturity from his early work. In his themes of communion with the dead and the kinship of nature, he had established the possibility of a new voice in American poetry as clear as that of Theodore Roethke; but to attain it, he would have to win through to the clarity of Roethke's vision and to the resonance of Roethke's music.

The three major poems in *Buckdancer's Choice* are "The Firebombing," "The Fiend," and "Slave Quarters." All three have taken on narrative progression, and all three skip in great leaps backward and forward in time and space. A fourth narrative, "The Shark's Parlor," is a carnival of violence which falls short of success because the poet declines into his old habit of summing up at the end, in a moral which might have suited a poem of images but which is out of place in a poem of narration. "The Firebombing" explores the relation between the corpulent householder of 1965 and the napalm-scattering pilot on a run over Japan of twenty years earlier: "when those on earth / Die, there is not even sound. . . ."

> It is this detachment,
> The honored aesthetic evil,
> The greatest sense of power in one's life,
> That must be shed in bars, or by whatever
> Means, by starvation
> Visions in well-stocked pantries . . .
>   I swing

Over   directly over the heart
The *heart* of the fire. . . .

"The Fiend" is a dazzling performance in its characterization of a middle-aged Peeping Tom and his transcendent relationship with the women he peers at from trees and bushes at night. This poem is the first of more to follow that explore the realms of sexual aberrance: "It will take years / But at last he will shed his leaves   burn his roots   give up / Invisibility   will step out   will make himself known to the one / He cannot see loosen her blouse take off luxuriously   with lips / Compressed against her mouth-stain   her dress   her stockings / Her magic underwear." In these poems the mature technique makes itself manifest: long lines with stresses far apart, emphatic pauses punctuated by typographical spaces, frequent repetition of words and rhythms, looping syntax. Sometimes the old dactylic cadence appears, especially in short poems, but it is much altered in the direction of subtlety.

The full power of Dickey's poetry becomes apparent in the new part of his new book, *Poems 1957–1967* (Wesleyan University Press, $6.95). The breakthrough goes far beyond what might have been expected in the previous books. "I have had my time   dressed up as something else, / Have thrown time off my track by my disguise." The rhythms are now remarkable indeed, and flexible as acrobats:

> She was a living-in-the-city
> Country girl   who on her glazed porch broke off
> An icicle, and bit through its blank bone: brought me
> Into another life   in the shining-skinned clapboard house
> Surrounded by a world where creatures could not stand,
> Where people broke hip after hip.

Dickey's oldest theme, that of man's reincarnation as angel, returns in strange and novel form:

> I always had
> These wings   buried deep in my back:
> There is a wing-growing motion
> Half-alive in every creature.

It emerges again in "Falling," a very long but not really successful poem about a stewardess who falls from an airliner and strips as she falls. In "The Sheep-Child" he investigates a theme as old as the Minotaur, sexual relations between man and beast, in terrifying eloquence: "I saw for a blazing moment / The great grassy world from both sides, / Man and beast in the round of their need. . . ." In "Sun," "Power and Light," "Adultery" (". . . me with my grim techniques. Or you who have sealed your womb / With a ring of convulsive rubber"), he deals with domestic relations and the love-hate between man and woman. In "Encounter in the Cage Country" he returns once again to the animals, but with a wolfish intensity that is new:

> the crowd
>
> Quailed from me   I was inside and out
> Of myself   and something was given a life-
> Mission to say to me hungrily over
>
> And over and over   your moves are exactly right
> For a few things in this world: we know you
> When you come, Green Eyes, Green Eyes.

All of Dickey's development, and all of his thematic complexity, are wrapped up in one long poem which opens *Poems 1957–1967*. "May Day Sermon to the Women of Gilmer County, Georgia, by a Woman Preacher Leaving the Baptist Church" contains everything that Dickey, at this stage, can put into a poem. The new metric and syntax are there; the obsessive theme of death and renewal and repetition and eternity; the transformations of the earthbound, the archetypes of country life. It strains toward universality. Only time will tell whether it retains it; but this poem contains in one place everything James Dickey has been developing toward.

If American poetry needs a champion for the new generation, Dickey's power and ambition may supply the need. His archetypal concerns are universal to all languages and will no doubt carry over into translation; his sense of urgency is overwhelming; his volume, his range, his style, his technique, his process of maturing—all might supply W. H. Auden's five categories (and so might the number of bad poems he has written!). There is no need for pessimism, yet there may continue to be a danger of overblowing. Such writing as Dickey's requires a vast fire to keep the caldron boiling. If he were to encounter a slight recession of energy, such as that which seems lately to have overtaken Robert Lowell, Dickey's value as a poet might easily enter into a decline just at the moment when his reputation, like Lowell's today, has reached its apogee.

A Review of *Poems 1957–1967*

JOHN SIMON

"I place Dickey squarely above Lowell."

. . . It is hard to say anything in brief about the sprawling energies of James Dickey. Even his unsuccessful efforts, and *Poems 1957–1967* (Wesleyan, $6.95) contains quite a few, have a vitality and effervescence, a gladdening unwillingness to lie flat on the page. But at his best, this is one of our most untrammeled, irrepressible, yet never formless poets, one who is open to the largeness of life as much as to its detail, who is neither a lucubrator nor afflicted with logorrhea, neither too private nor too public. In Dickey's poetry, the country and the city coexist in the most mutually fructifying manner, and even his precosities are never effete. I place Dickey squarely above Lowell.

From *Commonweal*, LXXXVII (1 December 1967): 315. Reprinted by permission.

[From "The Great American Hunter, or, Ideological Content in the Novel"]

FREDERIC JAMESON

"... an adventure story like Dickey's ... causes you to posit the need for Leviathan, or the authoritarian state, to hold the disorder and the anarchy of individual violence and of human nature in general in check."

... To put it this way is in other words to raise the question of ideology, and of the relationship between ideology—conscious or unconscious, the reader's or the writer's—and the literary work itself ...

Such is the problem suggested by a reading of two recent works in a very old American genre, the wilderness novel, or the tale of the great American hunter. The first of the books I have in mind is James Dickey's bestseller, *Deliverance*, which tells the story of four town dwellers on a boating expedition through a wild area about to be submerged. The protagonists, however, suffer less from hostile nature than they do at the hands of human beings, if one may thus term men who are released by the very wilderness setting from the constraint of human law and the norms of human society, and whom the author evidently intends to represent that fundamental, bestial cruelty at the very heart of human nature ascribed by the maxim *homo homini lupus*. The heroes' eventual triumph over their pursuers, their laborious return to civilization, thus amount to a victory over Nature in general, so that the novel is by way of being an initiation ritual or *rite de passage*, if one can so characterize something that happens to middle-aged men. So from the very outset, in its choice of subject-matter, this book reflects a fashionable right-wing preoccupation, popularized by such writers as Robert Ardrey: that of the necessity of violence, both on the individual and the social level. For if violence is a necessary component of existence, or so the argument runs, if it is indeed the very heart of life itself, then modern civilization has robbed us of the supreme experience we can have as men. In this the primitive world was wiser, for the institutionalized rituals it prescribed for adolescents taught the ultimate lesson of bodily pain and fear. These rituals had much to do with the stability of the village structure, from which our modern restlessness for some indeterminable, yet absolute Experience—for some a Romantic, for others a typically American, phenomenon—was thereby effectively exorcized. The advantage of an adventure story like Dickey's lies in the way it permits the exercise of a kind of ideological double standard: on the individual level it allows you vicariously to experience and to satisfy this "ineradicable" instinct for violence, which is then the object of your critique on a social and political level, where it causes you to posit the need for Leviathan, or the authoritarian state, to hold the disorder and the anarchy of individual violence and of human nature in general in check. So the strategy of the adventure tale allows you to reconcile the apparently contradictory demands of your own individual license and your authoritarian political leanings simultaneously through the same series of events.

At any rate, Dickey's characters are out to prove themselves: "they tell me," says one of them, "that this is the kind of thing that gets hold of middle-class householders once in a while." So Dickey's wilderness expedition would seem to emerge from some more basic dissatisfaction with the structure of middle-class life (the dullness of routine, the renunciations of family living, the nagging frustrations of work and of the reality principle), if not, indeed, from some "insufficiency principle at the very heart of life itself" (Georges Bataille, quoted in epigraph to *Deliverance*). In actual practice, however, you never do prove yourself in general, you always try to prove *something* to yourself in particular; and one cannot long for Experience without locating it symbolically within some individual experience of a concrete and determinate kind, which is to say that what looked metaphysical at the outset is nonetheless in the long run obliged to realize itself in a social world through actions and choices invested with social and historical values. So when we observe Lewis, the ringleader of the expedition, it is not so much his *ennui* as his sheer technical and instrumental capability that strikes us: "Lewis was the only man I knew who could do with his life exactly what he wanted to. . . . He was one of the best tournament archers in the state and, even at the age of thirty-eight or -nine, one of the strongest men I had ever shaken hands with. He lifted weights and shot arrows every day in a special kind of alternating rhythm and as a result was so steady that he could easily hold a sixty-pound bow at full draw for twenty seconds. . . ." Such an account makes it clearer than in most sports stories (e.g., the mystiques of Hemingway and Faulkner) that the sport is not only a symbolic realization of some deeper project (as in the killing of animals), but also a preparation for something, a way of training the body and the self for some impending, if often imaginary, ordeal.

So we are only mildly surprised when we find out what it was for which Lewis was preparing himself; and the prudent reservation of Dickey and of his narrator is just a precautionary measure: " 'I just believe,' Lewis said, 'that the whole thing is going to be reduced to the human body, once and for all. . . . I think the machines are going to fail, the political systems are going to fail, and a few men are going to take to the hills and start over.' . . . What kind of fantasy led to this? I asked myself. Did he have long dreams of atomic holocaust in which he had to raise himself and his family out of the debris of less strong folk and head toward the same blue hills we were approaching?" But this is Dickey's form of irony, his way of having his cake and eating it too: those of us who don't swallow Lewis' motivation can identify with the narrator and with his bemused reaction. A process of *displacement* is involved, in the Freudian sense of the word: the rational surface of the mind accepts the objection, while the unconscious remains symbolically and unconsciously committed to Lewis' enterprise.

Surely, however, the technological fear cannot be a primary one. I have always felt that the terror of atomic destruction, which is no doubt for some an existential reality, only masked some deeper social and political apprehension. And as for the fear of technological breakdown, reflecting as it does the computerization of modern industry, the decentralized systematization of monopoly capitalism, the net drawing tight, sweeping everything into an irrevocably total organization, here surely, it is the very *existence* of the great computerized industries which is the nightmare, and not the in any case distant and improbable prospect of their collapse.

The same ambivalence marks the presence of the ecological theme in a work like this. For the expedition was organized in the knowledge that this partially unexplored wilderness area would soon be flooded in order to make an artificial lake. In this perspective, we rejoin that old theme of the imminent destruction of the wilderness which Cooper sounded in the earliest volume of the Leatherstocking series, and which has in our own time received its strongest mythical expression in Faulkner's *Go Down Moses*. Yet the tragic spirit of such a theme is no guarantee of its intellectual adequacy: for the sense of tragedy springs from the feeling of the inevitability of the destruction of nature, and it is as consistent with Cooper's belief in the desirability of progress and the unavoidable necessity for civilization to displace the lower barbarous or savage forms of life, as it is with a Romantic hatred for civilization and the city in general. The first of these positions, indeed, can be squared with a systematic apologia for the worst business practices, the worst excesses of the acquisitive instinct, while the second is able to repudiate socialism itself in the name of a revolt against regimentation and a refusal of industrial organization and planning. Both "tragic" viewpoints thus remain imprisoned in the ideological myth which opposes Nature to Civilization, so that whichever alternative is chosen, it perpetuates the feeling that there is some radical incompatibility between individual life and the social order.

At this point, no doubt, it will be observed that Dickey's novel is in reality a *myth*, and that a myth-critical analysis of the book can quite adequately account for the disparity we have been feeling between Lewis' conscious motivation and the deeper logic of the wilderness journey. And, no doubt, it would not be altogether wrong to see the latter as a journey into the unconscious itself, back to primal origins: a descent into the underworld, from which, after a battle with ogres or giants, limping painfully, one man lost and two others disabled, the heroes are at length able to make their way back up into the light of day, bearing with them a story which can never be told. In the process, the most essential function of myth has been fulfilled: the creation of the Hero—not the Hercules of the outset, the henceforth crippled Lewis, who is as it were a mere traveling companion and elder Mentor—but rather the narrator himself, on whom the entire responsibility of the return journey falls, and who may thus be seen as a representative of some newer generation of more human and less legendary heroes.

Yet we must observe, in this context, that the characters—and with them the writer and the reader—never do make it all the way back to the earth's navel, to the place of primal origins: we have to do here, in short, with a myth incompletely realized, with a kind of imaginative short-circuit, in which, for whatever reason, the deeper logic or intent of the mythic wish-fulfillment finds itself abruptly blocked by the intrusion of alien realities or impulses.

On one level, of course, such imaginative incapacitation is part of Dickey's sociological raw material, and it is hardly astonishing that his characters— these slick and typical professional men of the post-industrial world, men sophisticated enough to choose the good life of small business and a relatively rural environment, and to make the money they need at the same time that they appreciate folk music and camping—are constitutionally unable to shed their America for something radically different. In this sense the cheapness of Dickey's style, the meretriciousness of his imagination, only faithfully reflect the shallowness of his characters as of contemporary American life in general. Such is indeed the burden of his own prize poem, "The Firebombing," where the World War II saturation bombing of Japan serves as the archetype for the pathological indifference, the numbed gum-chewing ataraxia of such American push-button warmaking, for which only middle-class suburbia is real:

> It is that I can imagine
> At the threshold nothing
> With its ears crackling off
> Like powdery leaves,
> Nothing with children of ashes, nothing not
> Amiable, gentle, well-meaning,
> A little   nervous for no
> Reason   a little worried   a little too loud
> Or too easygoing   nothing I haven't lived with
> For twenty years, still nothing not as
> American as I am, and proud of it.

Only Dickey's poem is *about* this phenomenon, it takes the lack of imagination as its object; whereas *Deliverance* presupposes precisely the exercise of that projective imagination, of that vision of where and what you are not, of which "The Firebombing" sung the absence. So from beyond the irrevocable boundary line of monopoly capitalism, a post-industrial America—as sealed and disinfected as an astronaut's capsule, brainwashed, as Norman Mailer will put it, "until it smelled like deodorant"—gazes with fatal incomprehension at other cultures and, indeed, at its own past as well.

Something of this inability to cope with difference is vividly conveyed to us by the climax of Dickey's story, where the heroes confront their human enemies; and, no doubt, to have your heroes rather than your heroines raped is a new twist posited as much on the conditioning and the shock potential of your audience as on any genuine deeper content or logic.

Still, when we look more closely at these new arrivals, something in their mode of narrative presentation catches our eye, something like a nagging distortion of perspective, an odd discrepancy in the form, some stylistic incongruity that alerts us to the presence of some deeper structural imbalance. The new characters suggest a combination of hillbilly inbreeding and degeneracy on the one hand and the most proverbial barnyard perversion on the other. Nor are we the only ones to receive these stereotyped impressions: " 'Escaped convicts' flashed up in my mind on one side," the narrator tells us, " 'Bootleggers' on the other." To see these figures juxtaposed beside the novel's heroes, those standardized plastic men of our own business society, is to have a curious feeling of aesthetic anachronism, of the mixture of historical styles: it is as though Dickey's subconscious had been rummaging inside the wrong box of costumes, had grasped the wrong set of characterological conventions by mistake; and it is an eerie experience, in among the brand new equipment, the bow-and-arrow set from Neiman Marcus, the electric guitars, and the suburban houses financed on the most modern credit plans, to come across these ghosts from an older past, from the Dust Bowl and Tobacco Road, faces that stare at us out of the old Evans and Agee album, that listened to Roosevelt over the old radio speakers and rode the Model-T Ford and voted for Huey Long.

Now perhaps we are in a better position to understand what kind of a confrontation it was for which Dickey's heroes had prepared themselves: it was the Thirties they went forth to meet, in some obscure way they journeyed into the wilderness to settle their accounts with the great radical tradition of the American past. Not technological breakdown, not some nagging sense of the unfulfillment of middle-class life, not atomic holocaust, not the heroic attempt to overcome nature or to find the very outer limits of the self, no, the new heroes whose legend *Deliverance* passes down to us are the frightened men of the modern American suburb, men for whom Nature is a kind of unconscious synonym of underdevelopment, and whose systematic and self-punishing gymnastics are, like the classic Western theories of counter-insurgency warfare, a way of beating the enemy at his own game.

The hillbilly figures are of course a disguise and a displacement: for if the 1930's still call to mind that older indigenous heritage of American resistance and insubordination from Roger Williams to Eugene V. Debs, the threat to the middle-class way of life today has taken another form: that of the peoples of the Third World, of the Blacks, of the intransigent and disaffected young. For a political fantasy, however, which does not wish to know its own name, these images of the Thirties provide an eminently suitable manifest content behind which the deeper logic of the story can be concealed. For the Thirties are dead, both figuratively and literally, and the triumph of the heroes over their class enemies can thus be draped in the mantle of historical necessity, the fantasy seeming to be confirmed by the very outcome of history itself. Even the political coloration of these substitute figures is useful camouflage, for since the beginning of the civil rights movement, the redneck as a political symbol has changed his meaning, and tends rather to set in motion associations of knownothingism and reaction, than of the agrarian populism of an older era: thus there is nothing in Dickey's symbolism itself which risks giving the game away and warning that you have passed beyond the bounds of a respectable and conventional political liberalism.

That the encounter should be couched in terms of violence and perversion is scarcely surprising: for the propertied classes have always understood the revolutionary process as a lawless outbreak of mob violence, wanton looting, vendettas motivated by ignorance, senseless hatred and *ressentiment*, terms which are here translated into degeneracy and general disrespect for life. As for the rape itself, however, some of Jean-Paul Sartre's analyses in *Saint Genet* suggest that as an event its choice is not quite so gratuitous as we might at first have thought: for in Sartrean terms, rape, in which the body is treated like an object and exposed defenseless to its enemies, is essentially a process of being *seen*. Being looked at is a rape, being raped is being looked at: such an interpretation suggests the deeper social import of that horrified powerless indignation of Dickey's heroes, who are thus seen as though for the first time by a hostile class which rises up against them as an equal, able to think its own thoughts about you and to see you for what you are with an inexorable severity that puts your own good conscience and your own comfortable images of yourself forever in question.

James Dickey's novel is thus a fantasy about class struggle in which the middle-class American property owner wins through to a happy ending and is able, by reconquering his self-respect, to think of himself as bathing in the legendary glow of a moderate heroism. But Dickey's artistic fault was not in expressing such content. For surely such fantasies are among the most inescapable facts about contemporary American daily life. And the therapeutic function of literature lies in its value as a "talking cure," as a way of bringing such buried fantasies to expression in the broad daylight of social consciousness, rather than wishing or arguing them away in some facile optimistic manner. Dickey's book is thus repellent for some reason other than that of its content as such, and I am defending something a little more complicated than the proposition that bad politics makes bad literature. What is the matter with Dickey's treatment of these social terrors is that he is himself possessed by them; he is as unaware, as profoundly unconscious, of their shaping presence as are his readers. His story is thus not an instrument of ideological demystification, but rather an outright political and social wish-fulfillment and as such it reinforces the very tendencies which it is the function of genuine art to expose.

[From "The Masculine Wilderness of the American Novel" A Review of *Deliverance* by James Dickey]

Carolyn Heilbrun

"... Dickey's ... achievement is one more version ... of ... the woman-despising American dream."

James Dickey achieved for the American novel its apotheosis of manliness. *Deliverance* captures in marvelously readable form the quintessential male fantasy. It is the latest in a series of fictional escapes into the "territory" where women do not go, where civilization cannot reach, where men hunt one another like animals and hunt animals for sport. Whatever Dickey's intention, his achievement is one more version—dare we hope it is the last?—of what Leslie Fiedler identified for us more than a decade ago in *Death and Love in the American Novel*: the woman-despising American dream. Dickey's only addition is sexual gymnastics. In *Deliverance*, we finally reach the moment for which a hundred years of the novel of masculinity have been preparing us. Out in the "territory," beyond the bounds of culture, the men rape each other. This innovation, however, is barely remarkable, sexual assault being as mandatory in today's fiction as it was forbidden in the day of Dickey's precursors: Melville, Fenimore Cooper, and Mark Twain.

With the wonderful accuracy of chance, Dickey's novel appeared in the centennial year of Charles Dickens's death—the similarity of their names making the coincidence resound as in a divine pun. For if Dickey's *Deliverance* is the ultimate version of the male-fantasy novel that forms the mainstream of U.S. fiction, Dickens's works are exceptional among non-American novels precisely in their similar refusal to allow full humanity to women. The male-fantasy novel of America and the novels of Dickens are alike in that they are profoundly anti-androgynous.

Androgyny—from *andros* (male) and *gyne* (female)—is an ideal which allows full humanity to a human being without confining him within the conventional expectations for his sex. Coleridge told us more than a century ago that "a great mind must be androgynous," and the androgyny of most

Originally published in *Saturday Review* (29 January 1972): 41–44. Reprinted by permission.

artists has frequently been commented upon. The ideal of androgyny, which does not address itself to the particular sexuality of individuals, desires for them many choices along the whole spectrum of experience. Seeking to free men from the compulsion to violence and women from the compulsion to submission, the androgynous ideal imagines for each human being the fulfillment of his unique destiny and also a less violent future for the world. Where novelists such as Dickey and Dickens deny humanity to women and by extension, to the feminine impulses in all human beings, they lock us up more firmly not only into our prison of gender, but also into a world that is now fatally dominated by the male fantasy ideal. . . .

Why was Dickey's novel such a popular success? When we have noted that he tells a good story, that the book is readable and well-paced, full of adventure and the thrill of the hunt, we must also recognize that there is something more: Dickey has given us once again that damnable American dream, that polarized world that Priestley so well described.

Ed, the narrator in Dickey's novel, has sexual intercourse with his wife the night before he takes off on his adventure. Even as he enters her, he thinks of a model, a perfect sex object he had observed in a photographic studio that afternoon: The girl, modeling underpants, had been otherwise nude and fondling a kitten called, of course, a pussy. "The girl from the studio threw back her hair and clasped her breast, and in the center of Martha's heaving and expertly working back, the [girl's] gold eye shone, not with the practicality of sex, so necessary to its survival, but the promise of it that promised other things, another life, deliverance." Longing to be delivered from his wife, whom, to be sure, he honors, Ed longs either for the masculine adventure in the wilds, or for the sex object with the pussy who, at the end of the novel, he says "would have liked to see . . . hold her breast once more, in a small place full of men."

When Ed has murdered a man in his wilderness adventure and is intrigued with the way the head of the body lolls and jerks, the only equally irritating phenomenon he can dredge up is his partner's secretary's mouth, "and her tiresome, hectoring personality." This is perhaps the only emotional reference to a woman throughout the whole sequence in the wilderness. Ed has fled with his buddies into the world of the American movie fantasy where it's "either him or us," where the need to kill is conveniently unavoidable, where murder and violence and the homosexual rape he calls "a kind of love" are all that can be mustered up in opposition to the "long declining routine of our lives."

When the most muscle-rippling character among Dickey's crew has his thigh smashed, Ed touches it to assess the damage and notices that "against the back of my hand his penis stirred with pain." Thus, the most ironic touch in Dickey's book suggests that in the manly escape into the wilderness, even the phallic principle is wounded.

How long must we wait before American novelists and critics, with their true gift of vision, will look clearly at this terrible masculine ideal from which our lives so sorely need deliverance?

A Radical Departure for James Dickey
[A Review of *Puella* by James Dickey]

SUSAN LUDVIGSON

"A surprisingly androgynous experience as real—and as idealized—as that of any male or female passage from child to adult."

Think of the towering, broad shouldered huntsman in the photographs: wide-brimmed Stetson shading the tanned face, bow and arrows gripped in one steady hand, "American Manhood" the invisible caption.

Think of the novel *Deliverance*, and the WW II poems, such as "The Firebombing," from the National Book Award-winning *Buckdancer's Choice*, or the much-anthologized "The Performance." Now here is *Puella*, his 11th collection of poems—a radical departure for James Dickey, whose image as a "man's man" is suddenly admirably enlarged. In *Puella* Dickey assumes the persona of his young wife Deborah, and in that role he explores and imagines a girl's growth toward maturity.

This isn't the first time James Dickey has written from a female perspective, of course. Who could forget his stunning long poem "Falling," in which a stewardess plunges from an airplane to her death. But here Dickey creates a sustained, book-length journey into, through, and beyond female adolescence. The choice of the Latin word "puella" (girl) suggests the mythic significance the poet intends for the life he conjures partly from fact, partly from romantic vision. The result? A surprisingly androgynous experience as real—and as idealized—as that of any male or female passage from child to adult.

Male writers who convincingly enter a woman's consciousness are relatively rare. Flaubert and James and a handful of others come to mind. Among contemporary poets, perhaps the most notable is Randall Jarrell, whose "Woman at the Washington Zoo" and several other poems are wonderful examples of the male writer transcending the limits of his own sex.

In *Self Interviews*, published a dozen years ago, Dickey acknowledges his affinity with Jarrell: "Randall Jarrell seemed so much like me. He had sort of the same background . . . there seemed to be something in the temperament

Originally published in *State*, Columbia, South Carolina (31 October 1982), G6. Reprinted by permission.

of the writer—I hadn't met him at that time—very much like the part of myself that I wanted most to set down on paper. There was a humanistic feeling of compassion and gentleness about him." Jarrell, a master of the persona poem in the female voice, suggests the difficulty of the task Dickey recently completed. In his poem "Cinderella" Jarrell writes: " 'What men want . . .' said the godmother softly— / How she went on it is hard for man to say."

Hard as it is, the effort to imagine the inner life not just of another person, but of the opposite sex, is worth the trouble. In *Puella*, Dickey does what many of us are trying to do—in poems and in living: to put ourselves so entirely into the minds and hearts and bodies of those unlike ourselves that we can truly empathize, truly know, through our own imaginative capacities, the joys and fears and failures of our fellow humans. To escape the limits of sex is to make possible a similar erasing of the boundaries of race, nationality, age—all those demarcations that separate us from each other. We can only applaud Dickey's emergence, in the fifth decade of his life, as a poet who speaks for a more encompassing humanity than one rooted primarily in male experience.

The voice in these poems remains, nonetheless, the distinctive voice of the James Dickey we know: here are the driving, recognizable rhythms of the loosely dactylic line (not real meter, but the dactyl and its mirror twin, the anapest, recur often enough to feel dominant). Here too is the romantic vision typical of many of Dickey's past poems (the subtitle for one poem is "Deborah as Winged Seed, Descending with Others," and for another "Imagining Herself as the Environment, She Speaks to James Wright at Sundown").

In "Deborah as Scion," the speaker explores her relationship with the female members of her own family:

> As I stand here going back
> And back, from mother to mother: I am totally them in the eyebrows,
> Breasts, breaths and butt:
> You, never met Grandmother of the fields
> Of death, who laid this frail dress
> Most freshly down, I stand now in your closed bones,
> Sucked-in, in your magic tackle, taking whatever . . .

We sense the authentic in this mythic search for identity, for one's place in the family, in the universe. At the end of the poem the persona speaks of the merging of these women:

> And we can hold, woman on woman,
> This dusk if no other
> and we will now, all of us combining,
> Open one hand.

> Blood into light Is possible: lamp, lace and tackle paired
>   bones of the deep Rapture
> surviving reviving, and wearing well
> For this sundown, and not any other,
> In the one depth
> Without levels, deepening for us.

The reader is drawn into the depth, into the sense of life deepening with understanding, with the prospect of wisdom.

And when, in "Deborah in Ancient Lingerie, in Thin Oak Over Creek," the speaker discovers her power to achieve, to be competent in boylike gymnastics as well as at anything else she envisions for herself, we share her triumph. Her insistent "I can do," echoed throughout the poem, is the affirmation too of the poet, who can make language the means to a break-through in perception, a risk not unlike Deborah's balancing on the oak limb.

Dickey once said, "You enter into the experience that you have imagined and try to realize it. And that entering and committing-to is what makes writing poetry so damned exciting." The successful imagining of another life, and of other lives, is equally exciting for the reader who asks Dickey's central question in *Puella*: "Who can tell who was born of what?"

Vatic Poesy
[A Review of *The Eagle's Mile* by James Dickey]

FRED CHAPPELL

". . . If there were a literary prize for Poetry That Has Shown Real Moxie, it ought to go to 'The Eagle's Mile.'"

James Dickey's poetry has been largely rooted in local personal experience and has enjoyed strong narrative interest. Even those malcontents who professed no love for his work had to admit that his poems never sounded like impenetrable translations from an impenetrable eastern European language, as so many contemporary American poems do. Now in his new book, "The Eagle's Mile," he lays himself open to this charge.

Mostly, though, the charge won't stick. For the most part, this new volume contains strong, highly original work, strikingly different from the work that built Dickey's formidable reputation. He had experimented previously, in a sheaf of poems called "Head Deep in Strange Sounds," toward some of the effects found here, especially in eight poems designated as "collaborations and rewrites" from other poets. But never had he established this idiom as basis for a book.

The idiom I refer to is the High Bardic, the vatic, the transcendent—the Pindaric Grandiose, if you will. It is the poetic attitude that sets for itself heroic visionary ambitions marching out to trample the limitations of ordinary poetic diction. It is the stentorian chant that gives forth lines like these from the title poem:

> In the eagle's mile
> Let Adam, far from the closed smoke of mills
> And blue as the foot
> Of every flame, true-up with blindside outflash
> The once-more instantly

Originally published in *State*, Columbia, South Carolina (9 December 1990), 6F. Reprinted by permission.

Wild world: over Brasstown Bald
Splinter uncontrollably whole."

Heady stuff. Not even the poet who wrote "The Shark's Parlor" has achieved quite this magnitude of intensity before. It is not harmed by its tonal resemblance to Gerard Manley Hopkins' work and is not much damaged by the errant little colloquialism "blindside" a word that appears in too many other poems here. Neither is it isolated in its intoxicated grandeur; almost every page of "The Eagle's Mile" will offer passages of similar delight and awe.

When he feels that his language is flagging, he tries to pump it up with a note of jarring slang ("I speak to you from where/ I was shook off'") or with tortured tropes ("play-penned/ With holocaust") or with disingenuous direct address ("Oh fire, come on! I trust you!"). A recurrent signal of loss of authority in many poems is the intrusion of a shouted affirmative: Yes, exclamation point: "Yes!"

These phrases are signs of anxiety rather than poetic excitement. Dickey is better whenever he slackens the decibel level and doesn't lumber about so heavily that he steps on his own diction. The opening of "The Little More" is fine and exact and convincing:

> But the little more: the little more
> This boy will be is hard
> For me to talk of
> But harder for him. Manhood is only a little more,
> A little more time, a little more everything than he
> Has on him now.

The poem continues in this elegant and moving tone until an interjected "Yes!" toward the end destroys the spell and reduces the last eight lines to a rubble of pointless verbiage.

There are evidences of strain everywhere. Besides the deliberate overuse of "blindside" and the obsolescent preposition "amongst" and the insistence on gerunds until the repeated ing-sounds ding like a pawnshop full of alarm clocks and the ubiquitous self-applauding "Yes!" and the words "eagle" and "glory" and "gold" stuck about like ornaments on Federal period furniture, there is some plain old "all-time" "winning hand" "simmering like a mainspring" bad writing. Here are the final lines of "Weeds": "Don't come down;/ Come forward. A man loves you."

If there were a literary prize for Poetry That Has Shown Real Moxie, it ought to go to "The Eagle's Mile." James Dickey has put everything on the line and has come off, on balance, a winner. He has suffered some pretty steep losses, but overall the book is a victory. If in some places he has not succeeded, there are others in which he has advanced beyond what he has done before and has done so in a new and unexpected fashion.

James Dickey shows us what his vatic idiom is capable of in such whole poems as "Gila Bend," "Night Bird," "Daybreak," "Air," "The Six," "Expenses," and "Heads." Then there are lines and phrases and sections of great force and beauty scattered throughout other poems. When he is good, he is good to a fine extreme. When he is good, he will set down a breathtaking passage like this one from "The Olympian":

> And all the time, all the time,
> Under the brown-browed, rose-ash glower
> Of the smog-bank, the crows, long gone
> Gray with the risen freeways, were thronging and hawing
> To be Doves of Peace.

When he is bad, he writes as badly as anyone else who attempts such tall flights. He must have foreseen the risks; he must have known that nonsense, silliness, and dull rhetoric are the abysses that gape beneath the poet as high-soaring glider pilot. On such steep windshears of artistic trial, a poet's critical faculties can find little purchase. He is likely to write sentences utterly daft: "Prison-paleness/ Over the streets between strobes/ Unfailingly." He will sometimes follow a pure and ringing image, "a scythe-sighing flight of low birds," with a lugubrious thudding locution, "I, oversouling for an instant // With them." He can set down lines embarrassingly banal—"Godfather, I say // To him: not father of God, but assistant / Father to this one"— without seeming to realize what he has said. He will plumb bathos to what one hopes is its limit; in one poem, he says of the sea that it is "Up front for all of us!"

Curiously, it is not his ambition that betrays him, but some old lapses of self-confidence.

ESSAYS

♦

James Dickey at Vanderbilt: A Memoir

CALHOUN WINTON

When James Dickey signed up for classes at Vanderbilt University in the summer of 1946, he saw around him a somewhat dingy collection of redbrick buildings, crowded helterskelter onto a hillside in residential Nashville. Summers were hot and humid, and in the winter black coaldust poured from nearby chimneys and smokestacks—pollution of a kind and degree that would outrage present-day undergraduates and mobilize them to action. The "city's western border," on which (according to the Alma Mater) Vanderbilt stood and still stands, had in fact long since proceeded westward itself. Vanderbilt was an urban university, and though the oaks and hackberry trees provided some green relief, it was not a prepossessing place. One went there for an education; that was why Dickey joined hundreds of other veterans in the long registration lines.[1]

At the end of the Second World War, Vanderbilt was generally regarded, along with Duke, Chapel Hill, and Tulane, as a premier university in the region—a school where one could get an education substantially as good as that offered at Yale, Bryn Mawr, or Princeton, and much less expensive. The combination of a high-quality education and a bargain price was what had made Vanderbilt attractive before the war to that brilliant galaxy of writers and thinkers who styled themselves the Fugitives. The quality of education was of course somewhat illusory in 1946. (Vanderbilt really was inexpensive, as we shall see.) But Vanderbilt's educational renown had *always* been a bit of an illusion; Cleanth Brooks recently spoke to me about the disappointment he felt when he actually got down to classwork there in the Golden Age.[2] In 1946 the university was coasting to a considerable extent on the reputation of the Fugitives and of its justly distinguished medical school.[3]

The aura was not all illusion, however—many first-rate faculty members taught there—and the point is that most southerners believed that Vanderbilt's excellence was self-evident: year after year it kept producing good doctors, good writers, Rhodes Scholars. It had to be doing something right.

This was the sort of school that would attract many a bright, ambitious veteran, coming out of the service resolved to make up for lost time. It also attracted, at least in the area of the arts and humanities with which I was

---

This essay was written specifically for this volume and is published here for the first time.

acquainted, a lot of veterans who weren't certain about just what they wanted to do with their new freedom, but were content to be around books and ideas for a while, to reflect and sort things out. There were elements of both ambition and reflectiveness evident in Dickey, when I first came to know him in 1949.

Vanderbilt in those days was an amazingly inexpensive place for a veteran. The GI Bill stipend was amply enough to cover Vanderbilt's tuition and fees, *and* to buy books. In addition, you were paid a modest monthly living allowance (105 dollars a month if you were married), and many veterans also had saved money in the military because there had not been much on which to spend their pay. If the veteran's faculty advisor approved a book, the G.I. Bill would pay for it. My benevolent advisor, Monroe K. Spears, approved just about anything he thought might contribute to my education, and that was plenty. I remember buying an approved copy of Wallace Steven's *The Man with the Blue Guitar* in the Vanderbilt Bookstore, on Jim Dickey's recommendation. Dickey grabbed the book out of my hands and read from the title poem as we stood there in the store aisle, accenting the reading to make his point: "Things as they are / Are *changed* upon the blue guitar."

This was before the postwar escalation in book prices; in 1949 Vanderbilt estimated the total cost of required textbooks per term at between 15 and 20 dollars.[4] Nashville and Vanderbilt were bookish places anyway for those so inclined, and by that time Dickey had built an impressive library collection of his own, emphasizing poetry and literary criticism. He lives among those books, and their followers, to this day.

Dickey entered Vanderbilt with some credits transferred from his first year at Clemson. He was able to escape the freshman class activities which still existed in residual form and, if he chose, the sorority and fraternity system, the "Greeks," which dominated campus undergraduate life. He chose to avoid it. The social side of college—fraternity beer busts, gym dances, cheerleader tryouts—he simply ignored.

Or perhaps there are transmuted echoes of his attitude toward this world in the poem Dickey published in the Vanderbilt literary magazine, *The Gadfly*. The poem, his earliest published work—and a good one—is entitled "Christmas Shopping, 1947." The poem is admirably analyzed elsewhere in this volume by Jim Elledge, who sees it as exemplifying the poet's feeling of isolation in the urban, materialistic environment. While I agree with Elledge's general analysis, I'd like to suggest a particular reading. "The bulging present fills / All calendars with gowns and tumbling clowns." Gowns and tumbling clowns; gym dances and cheerleaders?

Athletics, though, were another matter. Dickey's superior hand / eye coordination would get the attention of any athletics director today. In later years this coordination was demonstrated by his expertise with bow and arrow. Less familiar, no doubt, but related, is his astounding ability to throw playing cards into a hat, a skill honed (as he told me) by practice during those hours and days of waiting that everyone in the military service endured. Another way of killing service time is illustrated by his *Gadfly* poem, "Whittern and the Kite." We may imagine Dickey tossing cards at his flight helmet in the ready room, while Whittern enrages the "Clausewitz colonel" by flying his kite outside on the taxiway.

He had the necessary attributes for a wide receiver in football: he was big, and both quick and fast, and, as noted earlier, his hand / eye coordination was nearly perfect. At Clemson he had in fact played wingback for Frank Howard and Banks McFadden—wingback was the position which evolved into today's wide receiver. But he did not go out for football at Vanderbilt; instead he joined the track team, which was just then being revived after a wartime hiatus, as a hurdler. His brother Tom had been an Olympic-class sprinter at Louisiana State University, and though Dickey was not that fast he was good enough to win his letter. The only photograph of him which I have found in *The Commodore*, the Vanderbilt yearbook, shows him standing in his running gear with the track team, gazing somberly at the camera, next to John North, who was also captain of the football team.

Dickey was in splendid physical condition, lean and hard as flint, when I first encountered him in 1949. This was in Monroe Spears's seminar in eighteenth-century literature. It was the more surprising, therefore, when, as we were coming out of class one day, he leaned toward me and asked, "Cal, have you ever thought about physical *decay?*" This led to a discussion of bone imagery in the poetry of John Donne and John Dryden, moving to similar imagery in the work of various twentieth-century poets—bones were getting a considerable play among poets back then.

The curriculum which Dickey followed as an undergraduate major in English and then as a graduate student encouraged such eclecticism. It would no doubt be regarded as hopelessly old-fashioned today. All students took freshman composition and literature. ("One hour is devoted to the study of masterpieces; two hours are devoted to composition.")[5] Then majors had a sophomore survey of English literature, various elective courses, and a required senior comprehensive class. The senior seminar was conducted by faculty members specializing in different areas of English and American literature, each of whom taught a segment of the course: Walter Clyde Curry for Chaucer and the medieval period, Monroe Spears for the eighteenth century, Richmond Croom Beatty for American literature, and so on. This was a small-scale undertaking. In Dickey's senior year the entire English Department faculty consisted of only seven members: four full, two associate, and one assistant professor.

The necessarily superficial treatment of the material in the senior comprehensive had its virtues, however. As my wife, who was a year ahead of Dickey in the same curriculum, has observed, "At the end of the senior seminar you had a good idea of what you didn't know, and how to go about filling the gaps in your knowledge." Beyond certain distribution requirements, the undergraduate student was substantially free and was encouraged to pursue his or her own inclinations, or as the anonymous author of the *Bulletin* put it, to "elect those [courses] which will improve his general acquaintance with the several fields of knowledge" (p. 79).

Again, by today's academic standards this sentiment may seem quaint, trite, and laughable, but at least in Dickey's case it was effective: he *did* improve his acquaintance with the several fields of knowledge, such as astronomy. During the war he had studied astronomy in flight school, to the extent required for understanding aerial navigation. As it happened, astronomy has had a continuing, if somewhat tenuous, existence at Vanderbilt since the earliest days of the school: the little jewelbox of an observatory—demolished, alas, in recent years—was built in 1875 in time for the first full year of classes and was supervised by the great comet-finder Edward E. Barnard.[6] In 1948 astronomy was only a one-man division within the Department of Physics and Astronomy, but Carl Seyfert was an extraordinary teacher. Dickey enrolled in General Astronomy as a prerequisite to Observational Astronomy ("Theory and Use of Astronomical Instruments"), brushing up on the necessary mathematics. Under Seyfert's direction he gazed through the night skies at those strange constellations which had once been only navigational aids for him. "I have always wanted to energize what little I remember about the stars and galaxies into poetry," Dickey has said.[7] Astronomer and poet; for literature it was a fortunate conjunction of the stars.

Dickey's academic talents had meanwhile been spotted in the English Department as well. Betty Spears, wife of Monroe, was teaching a section of English 101, the required freshman composition and literature course—helping the department cope with the sudden flood of incoming students. The first paper she assigned was on Edward Donahue's story, "Head by Scopas." Working her way through the stack of themes, she came on one that gave her pause. "Monroe," she said, "I have a problem. I don't believe a student in freshman comp. is capable of writing this." Spears asked to see the paper, read it over, and pointed out several places that would not have survived an editor's blue pencil, though agreeing that it was an essay of outstanding quality. "What's the student's name?" Betty turned to the coverage. "James Dickey."

She recalls that Dickey sat in the front row, with his long legs folded in front of him, asked intelligent questions, but refrained from displaying his superior intelligence. When she returned the paper she suggested that he take her husband's literature survey course the following semester, which he did. Spears encouraged him to attempt differing verse forms, and the *Gadfly* poems show him doing just that. Monroe Spears, Dickey later recalled, had "a mind like a laser beam."[8]

This interaction between student writer and faculty member was unusual at Vanderbilt but not unique. Allen Tate had been admitted to the readings of the Fugitives while he was still an undergraduate.[9] Peter Taylor told me that Donald Davidson had taken him in hand during freshman registration and introduced him to John Crowe Ransom.[10] Taylor and Randall Jarrell were each writing as undergraduates (they had followed Ransom to Kenyon College before Dickey's arrival at Vanderbilt).[11] Fraternities and sororities dominated campus social life, but a small literary / artistic subculture existed there and had for a long time.

The Calumet Club had been founded in 1906 "to strengthen the literary spirit of the university,"[12] but it was for men only and though the Club continued, by the 1940s Vanderbilt was thoroughly coeducational. By then the focus of literary activity, with respect to publication, was the *Gadfly*, the student literary magazine "published quarterly," as its masthead stated, "by the students of Vanderbilt University." The *Gadfly*, as its name implied, was quite self-consciously out of the Vanderbilt social mainstream. The Spring 1948 issue, in which "Sea Island" and "King Crab and Rattler" appeared, has on its cover a sketch of a spotted horse, kicking vigorously backward. Laura Miles, now well-known as a painter, was art editor for that issue. Aside from the cover there was no visual art other than one typographic ornament, presumably due to the expense. Bertrand Goldgar, distinguished professor of eighteenth-century studies at Lawrence University, was then poetry editor and remembers accepting the poems, but recalls Dickey only as a tall figure striding across campus wearing his Air Force flight jacket.[13]

Dickey's last *Gadfly* poem, "Whittern and the Kite," appeared in the Summer 1949 issue. In that same issue is an essay by Marion Junkin, who was teaching art history and studio art in the Humanities Program—there was no art department. Entitled "The Case for Art," Junkin's essay presents a parable of Hershel, an affluent young man who attends university, joins a fraternity, and just after graduation marries "a delightfully stupid little orchid rack from a neighboring sorority." He goes into business and is soon "on the old tread mill—work-commute-home." "Hershel had absolutely no interest in poetry, music, pictures, sculpture, the drama, the novel or anything that might have given his spiritual nature the pleasures and satisfactions it deserved." Hershel ends up in Alcoholics Anonymous, divorced from his orchid rack. This parable struck close to home, to those of us who *were* interested in the arts. Lee Preston (he is now my colleague, professor of business and management at the University of Maryland), then non-fiction editor, accepted Junkin's essay.[14] Preston was also student manager of the University Theatre, which that fall presented *The Little Foxes*. I acted in it; according to the 1950 *Commodore*, it played "to capacity audiences." To those of us involved in the production, Hellman's play seemed to be a variation on Junkin's theme. It was worrisome.

The international situation was worrying, too. The Berlin Blockade was going on, and especially among the veterans there was a pervasive feeling that another big war was approaching, probably sooner than later, this time with the Soviet Union. Many of us, Dickey and myself included, had entered the reserves after service rather than accepting an outright discharge. If you joined a reserve or National Guard unit you could pick up some extra money. Those who had not been in the service faced the likelihood of the draft.

One way of dealing with all this was by avoiding it, by going on to graduate school. The G.I. Bill encouraged graduate study. The Vanderbilt Graduate School back then was small, but intelligently and humanely administered by Dean Philip Davidson. Course requirements were not onerous, though they included a thesis for the master's degree. In this context, graduate school looked like an attractive alternative, where one could continue—for a while anyway—reading and talking and listening to music and looking at pictures, a fate preferable to Hershel's, or to the service.

There were people worth getting to know at Vanderbilt in those days, but acquaintance was happenstance. One felt the lack of a central meeting place; no graduate student I knew set foot in the student union, which was the domain of the undergradutes. On the other hand, except in the classroom, few dividing lines existed among like-minded undergraduates, graduate students, and faculty (especially younger faculty), or for that matter among academic and nonacademic people. This had been true in the days of the Fugitives as well. In addition to those already mentioned, I remember Dan Young from Mississippi, Jesse Hill Ford from West Tennessee, Joe Bryant from Kentucky, and Louise and Donald Cowan from Texas, each of whom has gone on to individual distinction. Most of us lived in rented rooms, or if married, in small apartments carved out of the basements or upper stories of big old houses—there were many such houses on the west side of Nashville. Monroe and Betty Spears, for example, lived in a faculty apartment near the football stadium, a converted army barracks the rooms of which were so small you could almost touch opposite walls by spreading your arms. Parties were informal, crowded into one or another of these apartments, and the talk was spirited and good, or so it seemed, and still seems in retrospect: politics, religion, literature—especially literature, in our association. Friends of mine who were at Columbia and Louisville at the time have told me the atmosphere was much the same, allowing for local differences.

This was the association into which James Dickey brought his new wife. He had met Maxine Syerson in Nashville, and they were married on 4 November 1948.[15] Maxine worked in the downtown office of American Airlines; my earliest remembrance of her is in her airline blue uniform. She was a young woman of great beauty and considerable wit, but not much formal education—nothing beyond a convent high school. My wife was working downtown, too, at an advertising agency, writing copy for the Grand Ole Opry. When the two couples got together for the first time—I can't pinpoint the precise date—she and Maxine, as southerners say, hit it off right away.

As noted earlier, I had first met Dickey in Monroe Spears's seminar on Restoration and eighteenth-century literature. The course began during September heat—this was before general air-conditioning—and my first recollection of Dickey is as he was coming out of class in the Joint University Library, wearing a white T-shirt and khaki trousers, with a Phi Beta Kappa key hanging from his belt. Although he had declined to have his picture taken for the *Commodore*, he was justifiably proud of his academic accomplishments. Many of the Vanderbilt writers—Ransom, Tate, Warren, Brooks, Jarrell, Taylor—had been excellent undergraduate students as well.

It immediately became clear that some academic ability would be required in Spears's class. A very large number of graduate students—more than 20, as I recall—assembled for the first meeting. In graduate school only grades of A or B received degree credit. Spears surveyed the group. "I realize this is a graduate course," he began, "but let it be understood that I will not hesitate to give C's [low groans], D's [more groans], or F's [chorus of groans]." Enrollment dwindled right away, and the seminar became a proper seminar.

Teaching methods varied in the graduate courses. The two that Dickey and I took together offered contrasting styles. Richmond Croom Beatty was then in the closing years of a distinguished career as a scholar of American literature, all of which, since graduate school, he had spent at Vanderbilt. His year-long Seminar in American Literature presented a chronological survey of the major writers, as they were understood in those days: Irving, Poe, Hawthorne, Melville, Whitman, and so on. Reading was from a standard anthology, of which Beatty was coeditor, and the approach was lecture / discussion, with emphasis on lecture, or perhaps more accurately, commentary. Beatty impressed a graduate student as a serious, even somber teacher, seated almost immobile at his desk in the front of the classroom, speaking in a cracked, tobacco-scarred voice. I am ashamed to say that Dickey and I indulged in such juvenile activities as exchanging handwritten notes which commented on the idiosyncrasies of the author being studied, or of the teacher or fellow students. But Dickey respected Beatty's considerable learning and asked him to direct his master's thesis.

Monroe Spears employed a teaching style as different from Beatty's as can be imagined. He was of course much younger than Beatty, indeed not many years older than the other veterans in the class. Spears had completed his doctorate at Princeton before entering the service and in cold weather sported a camel hair topcoat, much admired by graduate students, from his days at Old Nassau. He was then at the beginning of an outstanding career in teaching and writing, which continues.

He tended to be active in the classroom, jumping up from time to time to write something that had occurred to him on the chalkboard, listening to student reports with a straight, serious face, as if receiving information of the highest importance, and then directing precise and pointed questions at the reporter. He had a way of keeping one somewhat off balance; no sly, exchanged notes in this class. Early in the seminar, I remember, he remarked as if casually, "By the end of the term I would expect you graduate students to be able to distinguish the couplets of John Dryden from those of Alexander Pope, without reference to their content." Dickey and I compared notes after class. "Wow," he or I said, "those pentameter couplets look pretty much the same to me." Spears was right, of course, and we did learn to distinguish them.

Spears was an effective teacher of all of the literary genres but it always appeared to me that his special forte was teaching poetry. He is himself a poet—though we did not know it at the time—and his subsequent scholarly and critical work on Matthew Prior and W. H. Auden seem to confirm the hypothesis. Among many other things, Spears's seminar focused on the formal and technical aspects of poetry, and I believe Dickey has always valued those strings of a poet's bow, even though his poetry of recent years has moved toward metrical freedom. Critics who complained of a poet's having "too much technique," he once told me, were all wrong. "I don't believe a poet can have 'too much technique' anymore than a brain surgeon can have too much technique."

He was working at his own poetry in those days, regularly, trying different line-lengths, rhythms, casting widely for imagery; the *Gadfly* poems and the unpublished poem "The Earth Drum," a copy of which he gave me at about this time, testify to this experimentation. The nature of the poetic symbol and the definition of poetic merit preoccupied him. Sometimes, sitting on the grassy sward behind the library, we would play literary games. "All right," one or the other of us might say. "Romantic poets: which one is the best?" Answer. "Why?" Answer. "How is this demonstrated?" "Best line of the poet's that you can remember." "*Worst* line." (The anthology of bad poetry, *The Stuffed Owl*, had recently been republished and served as crib notes for the latter category, though I remember that his nomination for the worst of Wordsworth was drawn from his formidable memory: "And at the Hoop we landed, famous inn.")

The literary symbol was a central critical concern of the time. Dickey was working his way through signification, both for his own poetry and for the master's thesis topic that he had chosen. As noted earlier, this thesis was to be composed under the direction of Richmond Beatty, but it was only incidentally in the area of literary history. The title was "Symbol and Image in the Shorter Poems of Herman Melville," and as one would expect, it was exceptionally well written. Some scholar competent in both Melville and Dickey studies should examine it. I remember being impressed by his treatment of the Civil War poems (and his citation to me of a *Stuffed Owl* candidate, a line from one of those poems which rhymed "cannister" with "bannister"). A passage from Dickey's thesis abstract provides an indication of his concerns and his approach. "In regard to Melville's verse, the method followed is that of pursuing a given image through a number of separate instances wherein it is invoked and attempting to determine whether the connotations of these images point to a common area of signification. A single poem, "The Haglets," is taken as the central document of Melville's system of symbols. . . ."[16]

In the spring of 1950 I was also writing a master's thesis, on Dryden's translations of Juvenal and Vergil, under the direction of Monroe Spears. The routine of classes and typewriters was broken by expeditions to Zibart's Book Store, two or three miles downtown, but well worth the trip. Zibart's had been at least since Fugitive times the focus of bookish Nashville; their regular advertisements in the *Gadfly* read "Come In and Browse," and Dickey took them at their word. The Dickeys had an automobile—an old white flivver—which provided transportation in warm weather to the Willow Plunge swimming pool in Franklin, or in springtime to the Gerst Brewery for bock beer. Maxine Dickey had found copper cups in which she prepared Moscow Mules on ceremonial occasions, somehow finding genuine ginger beer to mix with the vodka.

Spring turned into that summer of 1950, classes were over, the master's theses were in and approved. Jim had a job offer from Rice University which he decided to accept. I had been admitted to the doctoral program at Princeton. The tracks of our lives seemed set, but old Virgil had it right long ago: the Fates judged otherwise, *fata visum aliter*. The twenty-fifth of June 1950 came and went. Within a year we were both back in uniform.

Notes

1. Dickey is aware that I am writing this memoir but I have not discussed it with him. Monroe and Betty Spears read an early draft of this, for which I am grateful. Errors and interpretations are, of course, my own.

2. Conversation at the Katherine Anne Porter symposium, University of Maryland, College Park, May 1991.

3. See Paul Conkin, *Gone with the Ivy: A Biography of Vanderbilt University* (Knoxville: University of Tennessee Press, 1985), pp. 403–44. The new Chancellor, Harvie Branscomb, "offered a most depressing evaluation of Vanderbilt in the fall of 1946" (444).

4. *Bulletin of Vanderbilt University* (hereafter *Bulletin*) 49, no. 4 (General Catalogue), October 1949, 71. This was in a sample student budget.

5. *Bulletin*, 101.

6. Conkin, 47, 75.

7. As quoted in Ronald Baughman, ed., *The Voiced Connections of James Dickey: Interviews and Conversations* (Columbia: University of South Carolina Press, 1989), 90.

8. Baughman, *Voiced Connections*, 64.

9. See Paul Conkin, *The Southern Agrarians* (Knoxville: University of Tennessee Press, 1988), 14.

10. Personal conversation at the symposium for Taylor, Baltimore, May, 1991.

11. See William H. Pritchard, *Randall Jarrell: A Literary Life* (New York: Farrar, Straus and Giroux, 1990), 25–50.

12. *The Commodore* (yearbook), 1950, 291.

13. Personal conversation, Seattle, March 1992.

14. And neighbor and friend, to whom I am indebted for lending me his copies of *Gadfly* from which I have worked.

15. I use Ronald Baughman's chronology in *The Voiced Connections of James Dickey*, 5–8.

16. *Bulletin of Vanderbilt University*, No. 2: Abstract of Theses For the Academic Year 1949–50 (Nashville: August, 1950), 79.

James Dickey Between Wars:
An "Appreciation" of *The Gadfly* Poems

JIM ELLEDGE

Like an old codger who relives his life too often without introspection, I'm uncertain of the chronology in the development of my interest in James Dickey's poetry. I believe it blossomed one undergraduate day during 1969. I remember having been put off several months earlier by what I referred to in those days as Dickey's "showmanship" when he appeared and read his poetry on *The Johnny Carson Show*.[1] Shortly after Dickey's televised appearance, I complained to Allen Neff, a poet and one of my teachers, about what, in my youthful zeal, I considered to be Dickey's betrayal. I felt that if Dickey were a *real* poet, he would never have compromised his art by appearing, wedged between commercials for panty hose and aftershave, on one of the ultimate bastions of hype in our culture. Knowing me all too well, Allen tactfully showed me his copy of the limited edition of Dickey's *Two Poems of the Air*.[2] The volume was beautifully published on rice paper in Carolingian script in 1964, during Dickey's tenure as writer-in-residence at Reed College in Portland, Oregon. Not only did the stunning production of the volume impress me, but I was also dazzled by and had learned to revere, like many students of literature, the term "limited edition" itself. That it was autographed *and* numbered incited my fledgling interest.

Allen's tactful attempt to get me off my high horse and to teach me something about contemporary U.S. poetry worked. He later loaned me trade editions of Dickey's *Poems 1957–1967* and, after it, *Self-Interviews*. Skimming the collection of poems, my eyes landed on "Approaching Prayer," a poem unlike any I had ever read before (*Poems* 163–68). It rattled me, firing my own imagination with Dickey's narrator's transformation into two other identities during the course of the poem. Dickey, whose persona is that of a son who has come to pray in his dead "father's empty house," slips into "the grey sweater" his "father wore in the cold," attaches "The spurs of his [father's] gamecocks" to his heels, and drops "the head of a boar [he] once helped to kill with two arrows" over his head, figuratively metamorphosing for a few

This essay originally appeared in a shorter version in *Pikestaff Forum* 3 (1980): 12–13. Reprinted here by permission of the editor and author.

moments into both his father and the boar while, simultaneously maintaining his own identity. Thus garbed, the son inhales "the breath of life / For the dead hog," experiencing the animal's last seconds of life as it witnessed

> *A young aging man with a bow*
> *And a green arrow pulled to his cheek*
> *Standing deep in a mountain creek bed,*
> *Stiller than trees or stones. . . .*

"I have seen the hog see me kill him," the narrator reports, while

> Hoping only that
> The irrelevancies one thinks of
> When trying to pray
> Are the prayer. . . .

The poem's display of alienation, fear, and longing seemed utterly, frighteningly honest to me, an echoing word of the late sixties and early seventies, a time characterized by metamorphosis. One decade turned into another. A young and idealistic group shed its academic garb and donned the uniforms of patriots or, from the opposite point of view, the masks of traitors. Parents pitted themselves against their children, and vice versa, the bond of blood dissolving, and rancor taking its place. Skirmishes assumed a biblical degree of conflagration. *Assassination* and *massacre*, words once virtually foreign to American citizens, became as common in U.S. homes as television sets. I saw struggle everywhere and no escape. Only Dickey's poetry revealed an understanding and exploration of *becoming, transformation,* and *metamorphosis*—terms, I later learned, applied time after time to Dickey's works by his interpreters.

I was hooked.

Years later, a full-fledged aficionado of Dickey's poetry, I began research on a book-length bibliography of works by and about James Dickey.[3] Rereading his *Self-Interviews*, I chanced upon a statement he made about his undergraduate days at Nashville's Vanderbilt University which began to obsess and annoy me increasingly, like a pesky fly. "Nobody cared much about what poetry I had written," he mentioned. "I published a couple of little things in the student literary magazine, *The Gadfly*" (*Self-Interviews*, 40). Many poets begin publishing while undergraduates in student literary journals, but what surprised me was that no bibliography of Dickey's works inventoried his poems in the *Gadfly*. Weren't bibliographers readers of his work? Didn't they know the poems existed? Or did they feel that his earliest, and probably most immature poems should be excluded from their lists? Certain that the *Gadfly* poems would be at least tangentially important to contemporary or future scholars and critics of Dickey's oeuvre, I decided to track them down for my own record of his career.

Luckily for me, an anonymous librarian at the Joint University Libraries in Nashville quickly responded to my request for photocopies of anything by Dickey appearing in the *Gadfly*. I received four poems: the earliest, "Christmas Shopping, 1947" by Jim Dickey; "Sea Island" and "King Crab and Rattler" by James Dickey; and the last, "Whittern and the Kite," by James L. Dickey.[4] I realized, as I began to study the four *Gadfly* poems, that I was possibly the only person in nearly 30 years to have read them. The anonymous librarian who had responded to my request and who may have taken a few moments out of a hectic schedule to glance at them was the only other contender for that honor, I decided. I eventually completed *James Dickey: A Bibliography, 1947–1974* and its supplement with the help of the librarian in Nashville and others unknown to me.

In his introductory comments to Dickey's first collection, *Into the Stone and Other Poems*, poet-critic John Hall Wheelock stated: "His themes abstracted from their particularizations could be listed, roughly, as follows: family, symbolized in the dead brother, the uncle, wife, and son, the unborn child; death and dying as experienced through its occurrence in the family; solitude and union with nature, and a symbolic resurrection through return to society and to the family group; the life of the airman, overseas, in war-time; and, finally, love . . ." (*Stone*, 23). We can readily apply Wheelock's observation—"the life of the airman, overseas, in war-time"—to the *Gadfly* poems. All were published from 1947 to 1949, only a few years after World War II, during which Dickey flew in the South Pacific for the Army Air Corps, and more than a decade before Wheelock's remarks. All have been reprinted in the limited edition *Veteran Birth*, the collection's title implying that the four poems were born out of Dickey's GI experiences.

After publication of *Into the Stone and Other Poems*, interpreters of Dickey's work have often pointed out that the major themes Wheelock initially observed crop up time and time again, to the chagrin of some and the delight of others. Indeed, the theme of war appears in many of Dickey's later, individual works, such as "Drums Where I Live," the second poem of "Two Poems of the Military," in which Dickey's narrator, living near a military base where maneuvers are being held, reveals his inability to escape war:

> Someone said it is
> Comfort, comforting to hear them.   Not every
> Sun-up, neighbor: now and then I wish I had a chance
> To take my chances
> With silence.
>
> (*Strength*, 21)

War also informs entire books by Dickey, either overtly, as with *Helmets* or his novel, *Alnilam*,[5] or by implication, as with *The Zodiac*, a lengthy poem based on one with the same title by Hendrik Marsman, a sailor who died in the North Atlantic in 1940 (*Zodiac*, 7). The surname "Marsman" strengthens Dickey's poem's tie to war, a link which originated in Dickey's earliest work, the *Gadfly* poems, and which extends the whole of his published oeuvre.

"Christmas Shopping, 1947" opens inside a department store with Dickey describing shoppers in a passage that chillingly echoes the regimented and robotic "life of the airman . . . in war-time":

> Wingless, wayworn, aging beneath a perpetual
> folded sun, despair unsounded in the eyes' drum,
> these wheel in lax processional
> past the cold counter and listless stall. . . .

Disgusted by shoppers' mindless attention to materialism, the "desire in rayon, in cellophane the dream," as well as by the subsequent perversion of the season's true meaning, "the bartered birth," Dickey's narrator leaves the store, in an attempt to escape the crass commercialism around him, for the sidewalk where he sees "the day, the frozen intercourse of streets; / glass placid, grave glitter of guilt and gift. . . ." However, he escapes only partially at best. Although he's left the shopping spree behind him, outside he notices a traffic jam—a noisy, chaotic situation—then the tranquillity of storefront plate glass, its peace compromised by Christmas lights, tinsel, etc.—the "grave glitter of guilt and gift"—which decorate them. A pun on death and seriousness, *grave* suggests that the materialistic way individuals observe the birth of Jesus is deadly and serious, is "glitter" not gold, and originates in feelings of guilt and sin as expiation, not in feelings of love and generosity.

In juxtaposition to the materialism and inappropriate methods of celebration, Dickey relates what Christmas *is* about: "the lip, the sponge, the God-swung temple-lash." The true meaning has been forgotten:

> . . . here the current of the five wounds fails,
> the igneous cross no longer lights the mesh
> and marrow of the hugely living.   The bulging present fills
> all calendars with gowns and tumbling clowns. . . .

Two levels of movement exist within the poem. On one, Dickey travels from within to outside the department store. On the other, he moves from the general, "the day," to the specific, "guilt and gift," in essence from external to internal, physical to psychological, secular to sacred. Dickey's poem suggests that life in the U.S. in December, 1947 is dark, characterized by ignorance and the lack of Christ's influence, the Light, while simultaneously oriented toward materialism and the physical—"gowns"—not the spiritual, toward the entertaining or the absurd—"clowns"—not seriousness and awareness. In the poem's concluding three lines, the narrator escapes, if only in his mind, from what had surrounded and disgusted him. He thinks "of chestnut waters / linked back to back with autumn floating leaves, / the flow of stallions over cloud-white hills" in a fantasy that, in opposition to the Christmas shopping, implies freedom, naturalness, quiet, spirituality, even sensuality—qualities which, the reader assumes, the narrator finds lacking in the celebration around him, and even in contemporary life in general. Dickey has transformed his environment from one that was spiritually and psychologically debilitating, with other negative attributes, to one in which he may survive.

In his post-*Gadfly* work, Dickey rarely permits himself the type of social criticism which appears in the first 14 lines of "Christmas Shopping, 1947." However, many of Dickey's poems are anchored in "solitude and union with nature," to borrow Wheelock's phrase, as is the conclusion to "Christmas Shopping, 1947." In "The Dusk of Horses" (*Poems*, 113–14), for example, Dickey describes a hill—"The grass is white. / There is no cloud so dark and white at once . . ."—while watching horses ". . . feeding on solid / Cloud. . . ." The fog glazing the hills in the concluding image of "Christmas Shopping, 1947" and the low-lying fog in "The Dusk of Horses" enhance the feeling of aloneness in each poem, a comfortable rather than painful emotion. In "Christmas Shopping, 1947," Dickey's narrator welcomes the condition. In "Winter Trout" (*Poems*, 127–29), which describes a river's "surface full of gold flakes / Of the raw undersides of leaves," and associates that image with "the thing seen right, / For once," Dickey suggests that individuals who observe and interact with nature mystically attain an awareness others don't have, a concept which parallels the conclusion of "Christmas Shopping, 1947."

In another *Gadfly* poem, "Whittern and the Kite," a pilot named Whittern, ". . . malarial, his final mission bland / On the yellow sheets, squints from his beaked shade / Up . . ." at an airborne kite. In fact, all the other fliers around him similarly, simultaneously ". . . pause, look up. The exile's sapient nod / Lends to the handled air . . . guileless grace. . . ," and even the no-nonsense ". . . Clausewitz colonel, pledged and Undefiled, / Gut-sunk in battle-lure, and of a mind / Inimical to kites, stares like a loon. . . ." To these fliers, the kite is not ". . . Like an angel / In the air . . ." imagined by the GI in "The Wedding" (*Poems*, 32–33) nor like ". . . the Lord / Of their stolen voice in the air . . ." accompanying the child in "The Lord in the Air" (*Eye-Beaters*, 42–43). Instead, the kite that Whittern and his comrades watch represents at least one of two possible concepts.

On one hand, the kite symbolizes a war winding down—one "leashed, prolapsed and wavering-mild"—and leaving behind a war-wrung madness closely akin to, perhaps born of, the loss and loneliness that affects civilians caught up in military campaigns: "As if Headquarters jeeped bombed glades to find / Girls talking lilacs on the fiery noon." On another, the kite, a toy, becomes for the GIs a means of entertainment which offers the "*boys* who *play*" (italics added) a moment of peace, even innocence, in the midst of war, and allows for "humor" to exist in a now "boyish place" that had earlier been dead serious. Indeed, Dickey's mention of the "stark, manned light" and "handled air" suggests that the pilots not only influence the condition of the earth, but also the sky above it. As a toy, and thus an emblem of peace and innocence, the kite creates a strong irony in the poem, since it has taken the place of aircraft, which represent war and killing, if only for a short time in the aviators' lives. In effect, the pilots have momentarily abandoned their duty of flying bombers to fly a kite.

Even Dickey's brief epigraph to "Whittern and the Kite," which explains in part the GI's life as he had experienced it, suggests that the kite also permitted the pilots a needed respite from the boredom they faced between missions: ". . . three hundred combat hours entitled a pilot to return to the states. After all his time had been logged there was nothing for the pilot to do but wait for orders. Some of them . . . were hard put to find anything to do during this period. . . ." The epigraph calls to mind "The Jewel" (*Poems*, 28–29), in which Dickey also recounts the boredom that characterized the life of a GI during wartime—

> Forgetting I am alive, the tent comes over me
> Like grass, and dangling its light on a thread,
> Turning the coffee-urn green
> Where the boys upon camp-stools are sitting,
>   *Alone, in late night*

—and asks, in the poem's ultimate stanza, "Truly, do I live? Or shall I die, at last, / Of waiting?" Dickey has also commented about the boredom he faced during his war service elsewhere: ". . . I got interested in poetry in the Air Force, when I had a great deal of intense activity and then long stretches in which I didn't do anything except keep myself amused" (*Self-Interviews* 24). Even the last image in "Whittern and the Kite," that of a "fiery noon," corresponds to one of Dickey's more mature poems, "The Firebombing" (*Poems*, 181–88), in which the destruction of bombs—the

> . . . potential fire under the undeodorized arms
> Of . . . wings, on thin bomb-shackles,
> The "tear-drop-shaped" 300-gallon drop-tanks
> Filled with napalm and gasoline

—and the life-giving force of the sun are fused, the "potential," to use Dickey's word, for death or life revealed in one terrifying image: "Fire hangs not yet fire / In the air above Beppu. . . ."

In "King Crab and Rattler," Dickey's narrator reads a text—"A page that makes a simple counterfoil / Of cages in this stall of August heat / Spreads on an unused lectern of the mind"—in which a "Collusive crab and rampant snake," metamorphosed by the "therianthropic dusk," battle until the snake kills the crab "humped in his armored dark." The crab's shell, which the narrator describes as "escape is *in*" and "shell-harbored flight" and which should have protected its life, paradoxically offers no "escape," no "flight" but, instead, becomes its coffin. He then imagines, in the ultimate stanza, first a human body, presumably a dead GI's, lying at the ocean's edge then, farther from shore, a graveyard:

> Waves
> Clash over crab at throat and kelp-cold wrist.
> The rattler coils, (a tongue and pliant twist)
> His toxic ring on monumental graves.

Initially the crab and snake are simply animals, but they soon come to represent all animals, human and nonhuman, then to symbolize, in the last stanza, not only nature's ability to continue despite humanity's destruction of itself but consequently, nature's victory over humankind as well. Indeed, in the last stanza, Dickey portrays animals in a tableau of victory—the "crab at throat and kelp-cold wrist" and the "rattler [which] coils . . . / His toxic ring on monumental graves." They—certainly not the same crab and snake as those in the text the narrator reads, but rather those he imagines (or perhaps remembers having seen or is somehow watching)—are alive, not the soldier washed to shore nor those buried in "monumental graves." Dickey suggests that humankind's ability to wage war will eventually lead to its destruction; whereas animals, who only kill for food or protection, will survive. Their survival is tantamount to a mockery of humanity's destruction of itself.

Although Dickey set "King Crab and Rattler," a poem about death, in nature (a canal), unlike many of Dickey's later poems about death, such as "Armor," it is removed from the context of the family. However, by referring to the crab and rattler's battle in the "therianthropic dusk," Dickey hints that the animals nevertheless also represent humankind on *some* level. A few lines earlier, he had described their fight succinctly: "only the acts are human, never the wills." Both human beings and animals kill, Dickey realizes, and investigates more fully in "The Heaven of Animals" (*Poems*, 59–60), but human beings wage war and commit murder, acts of which animals are incapable, since they have neither intellect nor free will and respond only to instinct.

In "Armor" (*Poems*, 81–82), Dickey presents a different, though complementary view of the shell-as-armor concept: "When this is the thing you put on / The world is pieced slowly together / In the power of the crab. . . ." Throughout the poem, Dickey offers "the power" as one of metamorphosis, as if the armor the narrator wears allows him to become "the being / [He] was in a life before life." Similarly in the opening lines of "Drinking from a Helmet" (*Poems*, 173–78), Dickey combines in one image the boredom of GI life, expressed in "King Crab and Rattler" as the "unused lectern of the mind," with the paradox of armor being unprotective: "I climbed out, tired of waiting / For my foxhole to turn in the earth / On its side or its back for a grave. . . ." The narrator abandons the foxhole, meant to protect its inhabitant, before his opponent blows it up and it collapses on him, burying him alive. The battlefield he sees before him is strewn with soldiers' bodies, appearing as if "a graveyard / Was advancing after the troops," and once again, he focuses on the failure of armor to save:

> I shoved forward
> A helmet I picked from the ground,
> Not daring to take mine off
> Where somebody else may have come
> Loose from the steel of his head.

Once the narrator puts on the helmet he had retrieved, he metamorphoses into the dead soldier to whom it had belonged, the dead soldier's final perception becoming the living soldier's: "My last thought changed, and I knew / I inherited one of the dead."

"Sea Island," which appeared in the same issue of the *Gadfly* as "King Crab and Rattler," is a lovely but difficult poem, its meaning evasive. The first 12 lines describe a beach where "Once more the tide-trimmed shadows run / Afearing to the sunken sun . . ." and where "Like energies divorced from maps / The glossy misspent waves collapse." Since the first 12 lines of "Sea Island" are descriptive, one expects its concluding stanza to give some clue to the poem's theme. Its conclusion, however, also escapes exact interpretation and compounds a reader's frustration:

> A watcher on these mirror sands
> Grows Himalayan, understands
> Why jasmine birds in opal trees
> Assemble futures at his knees.

"Sea Island" appears to be about art and art's place in human life. Because of Dickey's use of words such as *afearing, sunken, divorced, misspent,* and *collapse,* the poem suggests that only in art—"jasmine birds in opal trees"—may one find the potential life offers since humankind has blighted nature through its involvement or obsession with war, as the opening quatrain seems to suggest:

> One harbor's history is the beam
> Swung from a searchlight's heavy dream,
> Where shrimpers ride from painted docks
> And night has water-killed the clocks

In fact, one could interpret such lines more specifically, as a condemnation of humanity's destruction of itself, as well as nature, since a "harbor," from the docks of which shrimpers have set out in search of their catch, has been the focal point of a searchlight, an image which conjures military or police actions. Dickey uses night as an ambiguous symbol. It may simply represent a state of nature—i.e., that time of the day after which the sun has set and before it has risen—or it may symbolize war's blight—ignorance, despair, pain, destruction, etc., on a variety of levels. Regardless, night has destroyed the "clocks," a human invention, and thus it has destroyed time, a human concept. In either case, night has defeated humankind. Only art, unlike war a creative and not destructive act, allows human beings the possibility of a future. Dickey depicts a similar harbor scene in "Facing Africa" (*Poems*, 103–104), one in which the play of darkness—"night" or "shadows"—and sea also appears:

> These are stone jetties,
> And, in the close part of the night,
> Connected to my feet by long
> Warm, dangling shadows
> On the buttressed water,
> Boats are at rest.
>
> Beyond, the harbor mouth opens
> Much as you might believe
> A human mouth would open
> To say that all things are a darkness.
> I sit believing this
> As the boats beneath me dissolve
>
> And shake with a haunted effort. . . .

Although he does not specifically cite "Sea Island," or any of his poems, as an example, Dickey has briefly acknowledged the existence of his early, stylistically difficult or obscure poems which he abandoned for a more accessible type: ". . . I slowly worked away from the extremely allusive kind of poetry I had been trying to write . . ." (*Self-Interviews*, 47).

A football star with professional potential, as Paul O'Neil has noted,[6] Dickey originally attended Clemson College in Clemson, South Carolina, in 1942. World War II interrupted his plans for an education. He left Clemson and was eventually stationed in the Pacific theater of the war, on the Philippine island Mindoro, the possible setting of "Whittern and the Kite," "Sea Island," and "King Crab and Rattler."

The four *Gadfly* poems were published during Dickey's undergraduate years at Vanderbilt University, from 1946 to 1949. He was decidedly different from many other students there and unlike students I had known during my own undergraduate days. Most of my 18 to 21-year-old male friends did their damnedest to stay out of the Vietnamese conflict by whatever means available: keeping their grade averages high, applying for conscientious objector status, dodging the draft, and even praying. Dickey was already an adult when he was an undergraduate, a married man between 23 and 25 years old, and he was between wars.

Dickey received his B.A. in English and was graduated from Vanderbilt University magna cum laude. The following year he received his M.A., also in English, from Vanderbilt. However, his civilian life was cut short once again. In 1950, having completed only the fall semester of teaching at Rice University in Houston, the Air Force recalled him to serve in the Korean War.

After his World War II experiences as an "air-man, overseas, in war-time," Dickey's return to student life at Vanderbilt demanded a great adjustment, not only because he was an older, married student but also because he was suddenly a civilian who had, only months before, dealt with life on a more serious, life-and-death level than many of his classmates ever had, as "Christmas Shopping, 1947" suggests. A remark by Dickey supports this: ". . . the little girls, recent high school graduates, were writing themes on 'What the American Flag Means to Me' or 'My First Day on Campus of Vanderbilt University' or 'What I Did with My Summer Vacation;' I wrote about the invasion of Okinawa" (*Self-Interviews*, 29).

The end of Dickey's hitch in the Air Force and his entering Vanderbilt signified the completion of a particular American rite of passage from adolescence to adulthood, that of the warrior. Had World War II never interrupted Dickey's life, his rite of passage would have been of the more usual sort, characterized by the passes of a football from one team to another, not the flight of bombers from friendly to enemy terrain. His attendance at Vanderbilt University marked a second rite of passage, into intellectual adulthood, a journey less dangerous than his Pacific night missions in Black Window aircraft.

As an undergraduate adult at Vanderbilt University, Dickey's priorities and abilities were worlds apart from his classmates'. His specific and mature concerns, realizations, and experiences already ingrained within him supported him in the educational process he underwent and in his newly discovered interest in writing. Because he began to write when, as an adult, he had a mature individual's sophistication, concerns, and realizations upon which to build, not just high hopes and a strong imagination, Dickey's war experiences, first recorded in the four *Gadfly* poems, strongly influenced his later work.

While the theme of combat recurs in his poetry, fiction, and nonfiction, Dickey's more recent work reveals that for him war is no longer a political struggle per se but a personal one, not an historical event but an emotional one. Dickey once saw the victor's prize as a treaty with another; now he reveals it as peace with oneself. The concluding lines to "Turning Away" (*Eye-Beaters*, 56–63), a poem from the middle stage of Dickey's poetic development, exemplifies this as well as any other poem he has recently published:

> Stand by this window
> As on guard
> Duty rehearsing what you will answer
> If questioned stand
> General deserter . . .
>
> Like a proof of character learned
> From Caesar's *Wars* from novels
> Read in the dark,
> Thinking of your life as a thing
> That can be learned,
> As those earnest young heroes learned theirs. . . .

Notes

1. Neal Bowers has written astutely and honestly on this aspect of Dickey's career in his *James Dickey: The Poet as Pitchman* (Columbia: University of Missouri Press, 1985).

2. James Dickey, *Two Poems of the Air* (Portland, OR: Centicore, 1964). The shortened forms of the titles of Dickey's books used in documentation within the text are: *Poems* for *Poems 1957–1967* (New York: Collier, 1967); *Self-Interviews* for *Self-Interviews* (Garden City, NY: Doubleday, 1970); *Eye-Beaters* for *The Eye-Beaters, Blood, Victory, Madness, Buckhead, and Mercy* (Garden City, NY: Doubleday, 1970); *Stone* for *Into the Stone and Other Poems* (New York: Scribner's, 1960); *Zodiac* for *The Zodiac* (Garden City, NY: Doubleday, 1976); *Strength* for *The Strength of Fields* (Garden City, NY: Doubleday, 1979). Unless otherwise noted, all biographical data is from the "Chronology" in Dickey's *The Voiced Connections of James Dickey: Interviews and Conversations*, ed. Ronald Baughman (Columbia, SC: University of South Carolina Press, 1989), 5–8.

3. The book was eventually published as *James Dickey: A Bibliography, 1947–1974* (Metuchen, NJ: Scarecrow, 1979). See also my "James Dickey: A Supplementary Bibliography, 1975–1980; Part 1," *Bulletin of Bibliography* 38.2 (April–June 1981): 92–100, 104; and "James Dickey: A Supplementary Bibliography, 1975–1980; Part 2," *Bulletin of Bibliography* 38.3 (July–Sept. 1981): 150–155.

4. "Christmas Shopping, 1947," *Gadfly* 3 (Winter 1947):59; "Sea Island," *Gadfly* 3 (Spring 1948):104; "King Crab and Rattler," *Gadfly* 3 (Spring 1948):104–105; and "Whittern and the Kite," *Gadfly* 4 (Summer 1949):26.

The *Gadfly* poems have since been reprinted in a limited edition volume, *Veteran Birth: The "Gadfly" Poems, 1947–1949* (Winston-Salem, NC: Palaemon, 1978), with some slight revisions. Dickey added two stanza breaks in "Christmas Shopping, 1947" and one stanza break in both "King Crab and Rattler" and "Whittern and the Kite." He reprinted them in *Veteran Birth* in the order in which they had appeared in the *Gadfly*.

Interestingly, the four *Gadfly* poems are not the only examples of Dickey's indecision over his byline. From 1951, when his work first appeared in a national, highly-respected journal, the *Sewanee Review*, until 1956, five of the nine poems Dickey published appeared under the name of James L. Dickey: "The Anniversary," "The Child in Armor," "The Confrontation of the Hero (April 1945)," "Of Holy War," and "The Shark at the Window."

5. James Dickey, *Alnilam* (New York: Doubleday, 1987).

6. Paul O'Neil, "The Unlikeliest Poet," *Life*, 22 July 1966, 68–70, 72–74, 77–79.

"The Firebombing": A Reappraisal

Ross Bennett

"The Firebombing"[1] is probably James Dickey's best-known poem and, with the possible exception of *The Zodiac*,[2] his most controversial. Once described as "the best poem produced thus far out of the combat of World War II,"[3] "The Firebombing" is an important major poem of our age. But critical opinion has been far from unanimous in its judgment. In 1967, Robert Bly's by now infamous review of *Buckdancer's Choice*[4] condemned "The Firebombing" totally. He argued that Dickey was "teaching us that our way of dealing with military brutality is right: do it, later talk about it, and take two teaspoonsful of remorse every seventh year. . . . If we read this poem right, we can go on living with napalm" (p. 75). Though Bly had in fact not read the poem right, still, despite the critical war that has raged between him and Dickey for more than a decade, his point of view remains in need of answer.

Another common error (though far less damaging than that of Bly) has led us to read "The Firebombing" mainly as an attempted expiation of guilt. This kind of emphasis is widespread, but is possibly best illustrated in Laurence Lieberman's essay, "The Deepening of Being."[5] Objections have also alleged its artistic failure. In offering a close reading of "The Firebombing," I intend to reassess the basis for evaluating this major poem and also to show that it demonstrates a mastery of formal control and technique.

Central to a proper understanding is appreciation of Dickey's manipulation of multiple narrative perspectives. Failure to recognize this structural device has led several critics to mistake the poem's intentions. In *Alone with America*, for example, we find Richard Howard insisting that "He the poet James Dickey, no other man, in a waking dream carries out a napalm raid on Japan."[6] As Robert Bly had argued:

All three ["Slave Quarters," "The Firebombing" and "The Fiend"] are obsessed with power, and driven by a childish longing for it, disguised only by the feeblest verbal veil. . . . The amazing thing is that none of the reviewers noticed what the poems were saying. Even reviewers as acute as David Ignatow, and

Ross Bennett, "The Firebombing: A Reappraisal." *American Literature*, 52:3, pp. 430–448. Copyright Duke University Press, 1980. Reprinted with permission of the publisher.

as aware of American ambiguities, praised the pointless violence of these poems, and accepted the poems' explanation of themselves at face value.

We can only lay this blindness to one thing: a brainwashing of readers by the New Critics. Their academic jabber about "personae" has taken root. Instead of thinking about the content, they instantly say, "Oh, that isn't Dickey in the 'Firebombing' poem! That is a persona!" This is supposed to solve everything.

. . . There are no personas. The new critical ideas do not apply at all. Readers go on applying them anyway, in fear of the content they might have to face if they faced the poem as they face a human being. (pp. 76–77)

There *is* a "persona" in "The Firebombing." In fact, there may be more than one. The poem is spoken by Dickey's middle-aged suburban householder, recalling moments twenty years earlier when he had been a bomber pilot "fulfilling / An 'anti-morale' raid" over Japan. Those sections of the poem, however, where the speaker is describing his present situation, or commenting on his visions of the past, are differentiated both in tone and imagery from the sections in which he recreates the actual memories of the firebombing raid, to the extent that we can think of them as two different voices, two different characters, dual protagonists in an interior drama.

Dickey deliberately encourages this illusion. When, in the beginning of the poem, the speaker describes himself as he was twenty years earlier, he speaks of that person as a distinctly different self; he calls him "some technical-minded stranger with my hands," and "the one who is here"; it is not until the thirty-eighth line that he calls the bomber pilot "me."

And what is the poet's precise role in all this? In "The Firebombing" Dickey's position is not exactly that of the artist sitting outside the poem "invisible . . . indifferent, paring his fingernails." Rather, it can be likened to that of a magus. He is very much involved in his poem as an experiment in the theatre of the spirit, as a process of personal self-discovery, as a quest; yet at the same time he is detached from it as an autonomous, self-contained work of art.

A similar relationship exists between Dickey, the poet, and the I-figure, or "persona" of his poem. Dickey explains in his essay, "The Self as Agent": "Every poem—particularly those which make use of a figure designated in the poem as "I"—is both an exploration and an invention of identity. . . . The poet . . . sits outside the poem, not so much putting his I-figure through an action, but attempting to find out what the I-figure will do, under these circumstances as they develop. . . . During the writing of the poem, the poet comes to feel that he is releasing into its proper field of response a portion of himself that he has never really understood."[7] That is to say, while the poet is immediately concerned with what his speaker says and does in the poem, the speaker of "The Firebombing" need not be identified with Dickey himself.

We ought not underestimate the effect of these various narrative perspectives. For example, the middle-aged, overweight speaker knows the limitations of the former self he has created: he knows that the pilot lacks compassion because he is cut off from the real consequences of his actions; he sees him as a victim of an imposed detachment which distorts perspective of the reality beneath him. Bearing in mind, however, that the firebomber is an invention of the suburban survivor's memory, and a projection of his present state of mind—another "erotic daydream," perhaps—the portrayal itself is subject to certain distortions. Similarly, though the man in the pantry is well aware of his own predicament (he realises that he in turn has been imprisoned by his present way of life and that he has himself in many ways become a victim), there are many elements in his story the full significance of which escape even this agonizingly self-aware narrator. A pattern of ironies is thus set up, which effectively distances us from the protagonist in the poem and which mediates judgment of the drama enacted by the interplay of the various "voices." By emphasising the essentially dramatic nature of Dickey's "The Firebombing," I believe we avoid some of the errors which can arise if we assume a stance perhaps more appropriate to so-called "confessional poetry."

The poem begins with two epigraphs, one from the contemporary German poet, Gunter Eich ("after the Catastrophe, each man will claim that he was innocent!"), the other from the book of Job. Most interesting in the light of this version of the poem's structure, they reinforce the idea that what follows is, after all, a poem, an artificial and created world. Also, the quotations interrogate each other, demanding an answer that the poem must supply. The text from Job, in particular, introduces what is to become a central unifying impulse of "The Firebombing," the theme of Trial by Ordeal. As in most of the poems collected in *Buckdancer's Choice*, the subject of the tests is the redemptive power of memory.

If memory is the immediate subject, what is really on trial is the power of the sympathetic imagination. Memory can distort and dislocate normally perceived reality and thus free the imagination from certain repressions and inhibitions. But how effectively can the poet's memory recreate the past? Does it have the potential to release *fully* those "portion[s] of himself that he has never really understood"?

In one sense, the lost selves of the past include not only the firebomber but also the firebomber's victims. The speaker remembers that he did not feel for them then; how can he achieve empathy with them now? Can he effectively diagnose the reason for failure in the past and, if so, can this knowledge help break down the spiritual paralysis in which he finds himself at present?

At the beginning of the poem the odds against the spirit appear insurmountable:

> Homeowners unite.
>
> All families lie together, though some are burned alive.
> The others try to feel
> For them. Some can, it is often said.

The flat, listless lines, with their tone of self-mocking irony, reveal the extent of the speaker's spiritual despondency. Spiritual defeat promises an easy way out. The speaker is trying to convince himself that it does not really matter how people have died because, in the end, all are united in the grave. Ultimately, this may be true, but he cannot escape so easily the realization that some families have been burned alive. In order to come to terms with their deaths he must show the importance of how and why they died and who burned them.

There is irony, too, in that these opening lines foreshadow the failure of the quest to follow. The Japanese victims have been united in death, but the only way they can ever be united with their destroyer is through the speaker's symbolic (or mystical) death. This is precisely what does *not* happen in the poem. Some families (that is, the ones who were actually consumed in the flames) have been "burned alive," but the survivors are now being "burned alive" in the purgatorial fires of a struggle that is doomed to fail.

Coming so soon after the epigraph from Job, the lines carry further ambiguities. The Jehovah of the book of Job is a God who represents omniscient judgment but does not appear to entertain any special sympathy for the plight of suffering man. Recalling this allusion has the effect of further foreshadowing the speaker's failure to connect in sympathy with the victims. The firebomber who played God is judged by his failure of sympathy, the same failure which condemns his successor to eternal suffering. Ironically, all the victims of the firebombing (past and present) shall be condemned to lie together, and none will be resurrected by the Fire of the imagination. The "some" who are "burned alive" can be read to refer at once to the actual victims and to the speaker: the thought of "others" who "try to feel / For them" identifies Dickey's speaker in the role of tribal poet who tragically fails to assume the burden of collective guilt.

If we admit the inference of a deliberate pattern of controlling ironies in these opening lines, then we must assume Dickey's foreknowledge that the quest is doomed to fail. If this is correct, it would appear that the commentators who have talked about Dickey's failure to achieve his intentions have missed the point. It is not the poet—nor the poem—that fails: it is the quest of the sympathetic imagination, dramatized *within* the poem, that fails. This is an important distinction to make.

Immediately following the speaker's first few words comes the first of the poem's dramatic juxtapositions of past and present, the beginning of the memory's first sortie. In contrast to the lassitude and desperation of the opening lines, we are now involved in language as energetic action:

Starve and take off

Twenty years in the suburbs, and the palm trees willingly leap
Into the flashlights,
And there is beneath them also

A booted crackling of snailshells and coral sticks.
There are cowl flaps and the tilt cross of propellers,
The shovel-marked clouds' far sides against the moon,
The enemy filling up the hills
With ceremonial graves.

There is a feeling of direct participation, of unmediated engagement, yet there is also a detached other-worldliness about the experience. There is a sense of watching the scene through a cinematic eye. The camera picks out objects willy-nilly from the foreground and the distance; objects leap from the periphery to the centre, momentarily, and are gone. Details from the natural world and the technological are commingled, are randomly assimilated by an unselective lens; the sounds of booted footsteps crowd the soundtrack. The effect is a calculated dislocation of ordinary perception; we see things through an "innocent" eye,[8] one that assimilates rather than selects or orders the details which impinge on it.

The transition into the next section is important. As if this random world were indeed seeking its own definition, the "somewhere" among these objects becomes a "glass treasure-hole of blue light." Here is the familiar enclosed world we find so often in Dickey's poems. We are inside a helmet, and the visor has clicked shut.

As helmet and *jagdmaske*, the cockpit has several functions. As part of the necessary honesty of the quest, the repressed lusts of the submerged self must be freed from the moral self's normal inhibitions. The helmet releases this necessarily irresponsible energy. It also protects the self from the energies of the world outside. The price of this protection is detachment. The enclosed world is defined by the "blue light" (which associates it with ominous moon-light on the far sides of the clouds) "tricked on" in the cockpit: this world of the imagination is possibly deceptive, a lunar world of hermetic isolation.

In the remembered flight, for which this section prepares us, the feeling of insularity is further developed. While he is still on the ground the pilot hears the sounds of boots crushing shells of snails, but his innocent "I" assimilates this detail and misses its implications. During the flight, the enclosed "I" becomes literally an *eye* and can hear no sounds at all.

This section also introduces several other important thematic motifs. The "glass treasure-hole," for example, resembles the suburban pantry; this is the first in a series of mirror-image patterns exploited throughout the poem. Also, with its associations of a pleasure-dome, the image of the cockpit foreshadows an important symbolic link between the references to Beppu (approached by way of rivers and across an "inland sea") and the return to base at Okinawa. The recognition of the "potential fire under the undeodorised arms / Of his wings" introduces inversions of the Icarus and Prometheus myths.

The next long movement of the poem (lines 21 to 71) deals with the remembered experience of flying; more explicitly, with the flight from Okinawa to Beppu. Ten minutes after take-off, and still gaining altitude, the bomber rises through the cloud layer and enters clear air above. But consider the imagery: the aircraft "burst[s] straight out / Of the overcast into the moon." It is as if it were being drawn through a vortex. There is an almost sexual connotation in the way it breaks through into the moonlit world beyond the clouds.

The scene, as it presents itself to his eyes, evokes a paradoxical mixture of wondering involvement and brilliant clarity of detachment. The moon is the presiding goddess in this palace of the imagination; everything (including the technology which has enabled his flight) is in thrall to her. Only five lines deal with what must have been the longest part of the journey in terms of actual duration, but it is as if the pilot has soared beyond the temporal and actual world and into a dream world where the clouds provide the only defining edges in a "stopped" landscape.

When the aircraft begins to lose altitude and enter the approach path to the target, the "re-entry / Into cloud" functions as a symbolic rite of initiation. In the cockpit the flyer feels as if he is at the centre of the universe. (In actual fact, the aircraft is moving across a landscape. In the vertiginous relativity of flight, however, it appears as if the landscape is moving around the aircraft. This disturbance of normal spatial relationships is analogous to the distortion of reality by art.)

The landscape below has a strange, two-dimensional appearance. The woods are illuminated with "one silver side," while the hillside's solid shape can only be inferred from the terraced rice-paddies on its side. The rice-paddies become yet another mirror, a further analogue of art, surrealistic in their effect, yet somehow less than real (distorting reality rather than reflecting it). The world within the cockpit is also dominated by the moon. The canteen of "combat booze" is "cratered"—a mirror-image of the moon's face. The intoxicant it contains ("bourbon frighteningly mixed / With GI pineapple juice") suggests a Dionysian draught, an accessory in the trance-like state of moon-madness.

The association of the flyer as the Queen Moon's fascinated, captive lover is further strengthened by the images of disintegration which accompany his rite of passage over the enchanted landscape. As his plane approaches its target area, the remnants of another self are sloughed off in the cloud and previous prescriptions of reality disintegrate ("Enemy rivers and trees / Sliding off me like snakeskin"). The flyer is reborn into an impersonal, unknowable god. He moves in "dark paint" and is "invisible," drawn on by "the moon's now and again / Uninterrupted face."

Sentries of the land of the dead, dogs asleep on the island below warn of the approach of the mad god. Their dream-senses are superior and inviolate; they are not victims of the tyranny of the senses and its inherent delusions. The dogs' "sleep-smelling" contrasts natural instinct and autonomy with the irresponsible intoxication of mask-power. They identify the agent of impending destruction with the pilot's Dionysian intoxicant: together it is an ". . . ungodly mixture / Of napalm and high octane fuel, / Good bourbon and GI juice." As mentioned before, the peculiar relativity of flight makes it appear as if the landscape were circling around the aircraft. This dislocation of normal perspective parallels the inversion of myths: it is not Prometheus who brings the gift of fire to a "town with everyone darkened" but a moon-mad Zeus who brings death. And there is the added irony: whereas Lucifer in his falling flight at least achieved self-knowledge, our Jehovah-like protagonist has had his human ego stripped away. In his insane selflessness, he looks down on a world of darkened man, and in his dream of pride he has indeed "an arm like God."

Several critics have suggested that the passages which deal with flight threaten to overwhelm those which dramatize the poem's central concern— the moral predicament of the present self; as Lieberman says, for example, "the moments of ecstasy threaten to overbalance the moments of agony" (p. 1). The poetry describing the flight *is* perhaps more superficially brilliant than in the section which now follows, where the present-day householder describes his situation. But, contrary to Bly's assertion (p. 74), this does not indicate a self-indulgence on Dickey's part. The world of flight has been deliberately overglamourized; the entranced innocence of the pilot's dream world deliberately made attractive in order to emphasize the dangers of that "innocence." The real strength of the poetry in these sections lies in the irony that undercuts the account; we are as much aware of the moon-goddess' treacherous deceptions as her charms.

Similarly, we see that in his fantasy the firebomber has become the wrong god. Unlike Zeus, Apollo, or Thor, he does not bring justice from destruction; he only wreaks willful, irresponsible destruction. He thinks he has divinity, but all he has is power. Dickey sees the difference: the poet is not intoxicated; he is responsible and moral. He knows that the fantasy is overpowering; he also shows that it is wrong.

Therefore, while it is certainly true that Dickey intends us to see the flight sections as compensatory fantasies on the part of the suburban householder, we should not regard them solely in that light. We must not forget that the excursions of the memory constitute a quest undertaken in order to discover the reason for the failure of the imagination in the past.

We might also emphasize that, at this point in the poem, it is not the "ecstasy" which overwhelms the "agony" but quite the opposite. The impassioned voice of the present interrupts the memory, breaking into the fantasy world with the compulsion of its demands:

> Twenty years in the suburbs have not shown me
> Which ones were hit and which not.
> Haul on the wheel   racking slowly
> The aircraft blackly around
> In a dark dream   that   that is

> That is like flying inside someone's head
> Think of this   think of this

In a remarkable (and characteristically grotesque) image, the speaker explicitly identifies the dream of flight as taking place in an inner, enclosed world, a world belonging to another, alien self. The process here is exactly opposite to that in "Drinking from a Helmet." In that poem the I-figure puts on a helmet which liberates the spirit of the dead "brother," a process which eventually enables him to say—like Whitman—"I was the man."[9] In "The Firebombing," the narrator takes off his helmet and proceeds to enumerate the things that now deny him sympathetic power; apparently trivial concerns of the present crowd in, distracting him:

> I did not think of my house
> But think of my house now
>
> Where the lawnmower rests on its laurels
> Where the diet exists
> For my own good   where I try to drop
> Twenty years, eating figs in the pantry
> Blinded by each and all
> Of the eye-catching cans that gladly have caught my wife's eye
> Until I cannot say
> Where the screwdriver is   where the children
> Get off the bus   where the new
> Scoutmaster lives   where the fly
> Hones his front legs   where the hammock folds
> Its erotic daydreams   where the Sunday
> School text for the day has been put   where the fire
> Wood is   where the payments
> For everything under the sun
> Pile peacefully up . . .

Details accumulate in a conscious parody of Whitmanesque assimilation. The house and garden and the comfortable appurtenances of respectable Sunday suburbia recall the "sabbath calm" of Beppu, but the similarity only emphasizes the vast, irreclaimable distance between them. The pantry, where he is "blinded by each and all / Of the eye-catching cans," is another enclosed world, a mirror-image of the cockpit. The pantry is the tragic prize and price of survival. Those very things which define the self have been assimilated, not to liberate the self but further shield, further confine it.

The firebomber, in his innocence, did not realize the cockpit was his prison. The survivor knows too well that his house is both prison and purgatory. Dickey subjects that I-figure to a process of relentless self-laceration. For him, it cannot be Peace Now, but the Fire and the Sword. The self is imprisoned in a stasis from which there can be no progress unless the energies of the imagination are channeled to destroy that self. In the passage that follows, Dickey shows the mind turned inwards to discover its "secret charge":

> But in this half-paid-for pantry
> Among the red lids that screw off
> With an easy half-twist to the left
> And the long drawers crammed with dim spoons,
> I still have charge—secret charge—
> Of the fire . . .

It is a tribute to Dickey's control here that he still maintains detachment. Hephaestus was given charge of the fire, but he was a crippled god, cut off from love. Denied the undifferentiated Fire of the imagination and love, he used fire as ego-destruction, not liberation. Dickey knows more than the fire / sky god his speaker allows himself to become in his fantasy.

Embarking on a second sortie of the memory, the narrative is resumed where the firebomber is approaching the target area itself. Once again, the language functions on a number of levels. Behind the flyer are "set up" the Southern Cross, Orion, and Scorpio. As in *The Zodiac*, the constellations become symbolic emblems for the possible apotheosis of the quest. Here, the Southern Cross perhaps stands for the passive, compassionate sympathy of Christ as Redeemer; the familiar figure of Orion—one of Dickey's favourite emblems— might be associated with the active Christ as the Harrower of Hell; Scorpio (whose original sign was the Phoenix) could suggest rebirth or resurrection through destructive energies turned back upon themselves. The next few lines, however, seem to foreshadow the failure of the quest:

> Fire hangs   not yet fire
> In the air above Beppu
> For I am fulfilling
>
> An "anti-morale" raid upon it . . .

In fulfilling a further raid upon the past, the memory will once again betray the potential of the mental Fire.

As the account of the bombing begins, the imagery again takes up the motif of the mirror. Reflections from water let the pilot observe the bombs. He does not see actual explosions, he does not see their destruction; he sees only the reflections of their flashes. In this highly over-mediated version of reality, the bombing becomes merely an exercise: it has no more relation to the human reality of the events below than a "chemical war- / fare field demonstration" has to actual war.

The effect of the passage is quite peculiar. It both heightens and lessens our sense of horror. We are perhaps reminded of the paradox implicit in Shelley's dictum, "Poetry is a mirror which makes beautiful that which is distorted."[10] The particularly nasty pun on the word, "late," for example, the terrible parody of baptism by fire, and the fact that the carp is a sacred emblem in Japan of longevity and reincarnation, are sick jokes indeed. But these details do not denote a "childish longing for power" (Bly, p. 76); rather, they suspend one's judgment altogether. Through one set of eyes the firebomber is a monster; through another, he is innocent. The language does "numb" us; there is "some kind of hideous indifference" (Bly, p. 74). But this is because Dickey wants us to see two things at once: we must see the explosions through the pilot's eyes—as totally unreal—yet we must also be able to see that order of vision as itself unreal. This can imply a great deal about *other* views of what has happened.

Through his account of the remembered firebombing, the speaker is made even more aware of alienation and estrangement. The recreation of these memories it itself an artistic exercise. He knows that he should feel remorse for the victims but, without genuine and substantive sympathy with them, this is merely a willed conviction:

> With fire of mine like a cat

> Holding onto another man's walls
> My hat should crawl on my head
> In streetcars, thinking of it,
> The fat on my body should pale.

Again, at such an important stage in "The Firebombing," it is amazing how Dickey deliberately risks the use of comic bathos to achieve a tragic effect. What are melodramatic clichés in the popular horror-story here succeed brilliantly by gathering together thematic motifs in ironic counterpoint. The image of the fire "like a cat / Holding onto another man's walls" seems rather contrived: it is precisely the effect Dickey wants. In drawing attention to itself, the simile is mimetic of how the pilot himself would see the fire; that is, in terms of an image rather than reality. We find the fire imitating the action of the suburban cat, suggesting a desperate attempt on the part of the speaker to humanize the remembered vision. Again, he fixates on the "walls" of the victims' houses because his own present circumstances are limited and defined by walls. In the same way, the helmet becomes a hat that "should crawl on my head" and the aircraft becomes a streetcar. Unfortunately, the more the speaker observes the similarities between present and past, the living and the dead, the more the gulf widens between them.

Once again, therefore, the sympathetic imagination has been denied; the memory only parodies assimilation:

> Gun down
> The engines, the eight blades sighing
> For the moment when the roofs will connect
> Their flames, and make a town burning with all
> American fire.
>   Reflections of houses catch;
> Fire shuttles from pond to pond
> In every direction, till hundreds flash with one death.
> With this in the dark of the mind,
> Death will not be what it should.

Not even the Japanese homeowners are "united" in this vision of death; not even their homes; it is only the "reflections of houses" that have been connected. Representations of individualities have been assimilated into the One through the mediations of a monstrous parody of art; the actual deaths of people are remembered merely as an art form and not as reality.

The speaker now explicitly realizes that the circumstances which inhibit his empathizing parallel those imposed on the firebomber. For example, the imaginative energies necessary to deliver the speaker from his state of moral inertia have to be induced by intoxication. Those moments when the realization of failure to connect in sympathy is most strong (when "my exhaled face in the mirror / Of bars, dilates in a cloud like Japan"), explicitly parallel the flyer's initiation into the dream world (the aircraft's "re-entry / Into cloud" where "Japan dilates around it like a thought"). The imagination does not necessarily bring us any closer to dealing with reality because the intrusion of distorting art perspectives may inhibit true vision; instead, we are led away from reality and into a world of illusion:

> The death of children is ponds
> Shutter-flashing; responding mirrors; it climbs
> The terraces of hills
> Smaller and smaller, a mote of red dust
> At a hundred feet; at a hundred and one it goes out.

What is needed, of course, is actual contact with the reality of their death; the imagination has to be able to get inside the houses where people died on fire. But in the insulated world of the cockpit there can never be real contact ("when those on earth / Die, there is not even sound"). The experience of the bombing is purely visual. As Wordsworth wrote, the eye is "the most despotic of the senses."[11] As it is closest to the intellect, it is also the sense most easily rationalized, providing the illusion that things have been thought through. The firebomber is "cool and enthralled in the cockpit." In this state of mind, even a source of potential danger to himself is assimilated into the art form—an anti-aircraft shell bursts like the petals of a flower.

This movement of the poem culminates in a passionate outburst:

> It is this detachment,
> The honored aesthetic evil,
> The greatest sense of power in one's life,
> That must be shed in bars, or by whatever
> Means . . .

This is no mere rhetoric. Here perhaps, the voice of the speaker comes closest to Dickey's own, in an impassioned denunciation of a flawed art, of a dehumanized imagination that has lost contact with reality. The description of the pilot as "cool and enthralled" draws attention to two separate processes of betrayal. The imagination has been deceived ("enthralled") by external beauty, and "cooled" by the conceptualizing mind. The virtue of art lies in detachment, Emerson suggested,[12] but here the speaker recognizes that the sympathetic imagination has been betrayed by an eye that has become predatory in its innocent detachment.

Here then, at least, is a step toward self-reintegration. In the recognition that they are both guilty of what is essentially the same crime—"the honored aesthetic evil"—the separate identities of the past and present selves finally merge. In contrast to the canisters in the pantry (whose shining surfaces "blind" the speaker and disperse the self), the blue light of the bar mirror unites the two selves across time.

Although the divided self has been partially reintegrated, however, there still has been no reconciliation with the firebomber's victims because the imagination is still incapable of real sympathy.

The final movement of the poem deliberately calls attention to itself as an excursion of language. The last images of the firebombing, for example, emphasize a tension between the recreation of the raid as the flyer saw it and the speaker's efforts to transform that vision. In a desperate attempt to free himself, the speaker identifies the bombs as innocent. The fire is humanized; it is "clinging and crying"; "another / Bomb finds a home / And clings to it like a child." But it is only rhetoric that gathers together the victims and their destroyer in a series of symbolic gestures. There is pathos, but no true sympathy. In its sense of willing the experience rather than embodying it honestly, the imagery is beautiful but false. As the narrative continues, the speaker is now conscious of the distorting power of the imagination; he is aware that redemption of the self requires redemption of a faulted art, through absolute self-honesty.

The departure from Beppu recalls the earlier images of disintegration. In significant contrast, the direction out of the vortex is now toward a new reintegration:

> Goodbye to the grassy mountains
> To cloud streaming from the night engines
> Flags   pennons   curved silks

> Of air   myself streaming also
> My body covered
> With flags, the air of flags
> Between the engines.

The flag imagery reminds us of military funeral rites and the ceremony of burial at sea. The old self identified with the highly specialized clothing and equipment of the bomber pilot is dissipated, giving way to a new self wearing air (compare another famous Dickey poem, "Falling"). It is a process of rebirth, an emerging from the amoral, enclosed world of the dream, a shedding of the trappings and emblems of the past self and its technology, the helmet of war.

A further mirror-image then follows:

> . . . Okinawa burns,
> Pure gold, on the radar screen,
> Beholding, beneath, the actual island form
> In the vast water-silver poured just above solid ground,
> An inch of water extending for thousands of miles
> Above flat ploughland.

This highly contrived passage parallels the images of Okinawa and Beppu (with the important difference, of course, that Okinawa "burns" only in the art-medium of the radar screen).

The speaker perhaps perceives the irony of the comparison, because this "illusory" reality can easily be dissipated by simply saying, " 'down,' and it is done." The reader is aware of a further irony. Throughout the poem we have observed an elaborate pattern of parallels, the comparisons between the victims and the survivor having emphasized the distance between them. They defeat empathy. Symbolically, however, the parallels have also drawn them closer together. Therefore, when the speaker says,

> All this, and I am still hungry,
> Still twenty years overweight, still unable
> To get down there or see
> What really happened

he is finally (and with complete honesty) acknowledging the failure of the sympathetic imagination. Denied redemptive empathy with the actual victims, the speaker himself is just as much a tragic victim as the dead; on the symbolic level, the firebomber had killed himself.

The speaker's final realization assumes a truly tragic dimension:

> It is that I can imagine
> At the threshold nothing
> With its ears crackling off

Like powdery leaves,
Nothing with children of ashes, nothing not
Amiable, gentle, well-meaning,
A little nervous for no
Reason   a little worried   a little too loud
Or too easygoing   nothing I haven't lived with
For twenty years, still nothing not as
American as I am, and proud of it.

Absolution? Sentence? No matter;
The thing itself is in that.

In other words, the price of survival is that the imagination can no longer deal
adequately with anything not familiar, cannot satisfactorily come to terms
with the world outside the self. The eyes of the victims and the eyes of
their destroyer can never meet; there can never be any exchange, any true
reintegration. What remains is a solipsistic vision of hell, a recognition that
the real enemy is the self. Although that self is always "amiable, gentle, well-
meaning," it is a self doomed to remain eternally divided.

As I read them, the last two lines of the poem show that the speaker partly
recognizes why this predicament is unresolvable. In remaining "American as
I am, and proud of it," he either consciously or unconsciously reveals his own
spiritual impotence as a personification of a basic flaw in the American
character—the refusal to relinquish the idea of a separatist ego. Ultimately,
this is both the cause and the effect of war. Honesty, integrity, patience, and
meaning well were not enough for Job, as long as he persisted in his pride.
The speaker in "The Firebombing" can no longer say, like Walt Whitman, "I
do not ask the wounded person how he feels . . . I myself become the wounded
person,"[13] because America is no longer innocent. In the speaker's inability—
or refusal—to humble himself, Dickey has shown how far the circumstances
of modern American life have betrayed Whitman's visionary ideal, and how
the impossibility of attaining that ideal must inevitably express itself in violence
and destruction.

As a final judgment on what is possibly James Dickey's most important
single poem—and possibly one of the best poems written in America since
1945—Dickey's own comments are accurate, precise, and incisive. In his
Playboy interview he says,

People talk about my poem "The Firebombing" as though it were written by
a man who loved to burn up children. They are either being perversely ignorant
or just ordinary, run-of-the-mill ignorant. That's not what it's about; that's not
the danger facing pilots. The danger is in the feeling of power it gives them to
do these things and not be held accountable for the carnage and the terror and
bloodshed and mutilation. To not even *see* it. I guess it's no longer the firebombing airplane that's the symbol of this sort of thing but something even farther

removed physically from the victims. It's the fellow who pushes the button for the ICBM. He is never even going to see the *cities* he reduces to atomic ashes. He might read about it later, but he is not held accountable or even called on to witness the result of this action.

Now that's the dangerous thing. That is what "The Firebombing" is about— that you'll never have to face up to the carnage and death and mutilation you have wrought. To you it just looks like a beautiful spectacle. And it *is* beautiful. You're far above it. You're looking down like the eye of God. It's really like fireworks. "The Firebombing" is about the worst guilt of all—the guilt of not being able to feel guilt over the things you ought to feel guilty about.[14]

While the quest for sympathy within the poem fails, the poem itself succeeds; while the quest is doomed because of a failure of the imaginative vision in art, the poem itself emerges as a consummate triumph of art. In other words, the poem triumphs because it succeeds in communicating the process of that failure. If H. L. Weatherby is correct in claiming that "most great poetry is tragic, dealing only with the impossibility of the vision,"[15] then undoubtedly we must include "The Firebombing" among those "great poems."

Notes

1. *Poems 1957–1967* (New York: Collier, 1967), pp. 181–88. All references are to this edition.

2. *The Zodiac* (Garden City, N.Y.: Doubleday, 1976).

3. Robert Huff, "The Lamb, the Clocks, the Blue Light," *Poetry*, 9 (1966), 47.

4. Robert Bly ("Crunk"), "The Collapse of James Dickey," *The Sixties*, 9 (1967), 70–79.

5. Laurence Lieberman, "James Dickey: the Deepening of Being," in his *The Achievement of James Dickey: A Comprehensive Selection of His Poems with a Critical Introduction* (Glenview, Ill.: Scott-Foresman, 1967), pp. 1–21.

6. Richard Howard, *Alone with America* (New York: Atheneum, 1969), p. 93.

7. "The Self as Agent," in *Sorties* (Garden City, N.Y.: Doubleday, 1971), p. 155.

8. The term is used in the sense established by Tony Tanner in *The Reign of Wonder: Naivety and Reality in American Literature* (Cambridge: Cambridge Univ. Press, 1967).

9. *Poems 1957–1967*, p. 178. Compare "I am the man, I suffer'd, I was there." Walt Whitman, "Song of Myself," line 832, *Leaves of Grass: Comprehensive Reader's Edition*, ed. Harold W. Blodgett and Sculley Bradley (New York: New York Univ. Press, 1965), p. 66.

10. "A Defence of Poetry," *The Selected Poetry and Prose of Percy Bysshe Shelley*, ed. Carlos Baker (New York: Random House, 1951), p. 500.

11. William Wordsworth, *The Prelude*, ed. Ernest de Selincourt, 2nd ed. (Oxford: Clarendon Press, 1959), p. 439.

12. "Circles," *Essays: First Series: The Collected Works of Ralph Waldo Emerson* (Cambridge: Harvard Univ. Press, 1979), II, 120.

13. "Song of Myself," line 845, p. 67.

14. "Playboy Interview: James Dickey," *Playboy*, Nov. 1973, p. 92.

15. H. L. Weatherby, "The Way of Exchange in James Dickey's Poetry," *Sewanee Review*, 74 (1966), 679.

Emerson in Vietnam:
James Dickey, Robert Bly and the New Left

ERNEST SUAREZ

James Dickey's career provides an especially clear example of the way history alters and informs the reception of a poet's work. Throughout his literary career, which began in the early 50's, Dickey has expressed the belief that volatile and violent qualities are an inherent and sometimes desirable part of the human condition, while the loss of aggressive, instinctual urges is a form of castration which cuts off access to the full realm of experience. However, in the late 60's Dickey's penchant for stating his views in extreme terms lead many critics to accuse him of possessing a brutal sensibility lacking social consciousness. Attacks on Dickey started in 1967 when Robert Bly, then co-chairman of American Writers Against the Vietnam War, called him "sick" and "sadistic" for his treatment of war in *Buckdancer's Choice*. Since then critics have often complained that Dickey's writings lack a moral arbiter. Dickey's use of violence in his writing has been widely viewed as symptomatic of this failure.

Without question, violence and aggression are integral parts of Dickey's vision, which finds its origins in the Emersonian tradition. Dickey sees history from a philosophically mystical vantage point that identifies violence and disorder as part of a larger scheme based on the primacy of the individual, a view for which the New Left literary establishment condemned him after the escalation of the Vietnam war. Examining these controversial elements of Dickey's poetry by situating them, and the adverse critical reaction to his work, within the historical backdrop of American culture and literature shows how the Vietnam war resulted in critics valuing the didactical over the dialectical and the communal over the individual. Dickey's complex metaphysics collided with the politics of a historical particular, the war, which generated a critical agenda that could not accommodate the philosophical underpinnings to his poetry. The poems I have selected to discuss—"The Performance," "Between Two Prisoners" and "The Firebombing"—are representative of Dickey's war poems, and point to an Emersonian transcendentalism that perpetuates the metaphysics of the major American visionary poets.

Originally published in the *Southern Literary Journal* 23.2 (Spring 1991): 77–97. Reprinted by permission.

* * *

Dickey's conception of the poet's function and effect on the reader distinctly parallels Emerson's.[1] For Emerson "the poet turns the world to glass, and shows us all things in their rightful series and procession"[2]; for Dickey "there is an essential connection . . . between the world and you, and it is as a divine intermediary between you and the world that poetry functions, bringing with it . . . an enormous increase in perception, an increased ability to understand and interpret the order of one's experience."[3] For both men the visionary act is integrative, allowing one to unify and transfigure experience, or, as Dickey matter-of-factly puts it, "evoke a world that is realer than real."[4] Like Emerson, Dickey wants his readers to draw upon long dormant psychic energies in order to discover a direct, active relationship to the world. Similar to Dickey's "energized man," the portrait of "Man-thinking" Emerson presents in "The American Scholar" describes not just a mind at work but an entire being actively using all of his or her faculties.[5]

In his first two books, *Into the Stone* (1960) and *Drowning With Others* (1962), Dickey presents poems that make up a primer for an aesthetics of renewal based on what Emerson called "symbolic perception," an ability to re-see the world again. The majority of these poems are relatively short, typically describing a brief experience during which the poem's first-person narrator undergoes a change resulting in a more unified and aware self. In essence these poems are short dramatic parables showing the reader the process of becoming "energized." Ideally, participation in what Dickey calls "creative lies" awakens in the reader the potential to realize a similar change.

"The Performance" (1960), one of Dickey's first compelling poems, illustrates his Emersonian emphasis. Dickey describes "The Performance," a tribute to a fellow pilot who was his "best friend in the squadron," as a poem in which "almost every word . . . is literally true, except that the interpretation of the facts is my own."[6] During World War II Dickey's friend, Donald Armstrong, was forced to crash land a P-61 while on a strafing mission on Panay. Japanaese soldiers captured Armstrong and beheaded him the next day.

Dickey stresses the force of the individual psyche, as the poem's narrator enters into a reverie in which he imagines Armstrong's death. The narrator remembers that the last time he saw Armstrong his friend was on a Philippine island practicing handstands. Though Armstrong staggers "unbalanced, with his big feet looming and waving / In the great, untrustworthy air / He flew in each night," he continues to practice in order to "perfect his role." The next day Armstrong is taken prisoner and executed. The narrator imagines Armstrong's performance before his captors:

> Doing all his lean tricks to amaze them—
> The back somersault, the kip-up—
> And at last the stand on his hands,

Perfect, with his feet together,
His head down, evenly breathing,
As the sun poured up from the sea

And the headsman broke down
In a blaze of tears, in that light
Of the thin, long human frame
Upside down in its own strange joy,
And, if some other one had not told him,
Would have cut off the feet

Instead of the head,
And if Armstrong had not presently risen
In kingly, round-shouldered attendance,
And knelt down in himself
Beside his hacked, glittering grave, having done
All things in this life that he could.[7]

Here the creative lie, portraying Armstrong doing gymnastic tricks, adds a sense of mystery to the situation, emphasizing the moment's revelatory quality. Armstrong perfects the handstand and dies in imagined glory—implied by the image in the last stanza of him being knighted as he is beheaded—"having done / All things in this life that he could." However, Armstrong's transformation only exists for the narrator, who is remembering the last time he saw his friend, but who was not present at the execution. The narrator creates a unity to his memory of Armstrong's life, but Armstrong remains unaffected. No anger or moral judgement concerning the justice of the situation is expressed, nor is Armstrong's death lamented; such issues are never addressed. Instead, war and death are accepted as givens, and the power of subjective perception is foregrounded.

Like his conception of the poet's function, Dickey's emphasis on the self is remarkably like Emerson's, which also makes the individual the locus of change. Both men view reality from the vantage point of the self, exploring "the force or truth of the individual soul" (*Selections from Ralph Waldo Emerson* 169), and maintaining that "The ruin or the blank that we see when we look at nature, is in our own eye" (*Selections from Ralph Waldo Emerson* 55). Such emphasis on intensifying the individual psyche is prevalent in much American literature of the fifties and the sixties, when a renewed interest in Emerson's work occurred.[8] Indeed, despite the impression often left by critics and Dickey himself concerning the wide gulf between Dickey and his contemporaries, Dickey participates in many of the trends of his time. David Riesman's *The Lonely Crowd* (1950), J. D. Salinger's *The Catcher in the Rye* (1951), Jack Kerouac's *On the Road* (1955), Sloan Wilson's *The Man in the Grey Flannel Suit* (1955) and William H. Whyte's *The Organization Man* (1956) were among the many books which expressed dissatisfaction with the tepid malaise they saw characterizing post-World War II American culture. All of these works priviledge individual expression over communal political action. Partly because he discovered his poetic aesthetic and his poetic raison d'être in the fifties, Dickey has continued to see poetry as a means of "energizing" the individual.

Many of Dickey's contemporaries, most notably the poets associated with the Deep Image school, expressed similar beliefs in the late fifties and early sixties. As Richard Sugg has pointed out, much of Bly's poetry "is squarely within the American romantic tradition of Emerson, Whitman, and Hart Crane."[9] Though the pressure of Vietnam compelled Bly and other Deep Image poets to apply their poetics of transformed individual consciousness to a more political canvas, the ideas behind the Deep Image movement, particularly its romantic emphasis on "inwardness" and discovering unknown regions of the psyche, did not initially involve political transformation. In fact, Bly had published and praised Dickey's work in his little magazine *The Sixties* and had lauded *Drowning with Others* in *Choice*.[10] The qualities in Dickey's work that Bly identifies as exceptional, such as creating radically subjective and original images to emphasize individual metamorphisis, are those associated with Deep Image poetry.

But while other visionary poets in the sixties—Bly, Allen Ginsberg, Galway Kinnell—eventually began presenting themselves as radicals trying to initiate some fundamental change in society, the transformations of self Dickey continued to advocate in his poetry had nothing to do with concrete changes in the social and political sphere. Though Dickey became deeply involved in anti-war candidate Eugene McCarthy's presidential campaign, he continued to associate much of the nonconformity expressed in the sixties with a fifties-like dissatisfaction with American culture. Indeed, Dickey's views on the New Left counterculture typify his tendency to concentrate on paradoxes. Dickey believed that the anti-war counterculture's formation largely was motivated by individuals' search for meaning, even though it involved mass political protest. On *Firing Line* Dickey expressed that there was no "proof" "humanly capable of being given" that would justify the "sacrifice" of "50,000 American lives and untold billions of dollars" in Vietnam, and that "one must pay attention" to "the public opposition to the war," but he also insisted that Vietnam served as a source of identity for the young: "Vietnam in a sense identifies them. They have an identity which they were afraid of being raped of by middle-class America and the situation in which most of them grew up. The war is something that's important to them because it gives them an identity both as a group and as individuals, just like long hair."[11]

In 1971 Dickey professed that "all the revolutions and revolutionary activities of the past ten or fifteen years" were "protests of the increasing trivialization of life."[12] In 1972 Dickey even evoked the spectre of Wilson's *The Man in the Grey Flannel Suit*: "I like the hippies . . . I think those outlandish costumes they wear are very colorful and nice . . . they are dead set against this business of being shoved into the gray flannel suit and the gray flannel image. They want to be themselves, even if they don't know who themselves are. They're looking, and I can't help thinking that's a good thing" (*Night Hurdling* 420).

Dickey's allusion to Wilson's book, his claims that the tumultuous upheavals of the sixties were reactions to the "increasing trivialization of life," and his view that young people "were afraid of being raped . . . by middle-class America," all describe sixties nonconformity in terms characteristic of reactions to revolts against Eisenhower Republicanism in the fifties. Rather than solely provoked by the policies of the Vietnam era, Dickey thinks the sixties anti-war and counterculture movements also emerged from a pervasive sense that social existence had become meaningless. Although the political circumstances surrounding Vietnam provided a channel or focus for widespread discontent, Dickey believes that in contemporary America nonconformity and rebellion are largely motivated by a quest for identity.

Consistent with this belief, Dickey's concerns involve examining the relationship between romantic individualism and power. In Dickey's work we discover a strange brew of existentialist and romantic philosophy that helps account for the virulent critical reactions he drew in the late sixties. In 1989 Dickey told me that, when he met Ivor Winters, Winters said that Dickey was "essentially an American decadent romantic poet following Emerson."[13] Dickey called Winters a "fascistic type" and praised Emerson's directives priviledging intuition over reason, declaring that "honest reaction to experience, intuitive reaction—nothing is of greater consequence than that" (122). Dickey also stated that he liked Emerson's idea that one could "have a direct line to God," but that he cannot believe its literal truth. Dickey finds no moral guide in Nature, unlike Emerson, who posited the existence of an "Oversoul" with which the individual conspired to serve as a moral center. The "real god is what causes everything to exist, like the laws of motion," but the idea of a moral force—especially in respect to human notions of morality—governing the universe, Dickey called "absurd" (122).

Winters' essay "The Significance of the Bridge by Hart Crane" helps elaborate his comment to Dickey and directly bears on many critics' reactions to Dickey. Winters blamed Emersonian ideas (via Walt Whitman) for leading to Hart Crane's death. He believed Crane was essentially a religious poet, but one whose religion entailed an absolute faith in impulse and intuition, rather than in any rational conception of God or morality. Winters felt that the "social restraints, the products of generations of discipline, which operated to minimize the influence of Romantic philosophy in the personal lives of Emerson and Whitman, were at most only slightly operative in Crane's career," and that without such restraints "madness" and "suicide" were the "inevitable" consequence of putting the "doctrine of Emerson and Whitman" "into practice."[14] When Winters told Crane that he found Emerson's doctrines unbelievable, Crane declared "Well, if we can't believe it, we'll have to kid ourselves into believing it" (579). As Winters points out, Crane expresses much this same sentiment in "The Dance" section of "The Bridge" when the narrator pleads with the Indian medicine man to "Lie to us! Dance us back the tribal morn!"

When Winters called Dickey an "American decadent romantic poet following Emerson," he no doubt had these very ideas in mind. Dickey's emphasis on "creative lies" are his way of dancing the reader back to the "tribal morn." In "The Suspect in Poetry" (1960), Dickey indicated his acute concern with a poem's religious effect on the reader. "What matters is that there be some real response to poems: that for certain people there be certain poems that speak as directly to them as they believe God would" (*The Suspect in Poetry* 10). But Dickey, living in an age even farther removed from the "social restraints, the products of generations of discipline" than Crane, presents a religion of naturalistic forces and of *willed* sensation.

For Emerson transcendence means passing beyond generally accepted human limitations to discover that a connection with an "Oversoul" exists. This supernatural entity guides the individual, rewarding good behavior while punishing wrong doings. For instance, in "Compensation" Emerson sets out to refute doctrines which claim that "judgment is not executed in this world." Dickey's metaphysics are immanent rather than transient, however. Morality becomes a subjective construct devoid of a supernatural touchstone. Dickey believes that "man no longer has to depend on any supernaturalisms, nor *can* he rely on them . . . man is essentially what he has made of himself" (*Night Hurdling* 91). Dickey desires to reconnect with intuitive, basic forces, but finds no god or "Oversoul" to help mediate the process. Dickey's individual must engage in an action—artistic, psychological or physical—that *makes* a new reality spring forth ("Man is free to act, but man must act to be free"). But while Dickey believes in the importance of "intuitive reaction" in combatting existential *angst*, he also believes that such a response has a destructive side, in contrast to Bly and Ginsberg, who both see "impulse" as a saluatory purgative from an oppressive commercialized society.

Dickey's Emersonianism is not innocent but propelled into a value-free world where no objective moral standards exist. Dickey claims that the combination of "the need for some kind of adrenalin in your body" which gives "the sense of living on the edge," "significance to things," and the security and comfort which America's relatively affluent life affords can be "an intolerable match up" because it creates "the Lee Harvey Oswalds of the world" who "would rather be murderers than be the nothings that they are" (*Night Hurdling* 95–96). Out of Dickey's belief in this condition arise characters like "The Fiend," a clerk who escapes his inconsequential existence by engaging in vouyerism and murder. In such poems Dickey gives us the world Winters feared. While Dickey sees Winters' antidote to Romantic philosophy, rationalism and order, as creating the need for actions based on impulse, he also regards such actions as potentially diabolical.

On the surface, much in the New Left—irrational mysticism and the instinctual—should have been agreeable to Dickey, but his belief in people's destructive potential causes him to depict reactions against mainstream culture as a double-edged sword that can pare conformity but also wound. Dickey's beliefs are incongruent with Winter's ordered world of high culture and Bly's New Left counterculture. In *Deliverance* the suburbanites engage in an experience designed to help them break away from routine existence, but the cost includes death and rape at the hands of truly primitive men who follow their impulses without vacillation.

This volitale combination of contradictory messages, in which the "cure" is potentially a life-affirming *and / or* a destructive atavistic reawakening, unsettled the New Left literati, who had a tendency to embrace Utopian solutions. In sharp contrast to the New Left's idealism, Dickey presents a world where violence, love, pain, pleasure, death, and life are all vividly present and, at times, even indistinguishable. As a result, situations or emotional states in Dickey's poems are seldom characterized by one overpowering sensation, but present a mixture of contradictory forces.

Dickey's war poems reflect this tendency, frequently emphasizing the unique insight extreme, and often violent, situations can yield, rather than explicitly protesting against the existence of such situations. Typical of Dickey's war poems, "Between Two Prisoners" (1962) emphasizes the subjective reality of the individual and the paradoxical nature of the visionary moment. In the poem Dickey shows that the captor is in many ways just as trapped as the captive. To create the poem Dickey draws on information he obtained from Filipino guerrillas, who told him Donald Armstrong and another prisoner, Jim Lalley, were held in an abandoned schoolhouse and tied with wire to children's desks until they were executed the next morning. Though the first half of the poem concentrates on the prisoners' situation and reactions, midway through the poem the primary concern becomes the guards' actions and reactions. The poem opens with the narrator's declaration,

> I would not wish to sit
> In my shape bound together with wire,
> Wedged into a child's desk
> In the schoolhouse under the palm tree.
> Only those who did it could have done it.

The last line of this stanza provides a key to the poem. The line could be translated "Only those who have been cast in such a role know what such a performance entails." As the poem develops the extreme situation serves as a catalyst for revelation. This becomes equally true for the role the guard must perform.

The dramatic situation in which Dickey places the guard reflects his emphasis on paradox. The guard finds himself, as the poem's title indicates, caught "Between Two Prisoners." The prisoners develop a special communication between them, as "A belief in words grew upon them / That the unbound, who walk, cannot know." The guard, who has fallen asleep, also becomes privy to this special language. He can "hear, in a foreign tongue, / All things that cannot be said." As the prisoners talk to each other they gain vision. Out of the "deep signs carved in the desk tops" by the children who once inhabited the schoolhouse and the "Signs on the empty blackboard," a burst of colors appears, evolving into the shape of an angel "casting green, ragged bolts / Each having the shape of a palm leaf." The palm leaf suggests peace and reconciliation, and the figure of the sleeping guard, emitting "red," bloodlike tears, also becomes luminous, suggesting his spiritual salvation. The guard's redemption is also implied when the two prisoners' voices enter his consciousness as he sleeps. In the morning when the guard awakes he discovers "he had talked to himself / All night, in two voices, of Heaven."

Later, the guard suffers a fate similar to the prisoners':

> I watched the small guard be hanged
> A year later, to the day,
> In a closed horsestall in Manila.
> No one knows what language he spoke
> As his face changed into all colors,
>
> And gave off his red, promised tears,
> Or if he learned blindly to read
> A child's deep, hacked hieroglyphics
> Which can call up an angel from nothing,
> Or what was said for an instant, there,
>
> In the tied, scribbled dark, between him
> And a figure drawn hugely in chalk,
> Speaking words that can never be spoken
> Except in a foreign tongue,
> In the end, at the end of a war.
>
> (*Poems 1957–1967*, 78–80)

As in "The Performance," in "Between Two Prisoners" Dickey focuses on individual revelation without issuing an explicit moral pronouncement. His suggestion that the guard experienced a visionary moment similar to that of the prisoners', and that the guard's experience was even a result of his relationship with the prisoners, goes beyond absolving the guard of any "blame"; it indicates that the prisoners and the guard share a spiritual bond. The common bond of death and war brings the characters to this union. While the narrator asserts that such situations are not desirable ("I would not wish to sit / In my shape bound together with wire"), the knowledge the characters gain is made possible by the torturous events. The drastic circumstances push the soldiers' thoughts towards revelation, and the narrator reports this paradoxical occurrence without moral evaluation.

As I have suggested, Dickey's tendency to regard violent forces not as anomalies but as a part of existence is an attitude characteristic of American visionary poets. American visionary poets have traditionally experienced difficulty identifying "evil" in their designs because their purpose has been to understand and unify. In rapturous moments in his essays Emerson could make statements to the effect that once human "vision" was completely restored "so fast will all disagreeable appearances, swine, spiders, snakes, pests, mad-houses, prisons, enemies, vanish" (*Selections from Ralph Waldo Emerson* 56), but his more typical approach is expressed in poems such as "Brahma" or in these lines from "The Sphinx," where he views the dualities of existence as necessary components to the whole of life:

> Eterne alteration
> Now follows, now flies;
> And under pain, pleasure,—
> Under pleasure, pain lies.
>   (420)

While Dickey's extremes are more extreme than Emerson's, both men account for violence or pain by assimilating the negative features of experience into the general process of life. Dickey's narrator does not condemn "The Fiend" but simply describes him and his actions. For Dickey he exists as an undeniable component of the modern world. Whitman, Crane and Roethke all display a similar way of dealing with the negative—a look at representative poems by each of these writers—for instance "Song of Myself," "The Bridge," "Cuttings (later)"—would bear this out.

Until the sixties, the project of the American visionary poet, unlike Blake or Shelley, had not been to enact political change through prophetic Utopian visions; instead, the American visionary poet typically takes elements or emotions that seem disparate and reconciles them to show us a connection that already exists but is not apparent—something that we never realized or that must be re-established. Thus the American visionary poet tends to focus on what is already there rather than what could be, and the poetry tends to be more realistic than allegorical: there is no "Urizen" or "Prometheus Unbound" among the works of American visionary poets. For the American visionary poet the message that comes across is "what we have here is enough if we can view it in the right way."

This factor helps account for the decidedly *realistic* component to this essentially romantic genre. The almost journalistic observation and detail found in places in Whitman's, Crane's, Roethke's, and Dickey's work (e.g., catalogues, arrays, etc . . .) implies that a convincing and exact portrait establishes that what already exists in many ways *is* the vision. The creed of the American visionary poet is best expressed in a sentence from the "Preface" to the 1855 Edition of *Leaves of Grass*: "The poetic quality is not marshalled in rhyme or uniformity or abstract addresses to things nor in melancholy complaints or good precepts, but is the life of these and much else and is in the soul."

To some critics, Whitman's statement, like Emerson's and Dickey's decision to focus on the "self," might seem a passive acceptance of America's political and social circumstance. Visionary realism could be seen as a means of reinforcing, or even actively theorizing, the status quo. But such an interpretation fails to take into account that such poetry strives to reach a greater understanding of what exists; indeed, this understanding is the vision. For instance, "Between Two Prisoners" reveals that the captors and the captives share a human and spiritual bond, but are forced into the dilemma because of forces beyond their control. War and violence are situated within a dialectic that generates the visionary insight. This is what Dickey means when he asserts that his poems have "an implicit moral stance" (Suarez 122). But, as I will show, the Vietnam milieu resulted in much literary criticism priviledging the didactic over the dialectical, resulting in criticism where subtleties were lost or misinterpreted.

The rise and fall of Dickey's critical reputation provides an excellent example of how historical events shape critics' responses. During the mid 1960's Dickey's reputation underwent a meteoric rise because people read his poems as a critique of sentimentality. Critics praised his ability to deal with a wide range of emotions and experiences. *Into the Stone* and *Drowning With Others* were very well received, and *Helmets* (1964) was nominated for the National Book Award. *The Nation* claimed that unlike most poets, Dickey provides "the real tooth and claw."[15] *Atlantic* magazine declared that Dickey and Lowell were the only living "major" American poets (Davison 116–121); the *New York Times Book Review* heralded him as one of America's most important poets and the *Chicago Sun Times* pronounced him the most important critic of contemporary poetry.[16] These reviews, and many others, lauded Dickey's poetry and criticism for its honesty and integrity.

One such "honest" poem, however, significantly changed the direction of Dickey's career. In 1965 Dickey published "The Firebombing," in which a middle-aged American confronts his participation in "anti-morale" bombing missions of Japanese civilians. "The Firebombing," like "Between Two Prisoners," "The Performance" and all of Dickey's war poems, is based on actual experiences; they explore the various dimensions of painful events that did occur in order to furnish insight into those events. "The Firebombing" draws on Dickey's experiences as a member of the 418 Night-Fighter air squadron in World War II. Widely praised, the poem was the central piece in *Buckdancer's Choice*, which won the National Book Award in 1966, but a year later Bly put together an issue of *The Sixties* featuring "The Collapse of James Dickey" and condemning "The Firebombing." At the time Bly was co-chairman of American Writers Against the Vietnam War and was leading anti-war protests across college campuses nationwide. Perhaps because Dickey was working for a political candidate and living in Washington while serving as Consultant in Poetry to the Library of Congress, Bly claimed Dickey was "a toady to the government." Though Dickey was working for Eugene McCarthy, and had helped write several anti-Vietnam war speeches,[17] Bly declared Dickey was in favor of the war and denounced "The Firebombing" as "sadistic."[18] To Bly Dickey's visionary realism was an "easy acceptance of brutality," a quality he identified as "deeply middleclass" (75): "As a poet and a man, Mr. Dickey's attitudes are indistinguishable from standard middle-class attitudes. One cannot help but feel that his depressing collapse represents some obscure defeat for America also. He began writing about 1950, writing honest criticism and sensitive poetry, and suddenly at the age of forty-three, we have a huge blubbering poet, pulling out southern language in long strings, like taffy, a toady to the government, supporting all movements towards empire, a sort of Georgia cracker Kipling" (78–79).

Despite his work for McCarthy, which went largely unnoticed, Dickey's reputation never recovered among the anti-war literary community after Bly's attack. As sentiment in the academic and literary community began to turn against the Vietnam war in the mid-to-late sixties, denunciations like Bly's became increasingly widespread.

Bly's attack involved a number of ironies. Bly identifies Dickey with the "average American"—an image Dickey had cultivated in opposition to the elitism of poets like T. S. Eliot. In other words, Dickey, who had presented himself and been received as a bold new voice who would shake up the literary establishment, became the embodiment of the WASP establishment. The "standard middle-class" stance Bly vilifies Dickey for was the same antiacademic "honesty" for which had critics praised him earlier. Bly himself provides the best example of this reversal. In 1964 Bly had praised Dickey's war poems, insisting Dickey's "courage is so great" that "he does not fill" his poems "with phony Greek heroes as disguises, but instead places himself in front of the poem, under clear glass, where you can see him for good or bad" (Bly 1964, 57). But as the United States became the enemy of the New Left literary establishment, Dickey, who had assumed a Whitmanesque stance as a people's poet, became a symbol of middle-class prejudices. The "democratic" poet became the poet of the "ugly American."

Anthony Libby called Dickey a "poet of ultimate violence" and a "reptile brain," asserting that Vietnam had "solidified Dickey's conservatism, his sense that powerful countries, like great men, are unnecessarily weakened by extreme moral self-consciousness."[19] Frederic Jameson wrote that Dickey's work was "repellent" and "right-wing."[20] Ralph J. Mills declared that Dickey's poems had sunk into a "moral abyss," reflecting "an obsession with power and the imposition of will—and a total insensitivity to the persons who are the objects of this indulgence."[21] Anthony Thwaite asserted that in Dickey's work the "world that lies outside might as well not exist for all the notice that is taken of it," complaining that Dickey takes no notice that "a real and bloody war is going on." Thwaite insists that because in *Deliverance* Dickey shows "Southern hicks behave badly and inscrutably; so, by extension, do oriental gooks."[22] Martin Dodsworth claimed that unlike "decent men like Robert Bly" "James Dickey is the poet of [another] America, which can afford to hunt, shoot and fish expensively—cleaned limbed son of Atlanta, Georgia, veteran of the Korean war and the war before that, who has not yet written a poem about baseball but probably will . . . His poems subscribe heavily to the fantasy of a man's world—war, savage nature, bloody sex—and don't have much to do with people."[23] This negative reaction was not due, however, to a change in the thematic content of Dickey's work, as Bly and others claimed. As I have shown, violence and war themes were prevalent components in Dickey's work from the start, and he continues to write poetry and prose that, without making explicit moral judgements, explores what violent situations reveal about the human condition. What Vietnam *did* change was the literary establishment's and the academic community's attitude about war, and, more generally, all forms of violence.

The way in which Bly reads "The Firebombing" demonstrates the extent to which the Vietnam milieu shaped and distorted his perception of the poem, and also suggests how the war pushed many critics towards didactic assessments of literature. Bly claims that in the poem the "civilian population of Asia" are treated as "objects of sadism" and that the poem "makes no real criticism of the American habit of firebombing Asians." Bly feels the poem shows "an obsession with power" and that it "emphasizes the picturesque quality of firebombing . . . the lordly and attractive isolation of the pilot, the spectacular colors unfolding beneath" and a "hideous indifference" (Bly 1967, 73–75).

In the poem Dickey does emphasize the feeling of unlimited power the pilot experiences, but for a purpose much different from the one Bly suggests. To Dickey the poem is "about the guilt at the inability to feel guilt." He wants to show that "the detachment one senses when dropping the bombs is the worst evil of all":

"The Firebombing" is based on a kind of paradox based on the sense of power one has as a pilot of an aircrew dropping bombs. This is a sense of power a person can otherwise never experience. Of course this sensation is humanly reprehensible, but so are many of the human emotions one has. Judged by the general standard, such emotions are reprehensible, but they do happen, and that is the feeling. Then you come back from a war you won, and you're a civilian, and you begin to think about the implications of what you actually did do when you experienced this sense of power and remoteness and godlike vision. And you think of the exercise of authority via the machine that your own government has put at your disposal to do exactly what you did with it. Then you have a family yourself, and you think about those people twenty, thirty, forty years ago—I was dropping those bombs on them. Suppose somebody did that to me? It was no different to them. (Suarez 122–123)

Bly reveals his preference for the didactic over the paradoxical when he identifies the poem's opening as its only redeeming section, because it offers "some critcism of the pilot" by showing his "indifference" (Bly 1967, 73).

> Homeowners unite.
>
> All families lie together, though some are burned alive.
> The others try to feel
> For them. Some can, it is often said.
> > (*Poems 1957–1967*, 181–188)

But even here, Bly's interpretation is off because of his insistence on creating binary oppositions. In this case he wants the pilot to be either "good" or "bad," which does not allow him to adequately address the poem's dramatic situation: a suburban American trying to confront his inability to feel guilt at having bombed Japanese civilians twenty years ago. The poem is not criticizing the pilot, but exploring his present state of mind and contrasting it with the sensations he experienced as a pilot. The narrator's use of the word "lie" indicates he is looking at his own "safe" existence in the American suburb and seeing it as an illusion. Besides lying together, in the physical and communal sense, domestic life presents the falsehood of civilized safety. The declaration that "some are burned alive" indicates that the narrator is comparing his present life with the lives of the Japanese civilians, who were firebombed in their homes. When he declares that "Some can, it is often said" "feel" for the victims, it is not a criticism of the narrator displaying his "indifference"; instead these lines show the guilt he cannot feel—guilt at having participated in the bombing—and the guilt he does feel: guilt at not being able to feel guilt for having committed the violent acts.

Dickey continues to stress individual subjective perception, as the narrator begins imaginatively re-creating his own war experience in order to comprehend it and to feel the guilt he senses he must:

> Snap, a bulb is tricked on in the cockpit
>
> And some technical minded stranger with my hands
> Is sitting in a glass treasure-hole of blue light,
> Having potential fire under the undeodorized arms
> Of his wings, on thin bomb-shackles,
> The "tear-drop-shaped" 300-gallon drop tanks
> Filled with napalm and gasoline.

Though at first the narrator has difficulty associating his present self with the self he once was ("some technical minded stranger with my hands"), he feels a clear sense of power. The cockpit is a "treasure-hole" and he becomes part of the plane ("his wings"). Dickey's decision to equate the man with the machine suggests that violence is not a product of technology or "progress," but a part of the human animal. Civilization, whose "deodorized" world view covers up the destructive aspects of existence, has been left behind for an "undeodorized" reality that includes impending violence and destruction. The situation in which he is placed—an "anti-morale" bombing mission—allows these forces to become unleashed.

The narrator flies over the peaceful Japanese countryside, occasionally returning to his present, recalling that "Twenty years in the suburbs have not shown me / Which ones were hit and which not." He *wants* to remember so as to make the situation real and induce the guilt accompanying that reality. Recalling the calm with which the Japanese civilians lived below triggers a vision of his own current life:

Think of this   think of this

I did not think of my house
But think of my house now

Where the lawn mower rests on its laurels
Where the diet exists
For my own good   where I try to drop
Twenty years, eating figs in the pantry
Blinded by each and all
Of the eye-catching cans that gladly have caught my wife's eye . . .

But in this half-paid-for pantry
Among the red lids that screw off
With an easy half twist to the left
And the long drawers crammed with dim spoons,
I still have charge—secret charge—
Of the fire developed to cling
To everything: to golf carts and fingernail
Scissors as yet unborn tennis shoes
Grocery baskets toy fire engines
New Buicks stalled by the half moon
Shining at midnight on crossroads   green paint
Of jolly garden tools   red Christmas ribbons:

Not atoms, these, but glue inspired
By love of country to burn,
The apotheosis of gelatin.

Dickey uses this ironic vision of suburbia to show how "each and all" of the suburban trappings serve to "blind" the narrator from the horrible destruction in which he participated. He also uses this passage to demonstrate the narrator's realization of his continuing responsibility for the firebombing. Because the narrator cannot see "Which ones were hit and which not" when he attempts to imagine firebombing the Japanese, he tries comprehending his actions by bringing the war into the American suburb. He imagines *his* world being firebombed.

The situation's paradoxical nature is again emphasized as the narrator remembers experiencing aesthetic detachment as he watched the bombs burst upon Beppu, consuming civilian homes, "fulfilling / An 'anti-morale' raid":

> Ah, under one's dark arms
> Something strange-scented falls—when those on earth
> Die, there is not even a sound;
> One is cool and enthralled in the cockpit,
> Turned blue by the power of beauty,
> In a pale treasure-hole of soft light
> Deep in aesthetic contemplation,
> Seeing the ponds catch fire
> And cast it through ring after ring
> Of land: O death in the middle of acres of inch deep water!

Beginning this sequence with "Ah" gives the affect that the narrator is experiencing a sense of relaxation and relief. The bombs ("something") seem to fall almost by accident and they result in an exhilarating sensation. Though the narrator feels that "thinking of it, / The fat on my body should pale," he cannot bring himself to experience genuine remorse. What frightens him is not the destruction he wrought, but his inability to feel guilt at having participated in the civilian massacre:

> It is this detachment,
> The honored aesthetic evil,
> The greatest sense of power in one's life,
> That must be shed in bars, or by whatever
> Means, by starvation
> Visions in well-stocked pantries.

Despite his efforts, he remains "unable / To get down there or see / What really happened." The only thing he can keep doing is to try to imagine the atrocities in terms of his current existence:

> But it may be that I could not,
> If I tried, say to any

Who lived there, deep in my flames: say in cold
Grinning sweat, as to another
As these homeowners who are always curving
Near me down the different grassed street: say
As though to the neighbor
I borrowed the hedge-clippers from
On the darker-grassed side of the two,
Come in, my house is yours, come in
If you can, if you
Can pass this unfired door. It is that I can imagine
At the threshold nothing
With its ears cracked off
Like powdery leaves,
Nothing with children of ashes, nothing not
Amiable, gentle, well-meaning,
A little nervous for no
Reason   a little worried   a little too loud
Or too easygoing   nothing I haven't lived with
For twenty years, still nothing as
American as I am, and proud of it.

Absolution? Sentence? No matter;
The thing itself is in that.

Bly felt the poem shows "an obsession with power" and that it "emphasizes the picturesque quality of firebombing . . . the lordly and attractive
isolation of the pilot, the spectacular colors unfolding beneath" and a "hideous
indifference." Actually, the poem shows the hideousness of the indifference
the pilot felt—an indifference that, at the work's conclusion, continues to
make him suffer and feel guilt. The detachment that warfare can create
between one's actions and those actions' consequences is identified as "The
honored aesthetic evil." The visionary moment results in the narrator bringing
the war into the American suburb, making him feel responsibility for the
slaughter of innocent civilians.

In "The Collapse of James Dickey," Bly never mentions that the poem
concerns World War II, not the Vietnam war, nor does he distinguish between
the Japanese and the Vietnamese. That he simply uses the category "Asians"
indicates how the distinction between the two wars is blurred in his reading
of the poem ("The Firebombing," in fact, was completed by 1963, before the
Vietnam war received much negative attention in the U.S.). The manner in
which he interprets the poem's opening lines, viewing them as a criticism of
the pilot, further suggests what triggers his misinterpretation. Bly objects
because he thinks the "poem soon drops this complaint" against the pilot.
Like Libby, Thwaite, Mills, Jameson, Dodsworth and others, Bly wants Dickey
to engage in didactic moral outbursts. Bly wants "The Firebombing" to

condemn war and damn the pilot for having participated in it at all: "If this were a poem scarifying the American conscience for the napalm raids, it would be a noble poem" (74). But Dickey's narrator never questions the war's justness because he assumes that World War II was fought for a legitimate purpose. Dickey's narrator attempts coming to grips with the atrocities he *had* to commit in a war worth fighting. The experience makes him recognize the violence of which he is capable; the poem enacts an individual trying to comprehend his actions and subsequent emotions.

Dickey's career clearly demonstrates how history changes and determines critical assessments of a poet's work. During the Vietnam era what was once a voice of complex courage became in the minds of many the simple tool of the status quo, as numerous critics were unable or unwilling to go beyond the question of whether or not a poem presented an outright denunciation of war or violence. Thus Dickey's war poems are not revelatory of insensitivity and unconcern but of the way their philosophical underpinnings conflicted with Vietnam altruism. Understanding the romantic and existentialist tenets that inform Dickey's poetry are essential to comprehending how his visionary realism was misinterpreted, and demonstrates how a writer who unrelentingly pursued insight into deeply distressing and very real situations became a moral monster to the New Left literary establishment.

Notes

1. Hyatt H. Waggoner. *American Poetry from the Puritans to the Present.* (Baton Rouge: Louisiana State University Press, 1984), traces Emerson's importance to subsequent American poets. Waggoner includes brief remarks on the similarities between Emerson's and Dickey's conception of the poet. Robert Kirschten, *James Dickey and the Gentle Ecstasy of Earth.* (Baton Rouge: Louisiana State University Press, 1988), 16, briefly compares Emerson's and Dickey's relationship to romanticism.

2. Ralph Waldo Emerson. *Selections from Ralph Waldo Emerson.* Stephen E. Whicher, ed. (Boston: Houghton Mifflin Company, 1957), 230; hereafter cited in text.

3. James Dickey. "The Energized Man" *The Imagination as Glory.* Bruce Weigl and T. R. Hummer, eds. (Urbana and Chicago: University of Illinois Press, 1984), 164; hereafter cited in text.

4. James Dickey. *The Suspect in Poetry.* (Madison, Minnesota: The Sixties Press, 1964), 76; hereafter cited in text.

5. Dickey has long professed the desire to "energize" his readers by getting them to remain receptive to the full spectrum of psychic and physical life. He describes the energized individual as one who "functions with not, say, fifteen percent of his faculties, as advertisers and psychologists say the average man does, but, ideally, with a hundred percent, a veritable walking A-bomb among the animated or half-animated spectres of the modern world" ("The Energized Man" 165).

6. James Dickey. *Self-Interviews.* (New York: Doubleday and Co., 1970), 92.

7. James Dickey. *Poems 1967–1967.* (Middletown, Conneticut: Wesleyan University Press, 1967), 30–31; hereafter cited in text.

8. Spurred on by F. O. Matthiessen's *American Renaissance: Art and Expression in the Age of Emerson and Whitman* (1941), a wealth of now well-known books which claimed a central

position for Emerson in American literature were published during the 1950's and 1960's. Notable examples include Vivian C. Hopkins' *Spires of Form* (1951), Sherman Paul's *Emerson's Angle of Vision: Man and Nature in American Experience* (1952), Charles Feidelson's *Symbolism in American Literature* (1953), Stephen Whicher's *Freedom and Fate* (1953), R. W. B. Lewis' *The American Adam* (1955), Roy Harvey Pearce's *The Continuity of American Poetry* (1965), Joel Porte's *Emerson and Thoreau* (1966), Richard Poirier's *A World Elsewhere* (1966), Michael Cowan's *City of the West* (1967), and Hyatt Waggoner's *American Poetry from the Puritans to the Present* (1968). Significantly, Waggoner, who sees Emersonianism as the central influence on American poetry, concludes the most recent edition of his book (1984) by predicting that Dickey, along with Denise Levertov, will come to be regarded as the most important contemporary poets.

9. Richard Sugg. *Robert Bly.* (Boston: Twayne, 1986), 142.

10. Robert Bly. "The Work of James Dickey." *The Sixties* (no. 7, winter, 1964), 41–57; hereafter cited in text, and "Prose vs. Poetry." *Choice.* (no. 2, 1962), 65–80.

11. James Dickey. *Night Hurdling.* (Columbia and Bloomfield Hills: Bruccoli Clark, 1983), 149–150; hereafter cited in text.

12. James Dickey. *Sorties.* (Garden City, New York: Doubleday, 1971), 72.

13. Ernest Suarez. "An Interview with James Dickey." *Contemporary Literature.* (vol. 31, no. 2, 1990), 121; hereafter cited in text.

14. Yvor Winters. *In Defense of Reason.* (Denver, Alan Swallow, 1947), 589–590.

15. Michael Goldman. "Inventing the American Heart." *Nation* 204 (24 April 1967): 529–530.

16. Peter Davison. "The Difficulties of Being Major: The Poetry of Robert Lowell and James Dickey." *Atlantic* 220 (October 1967), 116–121 [reprinted in part in this volume] and X. J. Kennedy, "Joys, Griefs, and 'All Things Innocent, Hapless, Forsaken.'" *New York Times Book Review* (23 Aug. 1964), 5.

17. Letters between Dickey and McCarthy which demonstrate Dickey's involvement in McCarthy's campaign are on deposit at the South Caroliniana Library on the University of South Carolina campus. As these materials make clear, Dickey helped the McCarthy campaign by attending fund raisers and other events, and helping develop speeches.

18. Robert Bly ("Crunk"). "The Collapse of James Dickey." *Sixties* 9 (Spring 1967), 70–79.

19. Anthony Libby. "Fire and Light, Four Poets to the End and Beyond." *Iowa Review* 4 (Spring 1973), 121.

20. Frederic Jameson. "The Great American Hunter or Ideological Content in the Novel." *College English* 34 (November 1972), 181. [Reprinted in part in this volume.]

21. Ralph J. Mills. "The Poetry of James Dickey." *Triquarterly* 11 (Winter 1968), 238, 240–41.

22. Anthony Thwaite. "Out of Bondage." *The New Statesman* 80 (11 Sept. 1970), 311.

23. Martin Dodsworth. "Towards the Baseball Poem." *Listener* 79 (27 June 1968): 842.

James Dickey's Natural Heaven

Marion Hodge

James Dickey's message for the world may be, finally, that earth is all we have and all we will ever have of heaven. This is the meaning of "The Heaven of Animals," a text which acts as a nexus of concerns in *Poems 1957–1967*.[1] Especially prominent themes in this collection are the status of predation in animal life and the relationship between nature and culture.

The heaven in "The Heaven of Animals" is not an ultimate place, as are traditional human heavens; rather, it is a primal place. It is not the ultimate abode of the ultimate bodily form involved in ultimate activities; it is the earth, where natural beings kill to eat and struggle to reproduce their kind. "The Heaven of Animals" does not describe what will be in some higher realm; it describes what *is* in our own "natural heaven." The perfection shown in the poem is not perfection as we ordinarily think of it; it is the way instinctive beings live their lives right now in the natural world.

"The Heaven of Animals" is a metaphor for the timelessness of life on earth. It is not about the immortality of individuals, but rather the immortality of species. If any genesis is suggested, it is the continuous "genesis" of life and generation. This heaven is not a heaven of reverent joy, nor of potential come to fruition, nor of fulfillment after an existence of incompleteness, nor of unity after chaos, nor of wholeness after fragmentation, nor of security after threat. This heaven is not a place where negation of ego is rewarded. It is a place where the whole physical panorama of life on earth is condensed to its fundamental elements: killing and birth. In fact, Dickey's own comments about "The Heaven of Animals" support the natural heaven interpretation. In an interview reprinted in *Night Hurdling*, Dickey rejects a number of traditional ideas, and says, finally, that the poem is indeed symbolic of physical life on earth.

Of initial concern to Dickey is the tendency of those who use the cycle-of-nature trope to rationalize—or ignore—the suffering of individual victims. "[A]ll this talk about the cycle of nature," Dickey says, "must be a tough thing to hear if you're the animal that's getting torn to pieces."[2] Dickey's own trope in the poem, "the cycle's center," is perhaps used as a kind of moral

From *South Atlantic Review* 56, 4 (November 1991), 57–70. Reprinted by permission of the publisher, South Atlantic Modern Language Association.

bull's-eye to cause readers to zero in on individual suffering, for suffering is certainly suggested when the victims "tremble," "fall," and "are torn." Still, the matter of individual suffering is made problematical in the poem by the statements that the prey "feel no fear" and are "without pain." Why do they tremble if they feel no fear? Why do they feel no pain when they are torn apart?

Resolution of this paradox would seem to hinge upon the matter of individual identity, which is Dickey's subsequent concern in the interview reprinted in *Night Hurdling*. Dickey finds "grossly unfair" the belief that "animals have no souls, and therefore they're perishable, not like us wonderful human beings" (284). Interpreting "soul" as essential identity, Dickey says that a heaven of animals "wouldn't really be a heaven if the animal was deprived of his nature. I mean the killer must still be able to kill, and the hunted should still be hunted" (284). Finally, Dickey summarizes his understanding of the theme when he says the poem is "some kind of mystical vision of creation" (286). If "creation" means "this world," then heaven, as the poem puts it, must consist of the "knowledge" as well as the "acceptance" of our role as both death-dealer and mortal being.

Traditional heavens are perfect because they conceive of the individual as existing in a place where, except for that modification, the individual ego is maintained throughout all no-time. Traditional heavens are places of peace because individuals, no longer prey to others, experience no fear and because, no longer predators, they experience no guilt. As Joseph Campbell says, images of heaven have been based on life within the womb, without action and without temporality: "The state of the child in the womb is one of bliss, actionless bliss, and this state may be compared to the beatitude visualized for paradise. In the womb, the child is unaware . . . of any of the images of temporality. It should not be surprising, therefore, if the metaphors used to represent eternity suggest . . . retreat to the womb."[3] In contrast to such metaphors, the images in Dickey's heaven of animals are full of action, and temporality is directly mentioned: the predators' descent upon the prey "May take years / In a sovereign floating of joy." Dickey's heaven, then, from just this perspective, would not seem to contain typical paradisaical bliss.

Despite this difference, readings of "The Heaven of Animals" commonly compare the environment there with traditional human heavens. In addition, readers often see the violent predation in the poem as nightmarish. Paul Carroll, for example, interprets the heaven as "an eternal Eden for animals" in which there is a "total absence of conflict or discordancy," an absence that "suggests an orderly, even tranquil and universal concord."[4] Yet, there is the stalking, attacking, and tearing apart of prey by predator. Aware, then, of the awful paradox he has discovered—violent concord—Carroll understandably finds himself "in the middle of a nightmare" from which he wants desperately to escape (47). Heaven should be Edenic, a peaceable kingdom where predator and prey lie down together because there is no need to eat each other.

Calhoun and Hill, too, find themselves in the same kind of nightmare as they try to unravel the knot of "[t]emporal flow in the timeless setting" of Dickey's heaven.[5] The poem, they say, describes a "horrid cycle," but an incomplete one, because it lacks the final predation of scavengers—there are, they observe, "no vultures to rip away the flesh of lions and leopards" (44). In addition, Calhoun and Hill interpret the predation in ultimate terms, as "the perfection of the law of the jungle," and they describe this heaven as "a world in which the strong prevail without guilt, without compunction, only to savor joy and flight, the savagery of killing without the obligations of consequence" (44). The heaven depicted in the poem is horrid to these readers because it lacks the moral values of the heaven we have been taught by the ages to desire, the heaven of ultimacy, the heaven that eliminates moral responsibility because it eliminates the necessity for deadly action. A place where the leopard tears the zebra's throat without guilt is no heaven we have ever created. We have striven long, millenia, to separate ourselves from the law of the jungle, to disguise the origin of our food. "Kill" becomes, eventually, "cuisine." We are civilized.

In Campbell's terms, religion itself, and story, are founded on the paradox that we must kill in order to live: "The qualm before the deed of life—which is that of dealing death—is precisely the human crisis overcome [in myth]. The beast of prey deals death without knowledge. Man, however, has knowledge, and must overcome it to live" (180).

Nelson Hathcock, too, talks about "The Heaven of Animals" in terms of nightmare, or, rather, dream, saying that while Dickey's heaven "is one into which the yaks and leopards and buffalo awaken, it is also a heaven from which we have awakened and found ourselves human."[6] Hathcock argues that the animals in the poem are "generic beasts of prey descending upon the backs of generic prey" (53). The heaven of the poem, he says, is "uncomplicated by any question of good or evil" (52), the implication being that people are superior to animals because we have "awakened" into morality.

Other readers interpret the poem in similar terms. Joyce Carol Oates says the animals are "poetic constructions, Platonic essences of beasts wholly absorbed in a mythical cycle of life-death-rebirth . . . like Emerson's red slayer and his perpetual victim."[7] Robert Kirschten says the poem tells of the "cyclic movement of life, death, and rebirth" in a heaven which "contains no pain," where there is "no gory detail," and where "victims feel no fear."[8] Ronald C. Baughman sees the poem as a "perfected version of the predator-prey relationship," and says the "animals repeat their performance—without concern, without remorse."[9] Laurence Lieberman says the animals are "ideally beautiful and innocent, incapable of evil."[10]

It is true that there is no question of good or evil in Dickey's heaven of animals; the animals are indeed incapable of evil, and they certainly feel no remorse, but the reason is not that they have been translated into a realm that perfects their identities. The reason is that animals are not encumbered with such matters as they go about their lives of surviving—eating and avoiding being eaten—right now on earth. Animals kill without remorse because they must eat, not because they find pleasure in it. Furthermore, the argument that Dickey is ignoring the entire cycle by omitting scavengers from his heaven fails to consider that the predation is the symbol of *all* animal killing and eating. The predator in the poem is all predators and the prey is all prey. In nature, and so in the "heaven" of animals, a predator is also prey and an animal that is prey is also a predator.

When they write of "sanctioned carnage" (44) and of the poem being Dickey's "cold dream of domination" (45), Calhoun and Hill are reading from the perspective of traditional ideas of heaven. For the predation to be "sanctioned," there must be a moral power superior to that of the animals' amoral identities, and there is no indication in the poem of such a power. Moreover, there is no evidence that Dickey is suggesting that domination is the superior quality. The prey receive the final, emphatic attention, and in nearly half the poem, Dickey is entirely unconcerned with the predator and its prey, showing us animals in general and their heavenly environment:

> Here they are. The soft eyes open.
> If they have lived in a wood
> It is a wood.
> If they have lived on plains
> It is grass rolling
> Under their feet forever.
>
> Having no souls, they have come,
> Anyway, beyond their knowing.
> Their instincts wholly bloom
> And they rise.
> The soft eyes open.
>
> To match them, the landscape flowers,
> Outdoing, desperately
> Outdoing what is required:
> The richest wood,
> The deepest field. . . .

This passage emphasizes clearly positive qualities: softness, blooming, rising, richness, depth—not domination. It also emphasizes the importance of individual identity rather than domination; *all* the animals, not just the predators, get in heaven the environment that has given them their identities on earth, or, to say it as we have been saying it, the natural environment is all the heaven there is. How could it be possible otherwise, for them and for us, to maintain identity except among the places and actions that created the identities in the first place? A setting can be heaven only if the animals can keep their instincts, which developed in a particular environment.

James Dickey may be *searching* for heaven on earth, as Peter Davison says,[11] but it is clear that in several moments he has found it. The purest discovery is told in "The Heaven of Animals," but there are many other poems in which the natural heaven is found and entered.

In "Trees and Cattle" (*Poems* 37–38), for example, the way to heaven is shown to be the monism of movement Kirschten discusses (11–16), which is the active joining of disparate parts, the search for the sense that all are one. Most trees stand passively in the sun, "But some may break out" and "be taken to Heaven." The "sun," the "gold," the "crowning glory," the "spark / and fire," the "new light" all symbolize the blinding, suddenly overwhelming realization that all things and identities are finally one thing and one identity. The speaker has broken out of the darkness of individuality and now can "hover . . . / With the trees in holy alliance," the hovering being the stage intermediate between passive imperception and transcendent insight:

> Like a new light I enter my life,
> And hover, not yet consumed,
> With the trees in holy alliance,
>
> About to be offered up,
> About to get wings where we stand.

In this near-transcendent mood, the speaker understands what it is to be a bull—horns grow on his head—and he becomes aware of the importance of other creatures, earthly creatures, in the cultivation of his ecstasy:

> Continually out of a fire
> A bull walks forth,
> And makes of my mind a red beast
> At each step feeling how
> The sun more deeply is burning
>
> Because trees and cattle exist.

The vision dissipates, but the speaker keeps his gift of heaven; "[I]n some earthly way," he says, "I have been given my heart." The vision's continuing influence is shown by events occurring after the speaker turns away. He is aware of a tree that "leaps up / On wings that could save [him] from death." Like a protective canopy, halo, or crown, the branches of the tree "dance over [his] head." The speaker suggests the equivalence of nature and human nature when he says, "[The tree's] flight strikes a root in me."

While readers might agree with Calhoun and Hill that in "Trees and

Cattle" Dickey "allegorizes some transcendent reality" and "tries to unify space, time, and eternity in one indescribable concept" (18), and with Joyce Carol Oates that "[a] miracle of some kind has occurred, though it cannot be explained" (70), we might find a way of describing and explaining it if we read the poem within the context of the natural-heaven complex. There are images at the center of the poem similar to the "cycle's center" image in "The Heaven of Animals": "No leaf but is actively still; / There is no quiet or noise." As in "The Heaven of Animals," the stillness is *active*, a paradox that can be explained in terms of the relationship we have already noted between individuals and the species—while individuals are active as predators and prey, the species is motionless, living, by comparison to individual creatures, eternally. The bull, the primordial "red beast," "Continually . . . walks forth."

The wings on which the tree "leaps up" to heaven "could save" the man "from death" were he able to hold on to the elusive vision; that is, he would go to heaven, too, on the wings of the knowledge that the earth *is* heaven.

In "Walking on Water," too, heaven is described as union; here, however, rapture is not experienced by a person but by animals (*Poems* 39–40). A man remembers poling himself along the surface of the water as a boy while standing on a plank, a "miracle" to observers unable to see the slightly submerged plank. Now, the event is a natural miracle to the man because he sees the act as "an infinite step upon water," a sign of the infinite in the immediate. The man's union with the ocean animals is said to be their "spell" and "enthrallment" because they have stood still, "amazed" that the land creature has joined them in their domain, and has even conquered it. The union achieved through enthrallment is expressed most dramatically by the image of a shark, "A huge, hammer-headed spirit," a vicious predator, following the boy and so being "led by the nose into Heaven."

In "A Screened Porch in the Country," Dickey directly contrasts the natural heaven and the traditional one (*Poems* 96–97). The people sitting on the porch melt, in a way, into the land, the natural heaven, and join the animals there. Their shadows are thrown into the yard by the light of the house, an extension described by the speaker as the family being "laid down / In the midst of its nightly creatures," the animals that live around the house and, at night, come to the edge of the light. In fact, the animals are said to "Come to the edge of them," an image of near-union. The contrast of the two heavens is made in terms of light and blending, the family's

> bodies softening to shadow, until
> They come to rest out in the yard
> In a kind of blurred golden country
> In which they more deeply lie
> Than if they were being created
> Of Heavenly light.

As Ralph J. Mills, Jr., says of this poem, the "shadows come to possess" the people's "spiritual being or constitute its reflection."[12]

In "Fog Envelops the Animals" (*Poems* 62–63) a "river of Heaven" is formed by the confluence of "currents / And streams of untouchable pureness." The poem shows how the hunter's civilized identity is consumed by the fog and the predatory self is released: "Soundlessly whiteness is eating / My visible self alive. / I shall enter this world like the dead. . . ." In "this world" erupts a flame of transformation that causes the speaker to be united with the animals he stands among:

> In my hood peaked like a flame,
> I feel my own long-hidden,
>
> Long-sought invisibility
> Come forth from my solid body.
> I stand with all beasts in a cloud.

Then, coming quietly at the apex of the transformation, there is ecstasy, "the purest fear on earth."

When Dickey talks about this poem in *Self-Interviews*, his tone is that strange matter-of-factness characteristic of his analysis of his own work. There are only hints that he recognizes the mythic qualities there. "Fog Envelops the Animals" is one of the many poems that are, he says simply, "about hunting," necessarily violent to show respect for the hunted: "[A]n important relationship between man and animals has to be a life-and-death relationship. It's no good to take a camera into the woods and photograph animals. I think an animal is debased by that. I think you've got to go in there and try to kill him."[13] In his comments on "Fog Envelops the Animals," Dickey mentions "the cycle of the man who hunts for his food," and he admits that such involvement "may be playacting at being a primitive man, but it's better than not having any rapport with the animal at all" (111). The closest Dickey comes here to acknowledging the natural-heaven theme is this statement about spiritual regeneration: "I have a great sense of renewal when I am able to go into the woods and hunt with a bow and arrow, to enter into the animals' world in this way" (111). The natural-heaven theme does not appear very dramatically in this statement, but it does appear, for renewal is a result of union with the animal world in such poems as "Trees and Cattle" and "A Screened Porch in the Country."

Dickey speaks literally, too, about becoming invisible in the fog, at least until the final words, which are telling: "We all want to be invisible, at least part of the time, but most especially the hunter does. Concealment for the archery hunter is the greatest thing of all. In this case, the hunter, being exactly the same color as the fog, has total concealment. As long as he can see enough to shoot, but the animals can't see him, he's in heaven" (111). The hunter is in heaven when he cannot be seen by his prey, but more important, the hunter *in the poem* is in heaven because he has been so purified, baptized, in the white river of fog "Up out of the buried earth" that he is spiritually resurrected, reborn as an essential part of nature, nearly an animal himself.

A resurrection into the natural heaven occurs in "The Owl King," too, the story of an unformed soul's crisscross trek toward identity, the achievement of which is said to be heaven (*Poems* 70–77). Calhoun and Hill call the poem "a mystical journey" and say it is "actually about the interlocking—even the interchangeability—of the myriad spirits of the world" (30). With images of descent and penetration, the poet describes a blind child "going down / . . . Down, down the hill," crossing a flowing boundary, and ending up "there, on the other side," where, having arrived, the child is said to "own the entire world" (73). Heretofore, the child has owned only half the world, the human half, his essential role in the human world represented by the father's frantic search for the son who has wandered into the woods. Now the child owns the other half, the animal half, this ownership described in terms of embrace, union, joy, innocent nature, and heaven:

> The owl's face runs with tears
> As I take him in my arms
> In the glow of original light
> Of Heaven. (76)

This embrace symbolizes the child's embrace of all nature, his recognition of the dignity of every phenomenon and every creature, his union with "The self of every substance" (76). The owl's joyful tears would seem to symbolize nature's profound gratitude for the child's acceptance. Heaven is also reunion with the father, who, in calling for his son, is singing a "holy song":

> Father, I am coming,
> I am here on my own;
> I move as you sing,
>
> As if it were Heaven.
> It is Heaven. (77)

The child's soul is now formed, complete. He is no longer blind. He has discovered that heaven is the human partaking of the natural.

That earth itself is heaven is the prominent theme of "Falling" (*Poems* 293–99), which tells of a flight attendant—a servant, a functionary—who becomes a goddess as she falls from an airplane and strikes the ground, in which she becomes embedded. The theme of the natural heaven is reinforced by descriptions of the spiritual effects on farmers and others who observe the woman during and after her fall.

In "Falling," Dickey reverses the usual spiritual implications of the fall metaphor, thus suggesting, as I have indicated, that earth is the real heaven. The woman's fall is described as a transitional stage between spiritual blindness and illumination, a movement from death-in-life to fully realized life, even from sexual impotence to sexual power: as she descends "in the overwhelming middle of things" (293), she removes her clothes, becoming more primitive, more natural, naked like an animal; she watches "her country lose its evoked master shape" and "get back its houses and peoples" (295); she becomes "the greatest thing that ever came to Kansas" (297), causing farm girls to feel "the goddess in them struggle and rise" (296) and causing widowers and boys to feel the stirrings of sexual desire (297). The woman's fall constitutes "her brief goddess / State" (298), this brevity suggestive of the individual's role in the eternal round of life and death.

Her heavenly power is most forcefully manifested, however, after she has struck the ground, becoming part of the earth, as it were. Now the earth-goddess, mother earth, the woman transforms those who come near her body. The farmers in the area "fall" into the natural heaven when they "walk like falling toward the far waters / Of life . . . toward the dreamed eternal meaning of their farms / Toward the flowering of the harvest in their hands. . . ." (298). In fact, everyone who finds the woman embedded in the earth experiences spiritual renewal: "All those who find her," the speaker says, "remember / That something broke in them as well . . ."; as a result, they "began to live and die more" (298). Presumably, the "meaning" derived by the people is their new understanding of their place in nature and in the processes of life and death, "flowering" and "harvest." This understanding then allows them to both live and die more fully, like the predators and prey in "The Heaven of Animals," with acceptance and compliance. They now know that they and nature are one. As the woman's last words, "AH, GOD," indicate, the "fall" from servitude in civilization's machine to nature leads us to deity.

"For the Last Wolverine" (*Poems* 276–78) is Dickey's despairing, angry eulogy for the natural heaven and the poetry that is this heaven's voice as they are being destroyed by civilization. The poem ends with one of the most poignant pleas in the poetry of our time: "*Lord, let me die   but not die / Out.*" Our age is the first in which people have been able to watch—and have caused—the extinction of species. Dickey's poem is largely a dream of revenge for this murderousness; the poet imagines a terrible beast, a combined wolverine and eagle, attacking the fur trappers and road- and railroad-building crews who are threatening the environment, the implication being that the incursion of civilization into the wolverine's habitat is the animal's curse and doom. Furthermore, since the wolverine is made a symbol of the "wildness of poetry," civilization is the imagination's curse and doom as well, eliminating what "the timid poem needs," and so what timid modern life needs: the "mindless explosion" of "rage." The wolverine's doom is the doom of the natural heaven: "Lord, we have come to the end / Of this kind of vision of heaven." The earth is no longer heaven but, instead, deadening, destructive civilization.

Before the wolverine-eagle takes its revenge, the speaker imagines the wolverine gaining knowledge, an "idea," by eating, as its "last red meal," the heart of an elk. The knowledge gained is that the wolverine, being the last of its kind, can afford to confront its enemies directly, come out of hiding and take on the insurgents, fight to the inevitable end. And as this predatory meal is the source of the wolverine's courage, we have come full circle, back again to the "horrid dream" of "The Heaven of Animals," the nightmare of the natural world we must accept if we are to live fully.

But Dickey cannot maintain such a vision any longer; the enemy is too strong. The fight is hopeless. The wolverine will die out. The eagle will die out. Civilization will kill them. And civilization will kill the poet, too. The earth is no longer raw heaven, but, rather, cuisine, bloodless, cooked and flavorless.

And that is the ultimate meaning of the natural-heaven theme in James Dickey's poems—to live successfully, intensely, we must accept the natural world as it is, bloody as it is, and fight to keep our place in the processes of earth, here and now. Eating, which, on earth, means also to be eaten, is the symbol of an active powerful love of life, and love of the earth that is life's source.

Our way to heaven, Dickey cries in "For the Last Wolverine," is "to eat / The world, and not to be driven off it." According to some readers, however, Dickey himself has driven humanity from the world of "The Heaven of Animals." Oates thinks the poem is "all but unique in Dickey's poetry because the poet himself has no clear position in it, as if the unity of Being somehow excluded an active intellectual consciousness" (71). Baughman also thinks that consciousness, with its attendant morality, excludes humanity from the heaven of animals; people are "not psychologically equipped to participate in" what Baughman interprets as the "un-thinking, remorseless life-and-death cycle" (40). Lieberman thinks humanity is not good enough for the heaven depicted by Dickey; the poem, he says, "suggests that man is the only corrupt animal. If he were removed from earth, beatitude would automatically transpire, just as it must have prevailed before his coming" (16).

Too much is perhaps being inferred in these readings. The omission of people from Dickey's heaven does not, of itself, mean that the unity of existence is destroyed by humanity's consciousness. Omission does not necessarily mean exclusion; it means, possibly, that people are to be included in the natural processes as one with the animals, as predators even, without morally superior natures. We are not like animals, we are animals. It is not a matter of being psychologically unable to participate in a "remorseless" cycle of killing and eating; we do participate in the cycle. That we do not recognize our part in it, or that we try to make ourselves superior to it, proves the strength of our ancient fear and guilt. The point of the natural-heaven theme is to show us that we do indeed participate in the violent cycle and to suggest that the acceptance of our place in it would lead us to "heaven," a message that makes moot the question of humanity's corruption. Beatitude is what is; each being is a part of it.

In virtually every James Dickey poem, the sympathetic reader finds the poet's serious effort to say something fundamentally important. There is probably no less whimsical poet, yet there is no poet more joyful. This blend of seriousness and joy stems, at least in part, from Dickey's rejection of the traditional ideal realm built upon denial of life's physical realities, and from his own acceptance of those realities. But we should not think that joy easily achieved. As such poems as "Falling," "For the Last Wolverine," and even "The Heaven of Animals" demonstrate, much—the luxuries of civilization and the notion of an entirely free will—must be divested, and this divestiture sometimes happens only as a last resort. The woman in "Falling" becomes a goddess because there is nothing else she can do except fall to earth. The last wolverine achieves its ferocious nobility only because it is cornered. The predators and prey in "The Heaven of Animals" cannot choose any other course of action. Thus, an emotional-philosophical struggle pushing the poet toward visions of unity seems to underlie these poems. It is possible that Dickey's emotional-philosophical struggle arises from his knowledge that the creatures of nature, including humans, must kill and die but that he rejoices because he knows that species exist far longer than the individuals that compose them ("forever" he might say in his expansive "heavenly" mood) and because he knows that individuals are species' particular loci of uniqueness. Perhaps such knowledge explains the passionate regard for the dignity of each creature and of all creation—and for the union of the two—shown in the natural heaven images.

Notes

1.   James Dickey, *Poems 1957–1967* (New York: Collier, 1968), 59–60; hereafter cited in text as *Poems*.

2.   James Dickey, *Night Hurdling* (Columbia, SC: Bruccoli Clark, 1983), 284.

3.   Joseph Campbell, *The Masks of God: Primitive Mythology* (New York: Penguin, 1969), 65; hereafter cited in text.

4.   Paul Carroll, *The Poem in Its Skin* (Chicago: Follett, 1968), 43, 44.

5.   Richard J. Calhoun and Robert W. Hill, *James Dickey* (Boston: Twayne, 1983), 44; hereafter cited in text.

6.   Nelson Hathcock, "The Predator, the Prey, and the Poet in Dickey's 'Heaven of Animals.'" *Contemporary Poetry* 18.1–2 (1985), 56; hereafter cited in text.

7.   Joyce Carol Oates, "Out of Stone, Out of Flesh: The Imagination of James Dickey 1960–1970," *The Imagination as Glory: The Poetry of James Dickey*, Bruce Weigl and T. R. Hummer, eds. (Urbana: U of Illinois P, 1984), 71; hereafter cited in text.

8.   Robert Kirschten, *James Dickey and the Gentle Ecstasy of Earth: A Reading of the Poems* (Baton Rouge: Louisiana State UP, 1988), 23; hereafter cited in text.

9.   Ronald C. Baughman, *Understanding James Dickey* (Columbia, SC: U of South Carolina P, 1985), 39.

10.   Laurence Lieberman, *The Achievement of James Dickey* (Glenview, IL: Scott, 1968), 16.

11.   Peter Davison, "The Great Grassy World from Both Sides: The Poetry of Robert Lowell and James Dickey," *James Dickey: The Expansive Imagination*, Richard J. Calhoun, ed. (Deland, FL: Everett and Edwards, 1973), 46.

12.   Ralph J. Mills, Jr., "The Poetry of James Dickey," *The Imagination as Glory: The Poetry of James Dickey*, Bruce Weigl and T. R. Hummer, eds. (Urbana: U of Illinois P, 1984), 31.

13.   James Dickey, *Self-Interviews*, Barbara and James Reiss, eds. (New York: Delta, 1972), 110; hereafter cited in text.

"Dancing With God": Totemism in Dickey's "May Day Sermon"

Joyce M. Pair

Recent studies reveal James Dickey's early knowledge of anthropology, ethnology, and philosophy and provide a clearer reading of his early poem, first published as "May Day Sermon to the Women of Gilmer County by a Lady Preacher Leaving the Baptist Church" in *Atlantic Monthly* (1967). These influences—"the works of such anthropologists as Bronislaw Malinowski, Alfred Reginald Radcliffe-Browne," James G. Frazer, Jane Ellen Harrison, and Joseph Campbell,[1] among others—continue to be reflected in Dickey's teaching at the University of South Carolina.[2] Dickey still uses Jane Ellen Harrison's *Themis* (1912), a seminal work for Frazer and Malinowski, in the classroom. As Jaan Puhvel notes, Harrison provided "a strikingly simple and exclusionary definition of myth: myth, the verbalization of ritual, is 'the spoken correlative of the actual rite'."[3] Familiarity with these textual influences enhances the reading of "May Day Sermon" because they provide a basis for the anthropological / ethnological gestalt that empowers women in prepatriarchal systems of morality. Dickey describes the enclosure of women in the Appalachian region of North Georgia as well as the mythical background, what Malinowski calls the rite, ceremony, or social and moral rule that demands "justification, warrant of antiquity, reality, and sanctity."[4] In *Self-Interviews* Dickey says that the poem resulted from a statement by Edwin Arlington Robinson to the effect that the Bible read as a novel has God as the villain. Dickey reports that he has "seen a good deal of evidence" that God, whether by nature a villain or a hero, can be made a villain by villainous people.[5] To dramatize the cruelty of such people, in this case the men of a rural community who subjugate women in the name of religion, Dickey reimagines a legend about a house in Gilmer County in the northern, mountainous part of Georgia.

According to the legend, people avoid the house because of the parricide committed there years ago. The legend relates a daughter's murder of her father, who brutally whipped her for meeting a young lover; she elopes, only to die with her motorcycle-riding lover as they plunge off the road. Reporting these events is the fundamentalist Baptist preacher, a woman. The woman

This essay was written specifically for this volume and is published here for the first time.

preacher as spiritual teller represents both ancient goddess and modern guide to young women. As Malinowski notes, folk tales recited annually are " 'owned' by a member of the community," usually a good raconteur[6]; the Baptist preacher is the owner-orator of this sacred tale of myth of the Georgia hills. Dickey's sermon form, according to Christopher Clausen, "is as native as the characters, though it presents the same problem of restricting the author to the voices of people . . . who are too unsophisticated to embody their author's attitudes and still remain in character."[7] Dickey's figures, however, mythologize the everyday and everyday people; archetypes brilliantly converge in the fundamentalist Baptist woman preacher, who with her church parallels Athena and her temple.

The eternal drama of death and resurrection is expressed through these naive characters, the native North Georgia mountain people often captured in Dickey's poems, as well as in *Deliverance* and *Wayfarer: A Voice From the Southern Mountains*. The preacher places the timeless, Edenic lovers in the modern machine age; they "fell from life. . . . / Their legs around an engine."[8] Dickey hints that the magic of science, through the motorcycle and its invasion of the North Georgia paradise, brings death to the clannish mountain people who believe the couple returns each spring. Dickey has said that the poem is concerned with the "absorption of these details into the minds of a community"; it also has "something to do with the ingrained attitude of mythologizing that rural communities have. What originated as blood lust and religion, sex and escape has now become something of a legend, and the woman preacher who speaks the poem has taken that legend as her text, and also as her valedictory to the Baptist Church, which is in some manner connected with the events of the legend" (*Self-Interviews*, 183). The connection between the Baptist Church and its belief in primal sin and the blood lust, religion, sex, and death / resurrection of the legend, symbolized by the May Pole, forms the cultural connection of primitive to modern religion.

According to Jane Harrison, part of the nature of the communal or tribal totem is the idea "of the unit of a group," in special relation to another group of non-human objects.[9] In this case, fog, gamecock, snake, and neighbor / lover are community markers. Totemism's two sides, according to Malinowski, are "a grade of social grouping and a religious system of beliefs and practices."[10] The connection between these two exemplifies Dickey's visionary exchange between the known, the particular, and the unknown, the universal, what H. L. Weatherby has called "some rather mysterious process of exchange between a man and his opposites."[11] Juxtaposing the ancient May Day goddess-mother who kills her consort[12] to the less ancient Old Testament religion of the vengeful father-god who beats his daughter while "screaming / Scripture CHAPter and verse" (33–34), Dickey patterns timeless moments; he connects woman as Earth Mother, who has fallen victim to her patriarchal role, to Eve, whose sin-called clothes—"abominations / In the sight of the Lord" (27–28)— are removed by her father for her punishment in "the woods / That hold its primeval powers" (84–85). The May Day ritual, sanctified by the earliest primitive religions, and accepted for more than a millennium after the time of Christ,[13] is unsanctified by Christianity, and also by modern woman's need to overcome paternalistic restraints of her sexuality. The woman preacher privileges women's determination to exit the patriarchal enclosure where sexuality means guilt by describing the daughter's bursts of pain and defiance as she screams again and again, "YOU CAN BEAT ME TO DEATH / And I'll still be glad" (66–67), glad of her sexuality, glad of her springtime lover. Consistent with her goddess vision, the woman preacher has foreknowledge that the daughter's hair will be "full of the gray / Glints of stump chains" (97–98) if she remains in Gilmer County: she will be imprisoned in the Christian patriarchy of original sin.

Dickey's comparisons in "May Day Sermon" demonstrate the connection between the modern Baptists and the violence of the legend by creating a meta-mythology; the poem represents what Jaan Puhvel calls "a study of the study of myth."[14] "May Day Sermon" is a mythopoeic creation that exchanges the pagan divinity of the fertility cult with the newer, Christian myth to establish a protoculture. By creating a myth of two totemic clans, Dickey creates a tension between two religions which have similarities and differences: the Christianity of the Baptist mountain men whose sexuality is sacrificed to guilt and the fertility rituals to which the preacher calls the mountain women. Throughout the 360 lines of the poem,[15] Dickey uses a four-part totem: Christian paternalism and the tree, symbol of ancient Druidism, are combined to represent the animism of the fertility ritual. By opposing clan symbols while revealing the unity of their origins, Dickey's poem transcends the temporality of its North Georgia rural setting and mythologizes the legend of the two lovers. Primitive and modern humankind demonstrate the timeless unity of blood acts, the mind, and the spiritual consciousness. In the poem, the mystic symbols are an explicit totem, one that represents the Christian patriarchy of the father and the young male lover, and an implicit, totemic May Pole that represents the primitive matriarchy of the woman preacher and the female hero. The two totems are presented by the narrative voice of the woman preacher, fully informed of both views because of her soon to be ended connection with the Baptist Church, and because of her gender.

Dickey's selection of the female preacher-narrator and the parricidal daughter as protagonists establishes the frame of pre-Christian religious rituals that worshipped the Earth Goddess. In an early review of the poem, Maxine Rose recognized in Dickey's epistemology the "perceptiveness in this poem which transcends gender, but, at the same time, leaves a powerful impression at once sympathetic and empathetic toward women in society and their subjugation at masculine hands, particularly those of the church."[16] In spite of the misprision of women's sexuality by contemporary mountain Christianity, Dickey indicates that all time flows together in nature; therefore, fog, game-cock, snake, and neighbor / lover must finally flow into one ritual, the fertility ritual represented by May Day, assimilated into Christianity by God's injunction to Noah and his sons (Genesis 9:1) to "Be fruitful, and multiply, and replenish the earth."

The fusion of female images—daughter / priestess / lover—emphasizes life's flow, the Heraclitean (or Dickeyean) way of exchange.[17] As the father unchains his daughter from the barn centerpole, the place where "all things have heard—fog, gamecock / Snake and lover" the chants of the father and the screams of the daughter, the priestess shows the dual direction of flow in Gilmer County: "Each spring, each creek / On the Lord's land flows in two   O sisters, lovers, flows in two / Places." One place is the accustomed creek bed from which enveloping fog arises; the other is where roads lead out of "the farm of God / the Father" (184–88; 190–91). The choice to remain in Gilmer County or to escape the enclosure is presented to the unchained goddess, and her selection creates an illuminating moment, what Northrop Frye calls "a single simultaneous pattern of apprehension." The epiphany occurs within the changed barn with "its one pole of light paid out / In spring by the loft" (6–7), chiaroscuric light that brings the events out of the shadows to illuminate the retributive act: the Earth Goddess-daughter chained and whipped for all the sins ascribed to women entrapped in the enclosure of Christianity who is

> WHIPPED for the wind in the willow
> Tree   WHIPPED for Bathsheba and David   WHIPPED for the woman taken
> Anywhere   anytime   WHIPPED for the virgin sighing   bleeding
> From her body   for the sap and green of the year   for her own good
> And evil. (120–25)

At this point in the poem, Clausen notes, "the preacher begins referring to Venus," references which "become increasingly numerous and disconcerting as the sermon continues," commenting that "the emotion is insufficiently grounded in either the story or the dramatic circumstances of the poem."[18] However, given the proper anthropological / ethnological frame, Venus, the Roman name for the Great Goddess in her sexual aspect, grounds the emotion of the conflict between primeval goddess worship and the Christian patriarchal religion. J. H. Smith, in *Constantine the Great*, recalls the denouncement by early Christians of the temples "dedicated to the foul devil who goes by the name of Venus—a school of wickedness for all the votaries of unchasteness."[19] And educated Romans, envisioning the moment of death as a culminating sexual union, a "final act of the sacred marriage promised by the religion of Venus," have Ovid as spokesperson, wishing to die in the act of love: "Let me go in the act of coming to Venus; in more senses than one let my last dying be done."[20] Venus the Evening Star is also Stella Maris, Star of the Sea, a title assimilated to the Virgin Mary.

The eventual collapse of the barn, a reversal of the primeval goddess's capture by and assimilation into Christianity, reverses also the enclosure of women and animals, symbolized by the Ark, and releases the animals pent up along with Noah; "the animals are saved without rain" (342) as they, along with the goddess, are freed by the sacrificial murder. In 1970 Dickey commented that "May Day Sermon" was his best work at that time because "the mode of treating this subject matter—which encompasses animals, religion, natural scenery and sex-as-action—is as near as I have been able to get to the kind of lengthy intensity I have hoped for."[21] This intensity owes much to the poem's narrative movement from legendary event to religious homily to sexual climax as Dickey brings together the separate and unified strands of local legend, May Day primitive ritual, and Christianity.

The modern wreckage of faiths and values of Christianity is posed against the deposed ancient primitive rituals, revealing both continuity and discontinuity between two anthropological and ethnological poles which have changed the status of women. The May Day fertility rite and the preacher / daughter / priestess metaphor of Diana and her Triple Will restores man as part of nature, removing his concept of being apart from and above the other animals. Using I. A. Richards' distinction between the tenor and the vehicle of a metaphor, we may say that the tenor in Dickey's "May Day Sermon" is fertility, nature's need to replenish itself, while the vehicle is May Day itself, a festival which evokes a group of ancient images of Maya or Maia, the Virgin Goddess of Spring represented in ancient cultures by many names. May, the traditional month honoring "the Earth Mother's new garment, and of fornicating in plowed fields to encourage the crops," was ushered in by May Eve, known variously as Walpurgisnacht, Beltaine, or Baltein, when the god Baal, Bel, or Balder was burned in effigy.[22] These customs relate to ancient rituals of burning of the man who represented the god in his love-death or *Liebestod*. Juxtaposing ancient ritual with more recent tradition, Dickey's poem advocates a full and free life for women. Monroe Spears has commented that "[L]ike most Southerners," Dickey "has a strong religious sense: [H]is poems are often sermons or prayers or invocations. But his creed might be called natural supernaturalism, or fundamentalism so fundamental that it concerns man's relation to all other life forms."[23] These characteristics of the poetry are evident in "May Day" as Dickey foregrounds the eternal flux and flow through animals, religion, and sexual energy.

Making the poem into an oral history of Gilmer County and of primitive peoples, Dickey uses Harrison's definition of myth: what the preacher / priestess has to say is the spoken correlative of the actual rites described. To present her sermon on the anniversary of the lovers' elopement and deaths and on the occasion of her own farewell to the Baptist Church, the preacher takes as text a therimorphic totem. The woman preacher lashes the clan, identifying the primitive totem in which, according to James Frazer, "A man keeps his life"[24]: "Each year at this time [she preaches] I shall be telling you / of the Lord—Fog, gamecock, snake and neighbor—giving men all the help they need / To drag their daughters into barns" (1–3). Taking this four-part totem as the basis for her sermon, the preacher explicates her homiletic text; she applies her doctrine to the contemporary springtime, elucidating the elements that conspire against women:

> . . . I cannot help
> Telling you how he hauls her to the centerpole   how the tractor moves
> Over as he sets his feet and hauls   hauls   ravels her arms and hair
> In stump chains. . . . (12–15)

Only in the light of "totemistic thinking," Jane Harrison's term in *Themis*,[25] can such a relationship between these natural elements on one side—fog, gamecock, snake, and neighbor / lover—and the group or clan on the other side be understood. The anthropological / ethnological relationship that exists among these elements equates the Christian "Lord" with fog, gamecock, snake, and neighbor, as well as with the male members of the mountain clan.

Fog, the first totemic element, rises from the several creeks, and transforms man and his anthropomorphic God into a legless creature, the serpent who introduces sin into Eden and Gilmer County. Jehovah becomes the local copperhead snake as the fog connects Gilmer County to the Edenic garden with its four rivers and serpent. In her Baptist sermon, the woman preacher is

> Telling: telling of Jehovah come and gone
> Down on His Belly   descending   creek-curving   blowing His legs
> Like candles, out   putting North Georgia copper on His head
> To crawl in under the door in dust red enough to breathe
> The breath of Adam into. (15–19)

Here, the baptism of life-giving dew, as Harrison identifies it, becomes a foggy cover for the stealthy serpent which in Christian myth inverts the classical image of Athena with the serpent who is "the lord and luck of the house."[26] With water, condensed into fog, Dickey unites the modern patriarchal Christian community with its beginning, when God's spirit moved upon the expansive void and separated the waters.

The second and third totems, the gamecock and the snake, comprise equal parts of the idea of male sexuality as totem. According to Frazer, an animal species is the most usual form of totem, although plant species are by no means uncommon; even classes of material objects are occasionally found, and sometimes abstract qualities, including pride, are totems.[27] In Dickey's second and third totems the classes of objects form an objective correlative to male sexuality; the male group, the most powerful force to which the individual is subject, receives totemic expression. The fighting rooster, the "cock-of-the-walk," equates the coercive force in the mountain clan with male sexuality. Dickey, reminiscing about his father's career in North Georgia's Fannin County with fighting cocks, says that in a gamecock-fight, "if your cock is not killed—which they almost always are—but if you want to save him, you put him out on a walk with nothing but hens. Because what makes them fight is sexual pride."[28] The North Georgia gamecock thus unifies the modern clan with the serpent ancestor; both serpent and gamecock represent "the old Adam," the sinful sexual impulse. Dickey's description of the gamecocks recalls Freud's description of men in *Totem and Taboo*: "Sexual need does not unite men; it separates them."[29] The gamecock as totem animal also inhabits the concealing vapor that is the presence of the deity: in the "fog taking the soul from the body / of water gaining rising up trees sifting up through smoking green / Frenzied levels of gamecocks [are] sleeping" (71–73). The lovers, attempting to elope by motorcycle, leave the road and seem to fly through the tops of the trees, "Through cocks tightening roots with their sleep-claws" (316), clinging symbolically to the roots of the world and to the beginning of Biblical time.

Into this mythic place of creativity, imaging both the primeval forest and Eden, Dickey brings the elements of Christian guilt: the dust of red clay that is both *Adhamah* or earth and the unregenerate side of man, his sexual impulse symbolized by the phallic serpent. Because a totem is considered the tribal ancestor, the Edenic serpent seems rightfully chosen for the Baptist clan which masks its sexuality as an evil, inverting the ancient myth of the serpent as companion to the earth goddess. Woman's enemy, the Judeo / Christian God who has identified her as evil, becomes the totemic Georgia copperhead; he is sin or Satan crawling on his belly with legs disappeared into the ground fog. He is the cock trained to fight, the "neighbor" or father who, "the Lord's own man[,] has found the limp Rubber that lies in the gulley," and seemingly in religious ecstasy punishes his naked daughter (21–22). God is the lover as well, no paladin, who leaves the rubber, "the penis-skin like a serpent / Under the weaving willow" (22–23). Thomas O. Sloan, noting the conflation of sexual metaphors, comments that "All male images in the poem become fused, and so do all female images,"[30] resulting in dichotomous totems. The fusion of theriomorphic cock and snake with neighbor and fog reveals the community of sameness shared by the father and lover. The father, the fanatical Old Testament Christian as well as the primitive, dying nature god, uses his daughter as an instrument of climatic religious and sexual fervor. "[E]ach May," the preacher accuses, the mountain people hear the father's punishment of his daughter for her participation in the spring fertility rite and for her escape from virginity, a metaphor for the Christian entombment in the "black box" which holds the old time religion:

<pre>
                                        you hear her father scream
          like God
And King James as he flails   cuds richen   bulls chew themselves
          whitefaced
Deeper into their feed bags, and he cries something the Lord   cries
</pre>

> Words! Words! Ah, when they leap   when they are let out of the
>   Bible's
> Black box   they whistle   they grab the nearest girl. . . . (44–48)

His speech, like semen and acrimony, is discharged in bursts. In spite of his Christianity (or perhaps because of it), the father images the ritual deposed king, the Earth Goddess's sacrificed lover, symbol of the resurrected god; because of his religion, he may also be a disguised Yahweh, who, the preacher warns the Gilmer County women, must be differentiated from the ritual slain god who has worshipped women: "O sisters . . . you cannot sleep with Jehovah / searching for what to be, on ground that has called Him from His Book" (75–76). The local woman who, under Christians sanctions, "knows she was born to hang / In the middle of Gilmer County to dance, on May Day, with holy / Words all around her" (49–51) must distinguish among the magical powers of gods such as Zeus and the Christian God who can appear like a cloud. Without such knowledge, the goddess, like Leda, will be raped, as the preacher's question indicates: "Shall He [Jehovah] be the pain in the willow, or the copperhead's kingly riding / In kudzu . . . or the wild face working over / A virgin" (77–79). The symbolic willow reinforces the totem theme, for the willow is especially related to goddesses. It represents, for instance, the virgin form of Hecate, and "willow wands invoked the Muses, whose mountain was encircled by the Helicon, 'Willow-stream'."[31]

The snake, an ancient classical symbol as well as totem animal, connects the Gilmer County fundamental Baptists, sometime snake-handlers in religious ceremonies, to earliest primitive man. The tribe or clan expected aid from its totem animal, and it was assumed that a totem such as a poisonous snake would protect rather than harm. However, as Freud comments, "The appearance of the totem animal near a house was often looked upon as an announcement of death. The totem had come to get its relative."[32] Snake-handlers in today's Christian fundamentalist ceremonies expect that only evil men will be harmed by the snake, that God protects the righteous, allowing only sinners to be bitten. In "May Day Sermon" the events ensue from the first, snakelike warning the girl's father receives: "the Lord's own man has found the limp / Rubber that lies in the gully the penis-skin like a serpent / Under the weaving willow" (21–23). Thus, the serpent's sign anticipates the sacrificial killing of the father. Although the daughter's hand raises the hatchet, the arrival of the competing male provides the catalyst as lover and serpent become synonymous; the preacher's voice identifies the springtime lover:

> Sisters, who is your lover? Has he done nothing but come
> And go? Has your father nailed his cast skin to the wall as evidence
> Of sin? Is it flying like a serpent in the darkness   dripping pure
>   radiant venom
> Of manhood?   (126–29)

The oxymoron—radiant venom—clarifies the opposing views of sexuality represented by the two totems, snake as companion of the goddess and snake as symbol of Christian sin. According to the legend, with the lovers' annual return the recurring sounds may be the daughter's "sinful barn- / howling for the serpent" (322–23), both Athena's cry for her old companion and the farm girl's lusty call for her lover. With the change of the serpent from symbol of classical wisdom and luck to the Baptist serpent of sin the regenerative barn becomes a torture chamber.

Finally, for the fourth and all-encompassing totem element, Dickey draws symbolic parallels between the Old Testament–chanting father and the young man, target of the father's jealous, gamecock-frenzy. Old and young, neighbors in the sense of clan members, they are fellowmen. Their rivalry is between clan members, among which totemic exogamy prevents the father's sexual intercourse with his daughter. The old father and the young lover reenact the mythic drama identified by Frazer in *Totemism and Exogamy* and by Freud in *Totem and Taboo*, among others. In the advance from animism to a religious society where incest becomes prohibited, the old father stands in the way of the son's sexual demands upon family females.[33] The young males kill the father and, in their guilt, substitute the totem. Thus the taboo against killing the totem animal arises because it represents the father, and the taboo against sexual intercourse with family women is established by the young males to prevent their competing to the death. Parricide and incest are the two prohibitions of totemism. In this poem, the incest is implied through the father's sexually-climactic calling upon the Old Testament god as he beats his naked daughter. The father as "neighbor" is, finally, exchanged with the lover; after the beating, the totem becomes "fog, gamecock, snake and lover":

> Children, by dark   by now, when he drops
> The dying branch and lets her down   when the red clay flats
> of her feet hit the earth all things have heard—fog, gamecock
> snake and lover—and we listen. . . . (182–85)

Opposed to the totem of the Baptist clan of men is the May Pole and its priestess to whom *we* listen. Emphasis on the narrative "I" foregrounds the woman preacher, whose protagonist role merges with that of priestess and of daughter, as she calls women to the May Day fertility ritual. Robert Kirschten notes that the Baptist preacher is "a modern shaman [who] entrances herself and her flock"; the poem "becomes a fertility rite designed to restore earth and women to a 'natural' state of fruitfulness by purging the community of evil through the scapegoating of the girl's father."[34] Rejecting the Eve-sin, woman as earth mother sacrifices the father, a primitive goddess ritual assimilated into Christianity by the sacrifice of the Christian son. The sacrifice frees her from the patriarchal barn centerpole, an inversion of the May Pole. Rather than the ritual fertility dance that is her right, the daughter, before her release from the Baptist community, leaps in agonized dance as she is whipped for the sin ascribed to women, her sexual appeal to men: "for woman taken / Anywhere anytime" (121–22). Around this centerpole, this "sapling to which she is chained like a tractor," woman dances to the patriarchal tune:

> ". . . like a girl
> on the red clay floor of Hell she screaming her father screaming
> scripture CHAPter and verse beating it into her with a weeping
> willow branch." (32–35)

The Druidic symbol, nature as willow tree or virgin, cries out against the Baptist repression of natural regeneration, a repression cast off when the daughter murders her father with a hatchet, reversing the patrilineal succession in favor of pre-Christian ritual.

As Kirschten observes, with the death of the father nothing perverse remains: "The repressive sexuality of the Bible is expelled along with its representative."[35] With the death of Christian patriarchy, the nature goddess is again at home in her green world; neither she nor the animals remain controlled. The preacher describes the goddess's reversal of Noah's selective gathering of mated pairs; she is "Telling on May Day, children: telling / That the animals are saved without rain that they are long gone / From here gone with the sun" (343–45), as the daughter releases all creatures, freeing the animals as well as herself from oppression. Like "Diana of the triple will, the white goddess who always kills, and whose rebirth is only for herself," the daughter ". . . comes down putting her back into / The hatchet often often" (225–26).[36]

After she has killed her father, the daughter puts an icepick into one of his eyes, rendering him Cyclopean in death. Her father is more than simply repaid by being killed with the hatchet; he is repaid in kind with the phallic icepick going into one eye. The father, like her lover struck in one eye by a tree branch and left with "one eye of amazing grace" (245), mirrors primitive clans with incestuous habits while also recalling Jesus's Sermon on the Mount, where externalism in religion is condemned. As Malinowski notes in *Sex and Repression in Savage Society*, the Cyclopean families consisted of a principal male who monopolized the women, including his own daughters—hence the evolution of taboos, the murder of the father by the sons, and the practice of totemic exogamy. The "one-eye" image Dickey uses suggests that the father, in incestuous and / or religious passion, has, like the lover, an erect penis. In "Sleeping Out at Easter" Dickey's persona clearly awakens with arousing passion as he thinks, "One eye opens slowly without me," followed in Stanza Two by

> As the Word rises out of the darkness
> Where my right hand, buried beneath me,

> Hoveringly tingles, with grasping
> The source of all song at the root,[37]

emphasizing the relationship between sexuality and regeneration. Dickey's use of erotic pantheism while relying on religious imagery creates much of the lyric intensity in "Sleeping Out" and in "May Day Sermon," as well as in other poems.

In the Christian terms of the Sermon on the Mount, the slain father as one-eyed man fits into one of two categories: "The light of the body is the eye; if therefore thine eye be single, thy whole body shall be full of light"; or, "But if thine eye be evil, thy whole body shall be full of darkness. If therefore the light that is in thee be darkness, how great is that darkness!" (Matt. 6: 22–23). Even as the daughter slips up behind her father with upraised hatchet, "he is rambling / In Obadiah," wondering who will bring him down (221–22); thus, the father is identified with violence and assault, the North Georgia mountain with Zion, for "upon Mount Zion shall be deliverance, and there shall be holiness; and the house of Jacob shall possess their possessions. And the house of Jacob shall be a fire, and the house of Joseph a flame, and the house of Esau for stubble, and they shall kindle in them, and devour them; and there shall not be any remaining of the house of Esau; for the Lord hath spoken it (Obad. 1:17–18). Dickey's suggestion that the walls of the barn, like Dagon's temple (line 39), will be pulled down like the walls of Jericho and the city of Sodom emphasizes the temporariness of structures of evil men. Samson's vengeance on the Philistines occurs after their righteous celebrations of Dagon (Judges 16:23–30). Thus, the poem intimates that the one-eyed father has lived in great darkness rather than in great light.

The implicit May Day totem becomes explicit southern pine as the ghostly lovers return for the annual spring ritual. Again they experience the ritual death as the motorcycle flies from the curved mountain road: "except for each year at this time, their sound / Has died: except when the creek-bed thicks its mist   gives up / The white of its flow to the air comes off [and] lifts into the pinepoles of May Day" (259–62). Applying the example of their deaths to contemporary life, the preacher exhorts the women of Gilmer County to reject the totem-shackles of the Baptist religion for a more ancient, woman-centered religion; she urges them to "enter into the older world of springtime, pleasure, love and delight" (*Self-Interviews*, 194). The motorcyclist, initially the "green world lover," represents "a combination of the animal guide, or spirit" described by Annis Pratt in *Archetypal Patterns in Women's Fiction*.[38] The animal guide, or serpent companion to the goddess, can help the women deny the Eve-guilt and regain their goddess role "with nothing / To do but be" (357–58).

Around the implicit May Pole totem the woman preacher fuses with the daughter. The woman figure is the whipped girl dancing; she is a Bacchante, a *maenad* frenziedly applying her text to the details of the bloody beating of the daughter as well as to the murder of the father with its implication of the symbolic slaying of the old god. She admonishes the girls and women of Gilmer County to follow the new / old god, the springtime lover representing the Dionysian principle: "O women . . . I shall be telling you to go / to Hell by cloud" (292–93), evoking shape-shifting gods. Dickey's image of one of these ancient shapes, the sacrificial boar-god often used as a totem animal, emerges with the motorcycle as boar-god, or hog-god, appearing annually.[39] With godlike prescience the approaching motorcycle rider "feels a nail / Beat through his loins far away" (132–33), as he senses the father's nailing the discarded condom to the wall and perhaps the blood response to past and present god-sacrifices as well. Approaching the farm, "there is now this madness of engine / Noise in the bushes   past reason   ungodly squeal- ing   reverting / Like a hog turned loose in the woods" (141–43). Eloping, the lovers take no earthly road but "have roared like a hog on May Day / Through pines and willows" (288–89) until the ensnaring scuppernong vine sends them off the road.

The motorcycle engine in the mountain Eden is crucial as evidence of the modern loss of regenerative energy. As Joyce Carol Oates has commented, a central theme in Dickey's work is "the frustration that characterizes modern man, confronted with an increasingly depersonalized and intellectualized soci- ety."[40] Dickey himself has noted that in a technological society people have been reduced to "well meaning zombies."[41] However, in "May Day Sermon" even "the one-eyed mechanic," experiencing godlike renewal on his motorcy- cle, finds a spiritual life of the modern age, a reaffirmation of human sexuality.

The mechanic in "May Day Sermon" owes much to the motorcycle rider in "Cherrylog Road." First published in the *New Yorker* in 1963, "Cherrylog Road" explores the sexual energy of a motorcycle rider and a farm girl whose meeting in dilapidated, ancient cars rejuvenates a North Georgia automobile junkyard. By being natural women in the world, by demanding acceptance of their sexuality, the women of Gilmer County and everywhere replace Baptist guilt with redemptive sexuality, as both "Cherry Log Road" and "May Day Sermon" testify.

In releasing the women of Gilmer County from the Baptist Church, with herself as symbol of empowerment, the priestess adjures the women to regain their goddess role; they must, she says:

> Listen   O daughters   turn turn
> In your sleep rise with your backs on fire   in spring   in your socks
> Into the arms of your lovers: every last one of you, listen one-eyed
> With your man   in hiding   in fog where the animals walk through
> The white breast of the Lord muttering   walk with nothing
> To do but be. (353–58)

The priestess / preacher urges the women to walk Venus-like in the "spring laurel," imaging Daphne, whom Hera "metamorphosed into a laurel" when

Apollo attempted to rape her,[42] and "self-sharpened Moon," their own lunar goddess; freed from the patriarchal enclosure of the barn, they "walk through the resurrected creeks through the Lord / At their own pace the cow shuts its mouth and the Bible is still / Still open at anything   we are gone the barn wanders over the earth" (358–60), and wanders in search of renewed freedom. Dickey's poem makes the point that the religion of the Baptist community holds no more sway than the fertility rituals, that the Gilmer County women are capable of and justified in escaping from enslavement in the torture barn, that the barn again has the possibility for fertility, regeneration. As the women walk through the fog—that is to say, through the entrapping Lord—the wandering barn renews the search for other beliefs, other myths, old and new. The preacher / priestess apparently renews her search for freedom also. She indicates that she will leave the Southern Baptist community that, according to Maxine Rose, is "torn between the primeval tuggings of the ancient past and the conscious prudery so nourished by Southern fundamentalism in the 'Holy Bible Belt,' and the female entrapped in the demimonde between." The homiletic harangue, an accretion of biblical and ritualistic images, is directed, Rose comments, toward "all that is cruel, savage, and atavistic in men everywhere."[43] The primitive as well as traditional and Christian image of the barn as a place of regeneration, as life-giving stable, undergoes a powerful change in ambiance: in the beginning, before the eyes of the watching animals, the barn is a torture chamber for woman's sin of sexuality, for imagined sin that is Adam's weakness and, biblically, the cause of man's fall. Controlled by the patriarchy, the daughter / goddess often finds herself "Dancing with God in a mule's eye" (87); a tiny image in the eye of a sterile hybrid work animal, she is merely an entertainment. Cleansed, however, by the fertility ritual, she may free herself, and she and the barn regain validity as symbols of rebirth. Finally, the Diana of the Triple Will survives in "May Day Sermon" to empower modern woman.

The influence of Dickey's studies of the earliest cultures of animism and religion is reflected in equally powerful totem symbols. With his way of exchange of opposites—the Baptist Church and blood lust, religion, sex and escape—Dickey releases the matriarchy from the Christian patriarchy that would use God as the villain and separate spirituality from sexuality. Through his acceptance of the iconography of religions through the ages, Dickey participates in universals prior to the time of Christianity and accepts the possibility of redemption and regeneration through all religious ritual. The preacher's sermon is not the solitary act of an individual but rather an act that participates in various cultural processes that relate the North Georgia mountain community to America, to Europe before Puritanism, to the world before Christianity, and to the universe of time and space.

Even though Dickey's May Day goddess must die for her sexual freedom, accommodating herself to a masculinized ideology and model of the self that reinforces the conflation of sex and violence, the poem's symbolic frame suggests that freedom does exist for women, that self-redemption exists outside the patriarchal enclosure, perhaps for even longer than the six-month period of freedom Persephone attained. Dickey's significant change[44] in the title from lady preacher to woman preacher emphasizes the preacher's status as the third stage of the triple will—the crone, or wise woman—who empowers herself *and* her female flock, representing the first two stages of virgin and childbearers by giving the Word, reborn and purified. Although the lovers have disappeared in death, they reappear by entering the mouth of the preacher through the Word of the Classical *mythoi*, which confronts the Biblical *logoi*, the Word the father chants. Through use of the mythology that has given western culture the Bible—which, as Frye indicates, provides "the epic of which God is the hero, the central place," a sky-father[45]—and Classical mythology, which focuses on a sexual creation myth and an earth-mother, the poet juxtaposes the mythic story that tells of a beginning and an end with the older mythic story, that has no ending but rebirth and recreation.

Too often, Dickey's critics have ignored his empowerment of women, preferring a reading of biographical details about the poet's own vaunted machismo to a close reading of the poetry. However, throughout the *oeuvre* woman has most often been presented with regenerative power, with originality, and with selfhood. (Far too many allusions exist to trace here; however, "The Scarred Girl" "The Fiend," and "Falling" are three such works, especially the latter where, when the restrictive trappings of her uniform are removed, the stewardess becomes goddess.) In the more recent *Puella* (1982), winner of *Poetry* magazine's Levinson Prize, Dickey imagines the childhood, coming of age, and passage into womanhood of Deborah, his young wife. Since publication of this cycle of poems that traces all women's evolution symbolized by these three stages of Diana of the Triple Will, Dickey has been assigned a more receptive attitude toward women. However, close reading of the poems reveals that Dickey's development of one strain of feminist thinking, which views woman as life-giving goddess, has been continuous throughout his career.

Epitomizing the poet's presentation of woman, the preacher / priest / daughter in "May Day Sermon" occupies the timeless, genderless, Tiresias role; as *seer*, what she sees is the substance not only of the poem but of all flux and flow of time. Thus, Dickey makes his neo-romantic point that humankind needs to reunify in time and space the body, the mind, and the spirit through nature. Perhaps ultimately only one mythological universe exists, although every reader may see it differently. In recovering both myths through the folklore of North Georgia, the poet transfers the mythic center from hero to the reader, where it belongs. By doing so, Dickey presents an early and positive view of woman's sexuality and capacity for empowerment.

Notes

1. Arthur Gordon Van Ness, "Ritual Magic: James Dickey's Early Poetry" (Ph.D. diss., University of South Carolina, 1987), 10, *passim.*

2. For discussions of Dickey's reading and teaching, see, for example, Gordon Van Ness, "When Memory Stands Without Sleep: James Dickey's War Years," *James Dickey Newsletter*, 4 (Fall 1987): 2–13; and his "Ritual Magic," a seminal study of Dickey's early reading and formal study. Also, see Ken Autrey, "James Dickey's Poetry Course," *James Dickey Newsletter*, 4 (Spring 1988):2–8. For Dickey's use of these sources, see Robert Kirschten, *James Dickey and the Gentle Ecstasy of Earth: A Reading of the Poems*. Baton Rouge: Louisiana State Univ. Press, 1988.

3. Jaan Puhvel, *Comparative Mythology* (Baltimore: The Johns Hopkins Univ. Press, 1987), 15.

4. Bronislaw Malinowski, *Magic, Science and Religion and Other Essays* (1948; reprint, NY: Anchor Books, 1954), 107.

5. James Dickey, *Self-Interviews*. (Garden City, NY: Doubleday & Company, Inc., 1970), 183. Further citations will be included in the text.

6. Malinowski, 102.

7. Christopher Clausen, "Grecian Thoughts in the Home Fields: Reflections on Southern Poetry," *The Georgia Review* 32 (Summer 1978):299.

8. James Dickey, "May Day Sermon to the Women of Gilmer County, Georgia, by a Woman Preacher Leaving the Baptist Church," *Poems 1957–1967* (Middleton, CT: Wesleyan Univ. Press, 1978), lines 256–57. Further citations will be noted in the text by line number.

9. Jane Ellen Harrison, *Themis: A Study of the Social Origins of Greek Religion* (1912; reprint, Cleveland and NY: World, 1962), 120.

10. Malinowski, 20.

11. H. L. Weatherby, "The Way of Exchange in James Dickey's Poetry," *Sewanee Review* 74 (1966); reprinted in *The Imagination as Glory: The Poetry of James Dickey*, Bruce Weigl and T. R. Hummer, eds. (Urbana: Univ. of Illinois Press, 1984), 21.

12. Of the ubiquitous studies of on goddess worship, beginning with Sumerian literature from the early second millennium B.C. recounting Inanna's journey to the underworld, *Themis* by Jane Ellen Harrison (Cleveland and New York: World, 1962) seems to have contributed significantly to Dickey's background. Harrison, the first female scholar permitted to study the classics at Cambridge, first demonstrated that the pre-Hellenic, women's mythic stories provide the foundation of Greek culture. Robert Graves' *The Greek Myths* (Baltimore: Penguin Books, 1961), Frazer's *The Golden Bough* (New York: Avenel Books, 1981), Jessie L. Weston's *From Ritual to Romance* (Cambridge: Cambridge University Press, 1920) (particularly as referent for the myths of the dying king), and the works of Joseph Campbell provide basic information. Barbara Walker's *The Woman's Encyclopedia of Myths and Secrets* (San Francisco: Harper & Row, 1983) is an excellent current work. Annis Pratt's *Archetypal Patterns in Women's Fiction* (Bloomington: Indiana University Press, 1981); Estella Lauter's and Carol Schreier Rupprecht's *Feminist Archetypal Theory* (Knoxville: University of Tennessee Press, 1985) and K. J. Phillips' *Dying Gods in Twentieth-Century Fiction* (Lewisburg, PA: Bucknell University Press, 1990) are among many recent explorations of the goddess role in myth and literature. Northrop Frye's *The Secular Scripture* (Cambridge: Harvard University Press, 1976) provides an invaluable discussion of these mythological concepts within the framework of romance.

Especially interesting in its assignment of goddess figures into four positive and negative characteristics (1. rebirth and immortality and 2. vision and wisdom; 3. death, extinction through sacrifice (including ritual execution) and 4. madness, impotence, stupor through tendency to dissolve the personality, enchant, etc.) is the Jungian Erich Neumann's *The Great*

Mother: An Analysis of the Archetype (1955): 79–80, with an outstanding collection of illustrative plates of the earliest to recent goddess icons.

13. Graves, in *The Greek Myths*, vol. 1, cites the instance of May Day and the thirteen-month year:

> Even when, after careful astronomical observation, the sidereal year proved to have 364 days, with a few hours left over, it had to be divided into months—that is, moon-cycles—rather than into fractions of the solar cycle. The months later became what the English-speaking world still calls 'common-law months', each of twenty-eight days; which was a sacred number, in the sense that the moon could be worshipped as a woman, whose menstrual cycle is normally twenty-eight days, and that this is also the true period of the moon's revolutions in terms of the sun. . . . As a religious tradition, the thirteen-month years survived among European peasants for more than a millennium after the adoption of the Julian Calendar; thus Robin Hood, who lived at the time of Edward II [1284–1327], could exclaim in a ballad celebrating the May Day festival: "How many merry months be in the year? / There are thirteen, I say . . ." which a Tudor editor has altered to ". . . There are but twelve, I say. . . ." Thirteen, the number of the sun's death-month, has never lost its evil reputation among the superstitious. The days of the week lay under the charge of Titans: the genii of sun, moon, and the five hitherto discovered planets, who were responsible for them to the goddess as Creatrix. This system had probably been evolved in matriarchal Sumeria. (16)

14. Puhvel, 7.

15. The length of "May Day Sermon" (I count 360 lines) and the use of Venus as the Evening Star as well as the goddess may make one suspect an elaborate plotting of time and space in the poem. A favorite Dickey activity, initiated during his own World War II Air Force career (and a topic of some poems), is establishing himself and others in exact times and places through use of the sextant, the navigational instrument placed in the hands of Captain Whitehall and, briefly, the blind Cahill, in *Alnilam*, Dickey's second novel. In ancient times, when the fertility ritual was ordinary, the year was thought to contain 360 days; the oldest kind of calendar and the most widely used was the lunar calendar based on the civil month, which approximated the length of an actual lunar month. A person could make a close guess of the date by the phase of the moon. And, of course, in most languages, days of the week are associated with the seven moving celestial objects known to ancients: the sun, the moon, Mars, Mercury, Jupiter, Venus, and Saturn.

16. Maxine S. Rose, "On Being Born Again: James Dickey's 'May Day Sermon to the Women of Gilmer County, Georgia, by a Woman Preacher Leaving the Baptist Church,'" *Research Studies* (December 1978), 254.

17. In one of the many instances when Dickey has mentioned his acceptance of the philosophy of Heraclitus regarding the world's natural flow, he stated to W. C. Barnwell in a 1977 interview that he is "a believer in William James's doctrines of fluidity, the flux and flow of human experience," and in the idea that "[E]verything should flow; as Heraclitus says, 'You cannot step twice into the same river, for new waters are ever flowing in upon you.'" In "James Dickey on Yeats: An Interview," *The Voiced Connections of James Dickey: Interviews and Conversations*, ed. Ronald Baughman (Columbia: Univ. of South Carolina Press, 1989), 154–160.

18. Clausen, 300–301. Clausen's denial of a basis for the emotional force of this poem validates, in fact, the substantial need for the anthropological / ethnological interpretation which grounds it in opposing religious myths and the need for women to be empowered. Clausen says, in full:

> Summary and sparse quotation do not do justice to the rhythmic and emotional force of this poem, but perhaps they indicate its major weakness, which is that the emotion

is insufficiently grounded in either the story or the dramatic circumstances of the sermon. The enunciation of a pantheistic mysticism that glorifies sex by a Baptist preacher before a congregation in rural Georgia is unconvincing, not because such people are incapable of feeling such things but because the preacher is not given sufficient motivation or psychological depth to make such a reversal of conviction plausible. Nor is the daughter given any characteristics but red hair and sexual longing; the murder and disfiguring of her father are presented largely without preparation or comment, as if they were everyday occurrences. Again, the point is not that such things cannot happen. It is that if such characters are to behave so unusually and to bear such symbolic weight—it is, among other things the whole nature of Puritanism that is at issue here—they must be developed with a degree of characterization and incident that is impossible in all but the longest narrative poems. (301)

Dickey's characters and poem do, of course, bear the symbolic weight in this long narrative poem if the reader recognizes the symbolism.

19. Smith, cited in Barbara G. Walker, *The Woman's Encyclopedia of Myths and Secrets* (San Francisco: Harper & Row, 1983), 1043.

20. Walker, 1043.

21. Dickey, cited in Whit Burnett, ed., *America's 85 Greatest Living Authors Present; This Is My Best; in the Third Quarter of the Century*. (Garden City: Doubleday, 1970), 65.

22. Walker, 624. Mythic ritual associated with the May Day festival, described by Barbara Walker, indicates that in Scandinavia "May was dedicated to Maj, the Virgin, either Mary or the pagans' Virgin Mother, interchangeably. In Saxon England the month was called Sproutkale; the sprouting time of virgin-mother earth with her archaic Aryan name of Kale, Kelle, or Kali. Another name for the month was Tri-Milchi, improbably derived by the Venerable Bede from a theory that the Saxon cows gave milk three times a day in May. Alternatively, it meant the Triple Goddess's appearance in the form of three cows" (Gloss, 624). The tradition continued with "The May King of medieval romance [who] inherited the customs of Diana's sacred kings. He won the 'queen of a magic wood' (the Goddess) by combat with her previous king on the festival of Ascension Day in May" (625). And, William Fennor's *Pasquil's Palinodia* (1619) lamented the new puritanical laws against the rites of May" (626). Thus, the strands of "May Day Sermon" are united in the May Day festival with the appearance of the Goddess (preacher / daughter), the death of the father (old king), and the winning of the goddess by the new or May king (lover), as well as by the assimilation of these myths into Christian tradition.

23. Monroe K. Spears, "James Dickey: Southern Visionary as Celestial Navigator," *in American Ambitions: Selected Essays on Literary and Cultural Themes* (Baltimore and London: Johns Hopkins Univ. Press, 1987), 85.

24. James G. Frazer, *The Golden Bough: The Roots of Religion and Folklore*. 1890, one volume edition. (Reprinted, NY: Avenel Books, 1981), 2:339.

25. Harrison, 119.

26. Harrison, 267.

27. Frazer, cited in Sigmund Freud, *Totem and Taboo*, in *The Basic Writings of Sigmund Freud*, trans. and ed. A. A. Brill (NY: Modern Library, 1938), 886, *passim*.

28. James Dickey, "An Interview: James Dickey at Drury College." ed. with an introduction by Ronald Baughman, in *James Dickey Newsletter* 5 (Fall 1988), 17.

29. Freud, 917.

30. Thomas O. Sloan, "The Open Poem Is a Now Poem: Dickey's May Day Sermon." *Literature as Revolt and Revolt as Literature: Three Studies in The Rhetoric of Non-Oratorial Forms.* Proceedings of the Fourth Annual University of Minnesota Spring Symposium in Speech Communications, 3 May 1969. Reprinted in *James Dickey: The Expansive Imagination: A Collection of Critical Essays* (Deland, FL; Everett / Edwards, 1973), 94.

31. Walker, 1076.

32. Freud, 888.

33. Freud, 916, *passim*.

34. Robert Kirschten, *James Dickey and the Gentle Ecstasy of Earth: A Reading of the Poems* (Baton Rouge: Louisiana State Univ. Press, 1988), 137.

35. Kirschten, 138.

36. Northrop Frey, *The Secular Scripture: A Study of the Structure of Romance* (Cambridge and London: Harvard Univ. Press, 1976), 117. Frey's complete statement reads:

> The imagination, as it reflects on this world, sees it as a world of violence and cunning, *forza* and *froda*. The typical agent of cunning is a woman, whose main instrument of will is her bed: in the *Iliad* even the greatest of goddesses, Hera, decoys Zeus in this way in an effort to aid the Greeks. Thus the *forza-froda* cycle is also that of Ares and Eros, both of which, for human beings, end in Thanatos or death. Ares and Eros are functionaries of Venus, whose alternative form is Diana of the triple will, the white goddess who always kills, and whose rebirth is only for herself. (193)

The triple goddess may be Diana, Queen of Heaven, the Roman name for the Triple Goddess as Lunar Virgin, Mother of Creatures, and Huntress (Destroyer), or Artemis, her Greek name. The Cretan name of the Aegean Universal Mother or Great Goddess is Rhea, for whom an alternate name, Pandora, was used by Hesiod to convert Rhea "into an Eve-like giver of disasters to mankind," an idea based in the triple goddess's giving of all kinds of fate, "death as well as birth, suffering as well as joy, in her endless time cycles" (Walker 233, 857, *passim*).

37. James Dickey, "Sleeping Out at Easter." In *James Dickey: Poems 1957–1967* (Middleton, CT: Wesleyan Univ. Press, 1967), lines 4, 12–15.

38. Annis Pratt. *Archetypal Patterns in Women's Fiction*. Bloomington: Indiana Univ. Press, 1981.

39. The boar as god has an extensive background; it was and still is, symbolically, sacrificed at Yul (Yule) with an apple in its mouth, a symbol of its regenerated heart / soul; it was represented in the Jewish prohibition against eating pig's flesh, an inheritance from remote ancestors who had the wild boar as totem; it was featured in myths of dying gods like Tammuz, Attis, and Adonis, killed in swine form by boarskin-clad priests, and sacrificial boar-gods were chosen as lovers by the Goddess from among her priests (Walker, 112–13).

40. Joyce Carol Oates, "Out of Stone: Into Flesh: The Imagination of James Dickey," in Weigl and Hummer, eds., 65.

41. James Dickey, "The Energized Man," in Weigl and Hummer, eds., 163.

42. Robert Graves. *The Greek Myths*, (1955; reprinted Baltimore: Penguin Books, 1961), 1:198.

43. Rose, 255.

44. Dickey's more than 60 pages of working manuscript for "May Day Sermon," deposited in the Special Collections of The Washington University Libraries, reveal the evolution of the poem through many stages.

45. Frye, 181.

Form and Genre in James Dickey's "Falling": The Great Goddess Gives Birth to the Earth

ROBERT KIRSCHTEN

> The fables of the gods are true histories of customs.
>
> —Giambattista Vico

> I don't think that there's a deeper part of nature than a woman.
> The blood of women is connected with the moon, the heavens, everything.
> They bear the very seed of meaning and existence.
>
> —James Dickey

> Oh, golden flower opened up
>   she is our mother
> whose thighs are holy
>   whose face is a dark mask
> She came from Tamoanchan,
>   the first place
> where all descended
>   where all was born. . . .
> She is our mother,
>   the goddess earth.
>   She is dressed
> in plumes
>   she is smeared with clay.
>
> —Atzec Poem to the Mother of the Gods

A quarter of a century ago, well before many current intellectual trends became mainstream, James Dickey reaffirmed the multicultural brotherhood of his own poetic vision with Native Americans, when, in *Self-Interviews*, he lamented "the loss of a sense of intimacy with the natural process. I think you would be very hard-put . . . to find a more harmonious relationship to an environment than the American Indians had. We can't return to a primitive society . . . but there is a property of mind which, if encouraged, could have this personally animistic relationship to things. . . . It's what gives us a *personal* relationship to the sun and the moon, the flow of rivers, the growth and decay of natural

This article appeared in *South Atlantic Review* 58:2 (May 1993), 127–54. Reprinted by permission of the publisher, South Atlantic Modern Language Association.

forms, and the cycles of death and rebirth."[1] An exhilarating celebration of just those harmonious cycles, "Falling" is one of Dickey's best known and most spectacular poems. The lyric runs more than six full pages in page-wide lines with minimal punctuation to interrupt its accelerating whirlwind of energy while depicting the fatal fall of a twenty-nine-year-old stewardess from a commercial airplane over Kansas. Although this woman starts off as the victim of a tragic accident, her fall is exhilarating because she ends up as someone significantly different.

Critics have offered clues to this transformation. Joyce Carol Oates claims that the stewardess is "a kind of mortal goddess, given as much immortality . . . as poetry is capable of giving its subjects."[2] Monroe Spears notes that she "becomes a goddess, embodiment of a myth."[3] Joyce Pair, editor of the *James Dickey Newsletter*, observes that the stewardess is "a modern incarnation of the goddess of crops and fertility."[4] Even Dickey himself says that the stewardess has "a goddess-like invulnerability" (*Self-Interviews*, 175).[5] While these clues identify the stewardess as a goddess, there are few extended discussions of the poem that develop this premise.[6] My own seven-page analysis, written in 1983 as part of a chapter on sacrificial victims in a book-length study of Dickey's poetry, concurs with these opinions to some degree, suggesting that "we may best read 'Falling' . . . as a ritual reenactment of the primitive practice of killing a god of vegetation to ensure both the perpetuation of crops and the continuation of the human species itself."[7] However, after more extensive reading in mythological literatures, I believe that my initial assessment under-values the power and character of this woman and that a more detailed reading is in order. To say that the stewardess is merely a "sacrificial victim"—a term derived from Kenneth Burke and René Girard—renders her passive in a way that does not reflect her true dynamic and dramatic character. We need thus to trace more fully the process of empowerment (the "plot" or "form" of the poem) that the stewardess undergoes by looking at the kind of mythological activity (the "genre") this process resembles. By offering three analogies with goddesses from Native American, Asian, and Mesoamerican myths, we may best see "Falling" as an animistic, matriarchal, creation myth—in many ways, the emotional and cultural opposite of the patriarchal narrative in Genesis—whose particular rendering in Dickey's hands reveals further insights into his conceptions of women and nature. My claim is that "Falling" is Dickey's remarkable transformation of an airline employee into an analogue of one of the Great Goddesses of primitive seed-planting cultures, more specifically, Mother Earth, who, in the process of falling and dying, gives birth to herself and the earth.[8]

First Analogy: Bird Woman (or Lady of the Animals) and The Woman Who Fell from the Sky

After the stewardess falls out of the plane (line 7), she panics at first, then experiments with her fall. Dickey says, "She develops interest she turns in her maneuverable body / To watch it."[9] Not only does she begin to enjoy her fall, but she takes on the first in a series of new kinds of power, namely, the power of animals. At line 30, she changes from someone merely performing "endless gymnastics" into what I will call her role as "Bird Woman," for she now can "slant slide / Off tumbling into the emblem of a bird with its wings half-spread" (294).[10] Whether in "Reincarnation II," where we find "There is a wing-growing motion / Half-alive in every creature" (*Poems*, 248), or in "Eagles," where the poet says "My feathers were not / Of feather-make, but broke from a desire to drink / The rain before it falls,"[11] the empowerment of human beings through magical contact with animals is a long-standing commonplace in Dickey's work. This topic recalls two of Jungian psychologist Erich Neumann's observations when he discusses animals symbolic of ancient goddesses: first, that the "birdlike character of woman points primarily to her correlation with the heavens,"[12] and second, that in Creto-Aegean culture "the Great Mother as a nature goddess . . . was mistress of the mountains and of wild animals" and that "birds . . . symbolized her presence."[13]

In "Falling," Dickey's stewardess-goddess has "time to live / In superhuman health" (*Poems*, 294) by so taking on the properties of bird flight and vision that she becomes a variation of what is called in Pali Buddhism "the great woman rich in creatures":[14]

> Arms out   she slow-rolls over   steadies out . . .
>   trembles near feathers   planes head-down
> The quick movements of bird-necks turning her head   gold eyes
>   the insight-
> eyesight of owls blazing into the hencoops   a taste for chicken
>   overwhelming
> Her   the long-range vision of hawks enlarging all human lights
>   of cars
> Freight trains   looped bridges   enlarging the moon racing slowly
> Through all the curves of a river   all the darks of the midwest blazing
> From above. . . . (294)

By acquiring the "insight- / eyesight of owls" and "the long-range vision of hawks," the stewardess is not only rich in creatures but reenacts the role of a prehistoric goddess known as "the Lady of the Animals" who often appears in the form of a bird. Citing Marija Gimbutas's *The Goddesses and Gods of Old Europe*, Carol Christ tells us that Gimbutas found a "pre-Bronze Age culture that was "matrifocal" . . . presided over by a Goddess as Source and Giver of

All. Originally the Goddess did not appear with animals but herself had animal characteristics. One of her earliest forms was as the Snake and Bird Goddess, associated with water, and represented as a snake, a water bird, a duck, goose, crane, diver bird, or owl, or as a woman with a bird head or birdlike posture. She was the Goddess Creatress, the giver of Life."[15] Known in classical mythology as "Aphrodite with her dove, Athene with her owl, [and] Artemis with her deer," the image of the Lady of Animals, Christ notes, goes back in history beyond Homer to the Neolithic and Paleolithic eras. In the *Homeric Hymns* (c. 800–400 B.C.), "the Lady of the Animals is cosmic power; she is mother of all; the animals of Earth, sea, and air are hers; the wildest and most fearsome of animals. . . . [She] is also earth: she is the firm foundation undergirding all life" (166).

In "Falling," Dickey's Lady of the Animals not only possesses the vision of hawks and owls but also their "fearsome" power over prey and, most importantly, their powers and instruments of flight. With "a taste for chicken overwhelming / Her" and "the air beast-crooning to her warbling" (294–95), the stewardess arranges her skirt "Like a diagram of a bat" and thus "has this flying-skin / Made of garments" (295). These diverse animal traits dramatically enable her to change both her activity and her character. Her fall becomes purposive, no longer the formless result of an unintended accident, but instead "a long stoop a hurtling a fall / That is controlled that plummets as it wills" (295). As the velocity of her fall accelerates, conveyed brilliantly by Dickey's spectacular visual imagery, so too the stewardess' plummeting will-to-power increases. At one point, she alters the very laws of nature as she "turns gravity / Into a new condition, showing its other side like a moon shining / New Powers" (295; line 54). And shortly thereafter, she begins to become fully active by determining her own fate; that is, she will not "just *fall just tumble screaming all that time*" She will "use / It" (295; line 79).

While magically connected to animals, yet still in her human form, Dickey's stewardess also resembles a goddess who experiences a similar fall in an Iroquois creation myth called "The Woman Who Fell from the Sky." From JBN Hewitt's "Iroquois Cosmology," we learn that in

> regions above. . . . [where] Sorrow and death were unknown. . . . [A] tree had been uprooted . . . a hole was left . . . opened to the world below. . . . [A] woman-being . . . fell into the hole and kept on falling through its darkness, and after a while passed through its length. And when she had passed quite through onto this other world, she . . . looked in all directions and saw on all sides about her that everything was blue. . . . [S]he was now looking upon a great expanse . . . of water. . . . On the surface of the water . . . all sorts and forms of waterfowl . . . noticed her. . . . [T]hey sent up to her a flight of numerous water ducks of various kinds, which in a very compact body elevated themselves to meet her on high. And on their backs, thereupon, her body did indeed alight. So then slowly they descended, bearing on their backs her body.[16]

Though the birds and animals in Dickey's poem do not bear the stewardess on their backs, they form an entourage of accompanying support that shapes the very contour of her fall. Her alignment with hawks, owls, and bats changes her fall from a "tumble" to a fall like those of "sky-divers on TV," which, at least, hypothetically, offers her the hope that, "like a diver," she may "plunge" into "water like a needle to come out healthily dripping / And be handed a Coca-Cola" (295). In addition to her birdlike motion, the Iroquois woman-being, like the stewardess, shares a similar, creative relationship with the earth. When the Iroquois woman falls, there is no land below her, only water. To safeguard her from drowning, the ducks place her on the back of the Great Turtle. Beaver and Otter try to bring up mud from the bottom to fashion earth for her, but they die in the process. So does Muskrat. As he surfaces, however, mud is found in his paws, and this the animals place around the carapace of the turtle. When the woman awakes, she finds the mud, like Dickey's "enlarging" earth, transformed: "[T]he earth whereupon she sat had become in size enlarged. . . . [S]he . . . saw that willows along the edge of the water had grown to be bushes. . . . [S]he saw . . . growing shrubs of the rose willow along the edge of the water. . . . [S]he saw take up its course a little rivulet. In that way, in their turn things came to pass. The earth rapidly was increasing in size. . . . [S]he . . . saw . . . all kinds of herbs and grasses spring up from the earth and grow . . . toward maturity" (*World Mythology 2*, 146). Later in this legend, the woman-being gives birth to a daughter who in turn gives birth to a set of twins. The first twin, Sapling, tosses the sun and the moon into the sky and forms the race of mankind. The Woman Who Fell from the Sky is thus a kind of mother responsible for the creation of the cosmos, the earth, and humanity.

In "Falling" the stewardess gives birth to a special kind of "enlarging earth." After she determines to "use" her fall, the American landscape "enlarges" not only because she falls closer to ground; it becomes animated—animistic—and a tremendous source of revelation and energy for her. Dickey's earth is, in fact, created out of animated elements similar to those in Chinese and Babylonian creation myths in which reality is said to emerge out of original "chaos" when "all was darkness and water."[17] When the stewardess falls out of a layer of clouds, she beholds a new world likewise issuing out of "chaos" and "darkness and water": "New darks new progressions of headlights along dirt roads from chaos / / And night a gradual warming a new-made, inevitable world of one's own / Country" with "its waiting waters" (296). These "waiting waters," like those toward which the Iroquois woman falls, also come magically alive as the source of all life for Dickey's goddess. Even though, on a literal level, the stewardess stands little chance of diving safely into water, imagery of "the waters / Of life" is so pervasive that it constitutes a major element in the vast scenic receptacle of natural movement in the "new-made . . . world" that receives her. As she heads "toward the blazing-bare lake," this world of water is "new-made" and life-giving because of its tremendous potential for burgeoning energy. Like a life-saving rope that cannot aid her, "the moon" is "packed and coiled in a reservoir" (295), and in the agricultural and sexual worlds of fecundity that she will never know, "farmers sleepwalk . . . a walk like falling toward the far waters / Of life in moonlight . . . Toward the flowering of the harvest in their hands" (298). As nourisher and transformer, water is the vessel of life in the womb; its nutrients make it a medium for growth, and, of course, the sea is the source of life, but also, tragically, the destroyer. Water, thus, unites heaven and earth in the "Great Round" of life and death. By entering so fully into this perpetual cycle, Dickey's stewardess is the great Egyptian heaven goddess Nut who is, Neumann reminds us, "water above and below, vault above and below, life and death, east and west, generating and killing, in one. . . . The Great Goddess is the flowing unity of subterranean and celestial primordial water, the sea of heaven on which sail the barks of the gods of light, the circular life-generating ocean above and below the earth. To her belong all waters, streams, fountains, ponds, and springs, as well as the rain. She is the ocean of life with its life- and death-bringing seasons . . ." (*Great Mother*, 222). This realm is not the world of discursive consciousness. It is, rather, what Neumann calls "the primordial darkness" of "the Dark Mother," "the Nocturnal Mother," more specifically, "the matriarchal world of the beginning" of the creative unconscious "which "the patriarchal world strives to deny" (212). And with its "moon-crazed inner eye of midwest imprisoned / Water" (296), Dickey's night-world is far less the real Kansas than D. H. Lawrence's Etruscan universe in which "all was alive. . . . The whole thing was alive, and had a great soul, or *anima*."[18]

Dickey's animistic conception of nature radically opposes that of the machine-world of the airliner with which the poem begins. While simultaneously revealing even more about his main character, his animism recalls Carol Christ's statement: "To the Old Europeans the Lady of the Animals was not a power transcending earth, but rather the power that creates, sustains, and is manifest in the infinite variant of life forms on earth. Old Europe did not celebrate humanity's uniqueness and separation from nature but rather humanity's participation in and connection to nature's cycles of birth, death, and renewal" (169). Speaking in a similar vein about natural "connection" in *Self-Interviews*, Dickey paraphrases Lawrence's statement to the effect that "that as a result of our science and industrialization, we have lost the cosmos. The parts of the universe we can investigate by means of machinery and scientific empirical techniques we may understand better than our predecessors did, but we no longer know the universe emotionally" (67). Dickey's poetic answer to technological alienation characterized by "the vast, sluggish forces of habit, mechanization and mental torpor" is to build a universe populated not only by what he has called elsewhere "The Energized Man"[19] but, in this poem, what we may call the "Energized Woman." She is, among other things, a poetic adversary of contemporary commercialism. The Energized Woman is someone whose mind is "not used simply to sell neckties or industrial machines or to make cocktail conversation, but to serve as the vital center of a moving and changing, perceiving and evaluating world which . . . is that world of delivery from drift and inconsequence" (164). She does not dwell in an earth filled with the deadening rhetoric of advertising—Dickey even parodies advertising slogans: when opening *"the natural wings of* [her] *jacket / By Don Loper,"* the stewardess shifts in the same poetic line from the world of fashion to the primitive world of movement *"like a hunting owl toward the glitter of water"* (295). Rather, the Energized Woman lives in a world filled with the dynamic energy of "mana," which is, in Jane Harrison's description, "a world of unseen power lying behind the visible universe, a world which is the sphere . . . of magical activity and the medium of mysticism."[20]

Commenting on the Iroquois myth, Joseph Campbell sheds further light on Dickey's energized "Sky Woman" and this magical, mystical power she possesses. The Woman Who Fell from the Sky is, Campbell says, "a North American example of . . . a universally recognized, early planting-culture mythology, wherein by analogy with the seeded earth, the creative and motivating force (*śákti*) of the world illusion (*māyā*) was envisioned, and in fact experienced, as female (*devī*)." The Sky Woman is an "avatar from the Sky World to this earth, bearing in her womb the gift of a race of human beings, heavenly endowed to join in mutual regard the supportive animal population already present" (*World Mythology* 2, pt. 2: 153–54). She is also a Neolithic great moon goddess or moon-messenger. Gimbutas notes that the moon goddess was "essentially a Goddess of Regeneration . . . product of a matrilinear community . . . [who] was giver of life and all that promotes fertility."[21] Lamenting the fact that "There's no moon goddess now," Dickey once stated that, from a scientific point of view, the moon is "simply a dead stone, a great ruined stone in the sky" (*Self-Interviews*, 67). And so it is, at the opening of "Falling," that "the states" are "drawing moonlight out of the great / One-sided stone hung off the starboard wingtip" (293). As the stewardess acquires momentum, however, the ancient mythological connection between the moon and water comes magically alive, for the moon is transformed into "the harvest moon," "racing slowly / Through all the curves of a river" and into "a great stone of light in waiting waters" (294–96). This all takes place beneath and above a moon-bride who falls from "the heavenly rapture of experienced nonduality. . . . [T]he woman's fall is at once a death (to the sky) and a birth (to this earth)" (*World Mythology* 2, pt. 2: 156).

SECOND ANALOGY: MISTRESS OF ALL DESIRES AND JOYS,
OR GODDESS UNCHAINED

The role of the stewardess as Sky Woman continues throughout her fall, but, at line 94, her "shining / New Powers" take on an even greater scope. Dickey provides a clue to this stage of change in *Self-Interviews* when he says that he tried "to think of the mystical possibility there might be for farmers in that vicinity" (175). Not only farmers, we might add, but all who feel the influence of the moon goddess are drawn, as

> ... under her   under chenille bedspreads
> The farm girls are feeling the goddess in them struggle and rise brooding
> On the scratch-shining posts of the bed   dreaming of female signs
> Of the moon   male blood like iron   of what is really said by the moan
> Of airliners passing over them at dead of midwest midnight   passing
> Over brush fires   burning out in silence on little hills   and will wake
> To see the woman they should be   struggling on the rooftree to become
> Stars (296)

At this passage, the stewardess acquires a pervasive sexual power that animates sexual instinct in all those, women and men, who fall within her range. This power accelerates in the following lines when, defiantly, "to die / Beyond explanation," the stewardess rids herself of the restrictive trappings of her airline uniform, "the girdle required by regulations," and "the long windsocks of her stockings" (297). She is now Goddess unchained, and her flight is "superhuman" because her "mystical," sexual power is even more comprehensive. She is

> desired by every sleeper in his dream:
> Boys finding for the first time their loins filled with heart's blood
> Widowed farmers whose hands float under light covers to find themselves
> Arisen at sunrise   the splendid position of blood unearthly drawn
> Toward clouds   all feel something   pass over them as she passes
> Her palms over *her* long legs   *her* small breasts   and deeply between
> Her thighs (297)

From lines 94 to 141 (just before she enters the ground and becomes the earth's creative force), the stewardess' procreative powers lead to a stage of empowerment at which we may call her the "Mistress of All Desires and Joys" (Zimmer, 89) or the "Great Maya." Speaking of the Buddhist "mother-goddess or earth-mother" who "signifies the triumph of the feminine principle over the masculine," Heinrich Zimmer says, "The goddess, who consists of all the beings and worlds is herself the pregnant salt womb of the life sea, holding all forms of life in her embrace and nourishing them; she herself casts them adrift in the sea and gives them over to decay, and in all innocence rebuilds them into forms forever new . . ." (*Mystic Vision*, 87). She is the agreeable side of the hideous Indian goddess Kali, who after she drinks blood, changes faces and becomes "the world mother"; she bestows "existence upon new living forms in a process of unceasing procreation" (74). In "Hinduism," Zimmer says, "the male looks upon all womanhood . . . as the self-revelation of the goddess in the world of appearances" (93). And "in the secret orgiastic ritual of the Tantras, reserved to the initiate, the erotic sacrament of the sexes stands above the enjoyment of meat and drink as the supreme intoxicant by which men can attain redemption in their lifetime" (93). She has a "magic power, which fulfills and hallows, is embodied in everything feminine. . . . [A]ll [women] have a shimmer of superhuman dignity, as vessel and symbol of the supreme natural force (*śákti*) of the mother-goddess, to whom all things owe their existence" (96).

Terms such as "the supreme intoxicant" and "orgiastic ritual" lead to further considerations about the erotic aspect of Dickey's poetic method. This method centers on an intoxicating, dreamlike ecstasy signaled early in the poem as the stewardess falls "with the delaying, dumfounding ease / Of a dream of being drawn   like endless moonlight to the harvest soil / Of a central state of one's country" (293). Both nightmare and adrenalin rush, these dream-states run throughout "Falling," suggesting Nietzsche's Dionysian and Apollonian forces upon which art depends, "as procreation is dependent on the duality of the sexes, involving perpetual conflicts with only periodically intervening reconciliations."[22] Insofar as Monroe Spears notes in *Dionysus and the City* that Dickey's poetry is at its best when "basic Dionysian preoccupations . . . operate in proper balance with the Apollonian elements (259)," we would do well to take a moment to see how these two Nietzschean opposites—in "balance" and "perpetual conflict"—operate in "Falling."

The Apollonian or dream component of the poem can be found in the fantastic stream of explosive celestial images that flow about the stewardess as she falls and in the Olympian point of view from which she has a godlike scope of vision. Nietzsche claims that such dream-states conduce to extraordinary modes of holistic consciousness, a philosophic topic that runs throughout Dickey's poetry and is incorporated in two oxymorons at the end of the elegiac "The Eagle's Mile" where we find Justice William O. Douglas's "death drawing life / From growth / from flow" so that, in the poem's last line, he may "Splinter uncontrollably whole" (27). Of this kind of ecstatic dream vision, Nietzsche says,

> In dreams, according to the conception of Lucretius, the glorious divine figures first appeared to the souls of men, in dreams the great shaper beheld the charming corporeal structure of superhuman beings. . . . [F]or Apollo, as the god of all shaping energies, is also the soothsaying god. . . . The higher truth, the perfection of [the inner world of fantasies] . . . in contrast to the only partially intelligible everyday world, ay, the deep consciousness of nature,

healing and helping in sleep and dream, is at the same time the symbolical
analogue of the faculty of soothsaying and, in general, of the arts, through
which life is made possible and worth living.

(Birth of Tragedy, 22–24)

In Dickey's poem, what is prophetic (and "healing") about the stewardess's
visioning powers is not that she attains a truth that can be put in the form
of an oracle or conceptual proposition but, rather, that the panoramic faculty
of her eye and its streaming "openness"—that of Apollo, Nietzsche's "sculptor-
god"—result in her "accessibility" to the Dionysian powers of the "more than
human," to "metamorphosis and transfiguration" *(Dionysus and City*, 258–59).
That is, though she faces certain death, the energy from her Apollonian rush
of consciousness and its Dionysian content "prophesizes" (i.e., foretells and
foreshadows) an ecstatic, life-affirming reversal of her fate; for, not only are
"[h]er eyes opened wide by wind" so that she sees the earth approaching, but
also she is "lying in one after another of all the positions for love / Making
dancing" (294) in a vibrant Dionysian ecstasy.

The result of yet another of Dickey's monstrous combinations of poetic
"good / And evil" (294), the stewardess's drama explodes in power by representing her Nietzschean opposites in a "perpetual conflict" that produces a
stunning kind of frenzy (or ecstasy). The dramatic method involved here is, as
Nietzsche says, "the Apollonian embodiment of Dionysian perceptions and
influences," which produces "enchantment" as a kind of reverse irony. Instead
of the audience distancing itself from the central action by knowing more than
the performing character, the end of this ironic frenzy is "to see one's self
transformed before one's self and then to act as if one had really entered into
another body, into another character. . . . [H]ere we actually have a surrender
of the individual by his entering into another nature. . . . In this enchantment
the Dionysian reveller sees himself as a satyr, *and as satyr he in turn beholds the
god*. . . . [In] his transformation he sees a new vision outside him as the
Apollonian consumation of his state. With this new vision the drama is
complete" *(Birth of Tragedy*, 67–68). The stewardess becomes a goddess—as
does the reader, participating emotionally with her—precisely through this
Dionysian state of intoxicating new vision, itself a delirious peripety. Her
frenzy is a "rapturous transport," a "narcotic potion," which, like certain
varieties of mysticism, erases "all sense of individuality in self-forgetfullness"
(Birth of Tragedy, 67–69), or, we might add, like a mystical transport that
produces movement transfiguring the vulnerable self into a greater power,
when, for example, one feels the sensation of being intoxicated by speed:

> She is watching her country lose its evoked master shape　watching
> 　　it lose
> And gain　get back its houses and peoples　watching it bring up
> Its local lights　single homes　lamps on barn roofs　if she fell

Into water she might live   like a diver   cleaving   perfect   plunge

Into another   heavy silver   unbreathable   slowing   saving
Element (295)

Produced by Dickey's technical virtuosity in "Falling"—the long, Whitmanesque lines punctuated by caesura, his terraces of spectacularly ascending
rhythm, his striking image groups conveying the sensation of a free fall—his
Dionysian goddess of motion, like Nietzsche's, gives us the sensation that she
is "on the point of taking a dancing flight into the air. His gestures bespeak
enchantment. . . . [S]omething supernatural sounds forth from him: he feels
himself a god" (*Birth of Tragedy*, 27). Of such frenzy, Nietzsche says, "The
essential thing in all intoxication is the feeling of heightened power and
fullness. With this feeling one . . . compels [things] to receive what one has
to give. . . . "One enriches everything out of one's own fullness: whatever one
sees, whatever one wills, is seen swelled, taut, strong, over loaded with strength.
The individual in this state transforms things until they mirror his power—
until they are reflections of his perfection."[23]

The frenzy in "Falling" is not simple escapism; it is entrance into an
archetypal mode of motion that features the cycle of desire and death (Eros
and Thanatos) but transcends death by participating fully in this eternal cycle.
Whereas Dickey's stewardess-goddess fills boys' "loins with heart's blood,"
she will also soon become part of "the loam where extinction slumbers in corn
tassels thickly" (297). This concept of life-in-death fits Nietzsche's conception
of the "orgiastic," which underscores the fabulous life-affirming impulse of the
stewardess even in the face of her own death:

> . . . the orgiastic [is] an overflowing feeling of life and strength where even pain
> has the effect of stimulus. . . . Tragedy is . . . [the] repudiation and counter-
> instance [of pessimism]. Saying Yes to life, even in its strangest and hardest
> problems, the will to life rejoicing over its own inexhaustibility even in the very
> sacrifice of its highest types—that is what I called Dionysian. . . . [Tragic feeling
> is] Not to be liberated from terror and pity, not in order to purge oneself of a
> dangerous affect by its vehement discharge—Aristotle understood it that way—
> but in order to be *oneself* the eternal joy of becoming . . . even joy in destroying
> . . . [say] I, the teacher of eternal recurrence.
>
> (*Twilight of Idols*, 562–63)

In "Falling," this Yea-saying Dionysian power features a matriarchal component that is reflected in Nietzsche's own metaphor; he claims that this is a
world in which "nature speaks to us with its true undissembled voice: 'Be as
I am! Amidst the ceaseless change of phenomena the eternally creative primordial mother, eternally impelling to existence, self-satisfying eternally with this
change of phenomena!'" (*Birth of Tragedy*, 128)

This orgiastic power is not the power of domination or control. Rather, it is what Herbert Marcuse calls an erotic stance which reconciles Eros and Thanatos in "a world that is not to be mastered and controlled but to be liberated." In such a realm, the "opposition between man and nature, subject and object, is overcome. Being is experienced as gratification."[24] The stewardess's shedding of her clothes is, thus, an enabling ritual or dance, designed to affirm a social "order without repression" (166) and to amplify her basic bodily powers, as Dickey says, in a "last superhuman act" (297) that defies the death of the body and expresses what Marcuse calls "a non-repressive erotic attitude toward reality" (166). Instead of the functionary of a commercial airline, the stewardess is, in Marcusian terms, "[n]o longer used as a full-time instrument of labor," for her body is "resexualized" (201) such that "Eros, freed from surplus-repression, would be strengthened" and "[d]eath would cease to be an instinctual goal" (235). This transforming dance and ecstatic vision of sexuality are not limited to gender. Dionysian rapture as a sexual mode of holistic motion transcending death also attracted Theodore Roethke, who reveals this account in his notebooks:

> . . . I got into this real strange state. I got in the woods and started a circular kind of dance. . . . I kept going around and just shedding clothes. Sounds Freudian as hell, but in the end, I had a sort of circle—as if, I think, I understood intuitively what the frenzy is. That is, you go way beyond yourself, and . . . this is not sheer exhaustion but this strange sort of a . . . not illumination . . . but a sense of being again a part of the whole universe. I mean, anything but quiet. I mean, in a sense everything is symbolical. . . . [I]t was one of the deepest and [most] profound experiences I ever had. And accompanying it was a real sexual excitement also . . . and this tremendous feeling of actual power. . . .
>
> The *real* point is that this business of the dance accompanies exaltation of the highest, the human thing, and it also goes into the Dionysian frenzy, which in modern life hardly anyone even speaks of anymore. . . . [W]hen Vaughan says, "When felt through all my fleshy dress, / Ripe shoots of everlastingness," well, *that's* the feeling. You feel . . . that you are eternal, or immortal. . . . [F]urthermore, death becomes . . . an absurdity, of no consequence.[25]

That Dickey should feature this kind of movement in "Falling" comes as no surprise, for the "Delphic trance" and world of "perpetual genesis"[26] are aspects of Roethke's poetic vision that Dickey has long admired.

THIRD ANALOGY: MAIZE STALK DRINKING BLOOD

It is precisely these Nietzschean opposites in orgiastic combination—joy and destruction, tragedy and inexhaustibility, power and pain—in "Falling" that lead to our third analogy. The stewardess's flight ends abruptly when she enters the earth with a tremendous impact, which Dickey does not show, but represents symbolically with pronouns, "This is it THIS" (298; line 143), and which is all the more powerful and tragic for that indirect symbolization. At first glance, this moment exhibits a cataclysmic reversal of the life-force of her flight, for immediately after she lands, she is, terrifyingly:

>   impressed
> In the soft loam   gone down   driven well into the image of her body
> The furrows for miles flowing in upon her where she lies very deep
> In her mortal outline   in the earth as it is in cloud
>
>   (298)

She continues to live for a time after the impact; at the end of the poem, some thirty lines later, her last words are given in capitals: "AH, GOD—." Though she dies, this final poetic space, approximately one-sixth of the entire lyric, exhibits her full goddesslike nature and power in a way more compelling even than her fall. It bears repeating that Dickey does not dwell here on a mutilated woman. It is not her death that is his focus but a circle (or cycle) much wider in scope. In addition to our natural compassion for her death, our feeling for her issues from a deeper recognition of the universal in Dickey's dramatization of the intermingling forces of life and death. For those who find her, the poet says,

>   can tell nothing
> But that she is there   inexplicable   unquestionable   and remember
> That something broke in them as well   and began to live and die more
> When they walked for no reason into their fields to where the whole
>   earth
> Caught her
>
>   (298)

At this point, this contemporary airline stewardess bears comparison to the great Mesoamerican mother of the gods, Maize Stalk Drinking Blood. In a painting from Codex Borgia, Mexico (c. AD 1500) called "The Tree of the Middle Place," these striking images occur:

Rising from the body of an earth goddess recumbent on the spines of the . . . alligator . . . of the abyss, the Tree, encircled by the World Sea, is surmounted by a quetzal bird of bright plummage. Two streams of blood pour into the goddess, and from her body rise two ears of maize, a yellow and a red. . . . Personifying the fertile earth, this goddess of life out of death is . . . known as the Maize Stalk Drinking Blood, . . . [whose] skeletal remains were . . . regarded as the seat of the essential life force and the metaphorical seed from which the individual, whether human, animal, or plant, is reborn.[27]

This voracious image of death points to a different aspect of the stewardess and of Great Goddesses in many cultures, namely, their terrible power of destruction. As Erich Neumann says, "The Great Mother as Terrible Goddess of the earth and of death is herself the earth, in which things rot. The Earth Goddess is "the devourer of the dead bodies of mankind" and the "mistress and lady of the tomb." Like Gaea, the Greek Earth Mother, she is mistress of the vessel and at the same time the great underworld vessel itself, into which dead souls enter, and out of which they fly up again" (*Great Mother*, 162). The power of this goddess, also called the "Terrible Mother," is double-edged, suggesting not only death and destruction, but also new life, for out of the body of Maize Stalk grow two ears of corn, signs of regeneration and rebirth. Discussing the story of Demeter and Persephone in the Greek festival Thesmophoria, Joseph Campbell emphasizes this redemptive power in the Great Goddess when he notes that in certain, primitive Indonesian cycles "goddesses [are] identified with the local food plants, . . . the underworld, and the moon, whose rites insure both a growth of the plants and a passage of the soul to the land of the dead. In both the marriage of the maiden goddess . . . is equivalent to her death, which is imaged as a descent into the earth and is followed, after a time, by her metamorphosis into food. . . ."[28] These redemptive and sexual powers constitute one phase of the cycle of life and death through which humankind passes. Dickey's Goddess is Mother Earth giving birth and death to herself, for the goddess of sex is the goddess of death. Campbell notes that "The death god, Ghede, of the Haitian Voodoo tradition, is also the sex god. The Egyptian god Osiris was the judge and lord of the dead, and the lord of the regeneration of life."[29] And, commenting on the "primitive-village mythology" of certain New Guinea tribes that include the "death-feast" of a "divine maiden" who died by sinking "into the earth among the roots of a tree" to rise later in the sky as the moon, he discusses this dialectical pairing of sex and death: "[t]he plants on which man lives derive from this death. The world lives on death. . . . Reproduction without death would be a calamity, as would death without reproduction. . . . [T]he interdependence of death and sex, their import as the complementary aspects of a single state of being, and the necessity of killing and eating [—] this deeply moving, emotionally disturbing glimpse of death as the life of the living is the fundamental motivation supporting the rites around which the social structure of the early planting villages was composed" (*Primitive Mythology*, 177).

A considerably less violent figure than the goddess in "The Tree of the Middle Place" or the New Guinean moon-maiden, Dickey's stewardess nonetheless enters the earth in a way suggesting that she gives birth to a similar cycle of generation and decay and that her death is not, merely, the termination of a single, discontinuous individual:

> All the known air above her is not giving up quite one
> Breath   it is all gone   and yet not dead   not anywhere else

Quite   lying still in the field on her back   sensing the smells
Of incessant growth try to lift her (298)

By accretions of these cyclic moments of death-in-life, Dickey often builds his
poems out of magical circles, poetic "mandalas" (Sanskrit for "circle"); "Falling" also suggests the transference (and continuance) of the stewardess's fertile
powers in the comic totems of "her clothes" which, magically, are "beginning /
To come down all over Kansas": "her blouse on a lightening rod" and "her
girdle coming down fantastically / On a clothesline, where it belongs" (298).
Further proof that her "all-sustaining, all-nourishing" sexual power continues
is that it is felt sympathetically in the lives and in the fields of local farmers
who perpetuate and participate in her extraordinary energy when the erotic
dream sequence impels them to

                                                     sleepwalk without
    Their women from houses   a walk like falling toward the far waters
    Of life   in moonlight   toward the dreamed eternal meaning of
            their   their farms
    Toward the flowering of the harvest in their hands
                                                              (298)

When "Falling" is read aloud, the poem's cumulative energy is so overwhelming by the end of the performance that—although the death of the
stewardess is a necessary, realistic outcome of her accident—her death has
in it the feeling of a beginning. This beginning resembles the tremendous
burgeoning that Kenneth Burke sees as the "frantic urgency of growth"[30] in
Theodore Roethke's "greenhouse poems," where "Nothing would give up
life: / Even the dirt kept breathing a small breath."[31] What truly animates
Dickey's earth is the stewardess's cyclone of energy that is magically transferred
to the ground she enters. Rather than a death, her impregnation of the land
is the beginning of a new cycle of growth and decay. At poem's end, this cycle
has been put in full motion by the poet. The reader's or listener's poetic
experience of the stewardess's death is not a sense of cessation but of transformation. Just as the form of the poem is the reversal of the journalistic narrative
that begins the action by announcing the airplane accident, the stewardess is
never more alive than when she dies into her new life. Yet one more variation
on Dickey's favorite topic of poetic motion, the stewardess's death is a "fresh
enactment, here and now" of a "god's own sacrifice . . . through which . . .
she . . . became incarnate in the world process"; she is a constant reminder to
us that "sudden, monstrous death" is a "revelation of the . . . inhumanity of
the order of the universe" (*Primitive Mythology*, 181), yet we are also reminded
that "To see the twofold, embracing and devouring, nature of the goddess, to
see repose in catastrophe, security in decay, is to know her and be saved"
(*Mystic Vision*, 96).

SOCIAL AND POLITICAL ENDS OF "FALLING"

Because it involves an erotic component and the death of a woman, "Falling" has received a considerable amount of negative commentary. By way of completing an inquiry into the form, genre, and value of this poem, we may use the preceding analysis to address a number of statements about this poem and Dickey himself. Some of these statements assess not only "Falling" negatively but also Dickey's work in general.

First, there are the charges of sexual perversion and insensitivity to women. In *Thinking About Women*, Mary Ellmann states that Dickey's depiction of women is "unnerving":

> James Dickey's poem "Falling" expresses an extraordinary concern with the underwear of a woman who has fallen out of an airplane. While this woman, a stewardess, was in the airplane, her girdle obscured, to the observation of even the most alert passenger, her mesial groove. The effect was, as the poem recalls, "monobuttocked." As the woman falls, however, she undresses and "passes her palms" over her legs, her breasts, and "deeply between her thighs." Beneath her, "widowed farmers" are soon to wake with futile (and irrelevant?) erections. She lands on her back in a field, naked, and dies. The sensation of the poem is necrophilic: it mourns a vagina rather than a person crashing to the ground.[52]

Ellmann's charge that Dickey is victimizing women requires some time to sort out. With regard to her claim that Dickey shows an "extraordinary concern with the underwear of a woman," there is little "concern" about underwear that is "extraordinary" at all in "Falling." The stewardess's underwear, mentioned only twice in a poem of more than 175 lines and even then quite briefly, with no detailed description of the garments or lingering preoccupation whatsoever, emphasizes the transformation of a rigidly and commercially clothed woman who is nonetheless a goddess. In the first instance where "the underwear of a woman" appears, it is mentioned briefly in four lines and is part of the stream of clothes shed by the stewardess not to titillate men but to animate the earth sexually as part of her ritual defiance of mortality so that she may "die / Beyond explanation." When the underwear is mentioned, it is treated comically: "absurd / Brassiere" and "the girdle required by regulations." In the poem's second reference to underwear, it appears in one line only and, once again, in a comic context, with the stewardess's girdle described as "coming down fantastically / On a clothesline, where it belongs" (298).

Second, Ellmann's claim that the stewardess is "monobuttocked" misses the point. The passenger's view of her "monobuttocked" condition is never mentioned in the poem. We scarcely see the stewardess in the plane; she falls out at line 7, and there is not the slightest hint of her being "monobuttocked" until 118 lines later, when the girdle is "squirming / Off her." Rather than stressing the girdle's "obsur[ing], to the observation of even the most alert passenger, her mesial groove," the poem emphasizes the stewardess's act of removing the girdle and revealing herself as goddess. The poem says that the stewardess is *"no longer* monobuttocked" (my italics). The poem does not "recall" the view that Ellmann derides; instead, the poem describes the stewardess's liberation from the unnaturally confining, "monobuttocked" condition.

Third, Ellmann offers a brief comment on the stewardess's running her hands over her naked body (while farmers below her have "futile" and "irrelevant" erections) then dying in a field when she lands. Based on this excerpted narrative, Ellmann makes the most astounding claim that "The sensation of the poem is necrophilic; it mourns a vagina rather than a person crashing to the ground." As reductive an example of critical paraphrase as one is likely to find, Ellmann's summary, which most certainly does not conform to Dickey's poem, is the only evidence for her bizarre charge. Ellmann's rewriting of Dickey turns "Falling" into a narrative of punitive reparation for the stewardess's sexuality, independence, and strength, a narrative whose tendency runs totally opposite to the poem's true course; her paraphrase does not admit of the tremendous energy of the poem or the fabulous series of powers that the stewardess acquires. The key point Ellmann misses is, as noted earlier, that *Dickey's poem reverses the tragic journalistic narrative* (which begins the poem) by converting a mortal stewardess into an earth goddess who lives and dies in the perpetual, natural alternation of generation and decay. Ellmann's omission of the poem's subtext that reverses the text is a disastrous misreading that turns a goddess into an inanimate corpse. To say that the poem "mourns a vagina"—only one four-word phrase in the work, "deeply between her thighs," even remotely mentions this anatomical area—is perverse and preposterous.[33]

Instead of mourning a dynamic woman unfairly reduced to a body part, we do better to conclude with questions centering on the social and political values of Dickey's poem and to address these issues with the ideas of four strong, intelligent women. Does "Falling" challenge our traditional conceptions of divinity as masculine, inherited from a Judeo-Christian religious history? What implications does the metamorphosis of a woman into an earth goddess from so-called "primitive" cultures have for a contemporary Western audience? What does the poem, as an enabling, matriarchal, creation myth with its distinctive conception of nature, say politically to both women and men? And, finally, does Dickey's mythological conception of woman impose any limit on feminine power?

First, with regard to conceptions of divinity as masculine, Carol Christ thinks that the idea of goddesses is revolutionary. Goddesses "are about female power. . . . This power is so threatening to the status quo that the word *Goddess* still remains unspeakable even to many of the most radical Christian and

Jewish theologians" (*Laughter of Aphrodite*, 111). Joseph Campbell agrees with this traditional "image of female power": "There can be no doubt that in the very earliest ages of human history the magical force and wonder of the female was no less a marvel than the universe itself; and this gave to woman a prodigious power, which it has been one of the chief concerns of the masculine part of the population to break, control, and employ to its own ends" (*Primitive Mythology*, 315). That Dickey's matriarchal creation myth in "Falling" is literally a revolution—a reversal or turning around—of our Western biblical tradition of Genesis and its concept of woman can be buttressed by further testimony from Campbell, interpreting the Iroquois tale of the Woman Who Fell from the Sky:

> [T]he flight of ducks ascending to ease the woman's fall; the earth divers in willing sacrifice of their lives preparing hastily a place upon which to receive her; Great Turtle becoming also willingly, the supporting ground of a new earth, upon which . . . a new arrival from the sphere of Air, would rest . . . while the new earth took form around her—[all this] represents a point of view with respect to the relationship of man to nature, and of the creatures of nature . . . that is in striking contrast to that defined in Genesis 3:14–19, where man is cursed, woman is cursed, the serpent is cursed, and the earth is cursed to "bring forth thorns and thistles" . . . the basic and sustaining sense of the relationship to mankind of the natural world and its creatures in this Native American origin myth, is of compassion, harmony, and cooperation.
>
> (*World Mythology* 2, pt. 2: 156)

Using language from Christine Froula's article "When Eve Reads Milton," we may say that Dickey's goddess is the opposite of Adam's God, "who is a *perfected* image of Adam: an all-powerful *male* creator who soothes Adam's fears of female power by Himself claiming credit for the original creation of the world."[54]

The second question centers on current implications of the stewardess's divinity. Summarizing Rita Gross's article "Hindu Female Deities as a Resource for the Contemporary Rediscovery of the Goddess," Christ indicates five lessons that "the symbol of the Goddess" from "ancient mythologies" can "teach modern Westerners." Analogues to these points can be found in our analysis of "Falling":

> First, the Goddess's obvious strength, capability, and transcendence validate the power of women as women that has been denied in Western religion and culture. Second, Goddess symbolism involves the coincidence of opposites—of death and life, destruction and creativity—that reminds humans of the finitude of life and points to its transcendent ground. Third, Goddess religion values motherhood as symbolic of divine creativity, but without limiting female power to biological destiny. Fourth, Goddess symbolism also associates women with

a wide range of culturally valued phenomena, including wealth, prosperity, culture, artful living, and spiritual teaching. Fifth, the Goddess requires the explicit reintroduction of sexuality as a religious metaphor in a symbol system where God is imaged as both male and female.

(*Laughter of Aphrodite*, 154–55)

Also addressing the meaning of a primitive goddess for a Western audience, Christ lists four reasons "Why Women Need the Goddess" (one of her chapters is so titled) that may serve us as descriptions of the social ends affected by the enabling, mythic drama in "Falling":

First, the Goddess is symbol of the legitimacy and beneficence of female power in contrast to the image of female power as anomalous or evil in biblical religion. Second, the Goddess validates women's bodily experiences, including menstruation, birth, lactation, and menopause, and validates the human connection to finitude, which has been denigrated in Western religions. Third, the Goddess symbol in the context of feminist goddess worship values the female will, which has been viewed as the origin of evil in biblical mythology. Fourth, the goddess points to the valuing of woman-to-woman bonds[,] . . . which is celebrated in the story of Demeter and Persephone. . . . The symbol of Goddess . . . legitimates and undergirds the moods and motivations inspired by feminism just as the symbol of God has legitimated patriarchal attitudes for several thousand years.

(*Laughter of Aphrodite*, 155)

Third, speaking of "the ritual poem in feminist spiritual circles," Alicia Ostriker offers a suggestive conception of "ritual" that articulates the kind of potential political effects we sense in Dickey's ritualized form: "For poet and reader-participant alike, ritual poetry implies the possibility of healing alternatives to dominance-submission scenarios. It suggests nonoppressive models of the conjunction between religion and politics, usually by re-imaging the sacred as immanent rather than transcendent, by defining its audience as members of a potentially strong community rather than as helplessly lonely individual victims, and by turning to nature (seen as sacred and female) as a source of power rather than passivity."[33]

Finally, to those who argue that Dickey's treatment of the Great Goddess confines female power to maternity, we counterargue by offering a summarizing definition of the stewardess in terms of the active powers she employs. Ranging from emotional to athletic to perceptual, these capacities far exceed nourishing or bearing only. Her dramatic character may be briefly outlined in a series of gerunds that disclose the plot of her transformation from that of victim to Energized Woman: falling out of the plane; blacking out; screaming; despairing; developing interest in her fall; dreaming; slanting; tumbling; diving; flying, seeing, and tasting like a bird; controlling her fall; arranging her skirt like a bat and thus changing the shape of her fall; energizing and watching the earth magically grow below; being born out of "chaos"; planning superhumanly; using her fall; feeling the Goddess in her and other women emerge; affirming her fate; shedding her clothes "to die / Beyond explanation"; sexually animating herself and hose below; landing; living into her dying; breathing "at last fully . . . AH, GOD—"; and, finally, dying into a new round of living. In "Falling" Dickey's Energized Woman, like his "Energized Man," acquires, in this writer's own words about the power of poetry, "an enormous increase in perceptiveness, an increased ability to understand and interpret the order of one's experience. . . , bringing only the best of oneself: one's sharpest perceptions, one's best mind, one's most hilarious and delighted and tragic senses" (*Imagination as Glory*, 164–65). Exchanging electrifying traits of goddesses from a plurality of cultures and religious traditions, "Falling" is James Dickey's exhilarating, mythopoeic celebration of tragedy transformed into delight and ecstasy, with a woman at the center of creation.

Notes

1. James Dickey, *Self-Interviews* (New York: Dell, 1970), 68–69; hereafter cited in the text as *Self-Interviews*.
2. Joyce Carol Oates, "Out of Stone, Into Flesh," in Harold Bloom, ed. *Modern Critical Views / James Dickey* (New York: Chelsea House, 1987), 101.
3. Monroe Spears, *Dionysus and the City, Modernism in Twentieth Century Poetry* (London: Oxford University Press, 1970), 257; hereafter cited in the text as *Dionysus and City*.
4. Joyce Pair, qtd. in Michael Hirsley, "On Wings of Words." *Chicago Tribune* 10 May 1987, sec. 10: 8–10 +, 29.
5. There is considerable evidence that Dickey has read extensively in anthropology and is strongly influenced by non-European poetry and song.

I've tried to come into conjunction in one way or another with Eskimo dance rituals and Bantu hunting songs and that sort of thing. And the revelations of those so-called folk as far as poetic imagery is considered are marvelously rich and evocative. They have nothing to do with Alexander Pope's use of the heroic couplet or Wordsworth's use of Milton's blank verse or any of that sort of thing . . . those people are saying something out of a condition with which they are in a precarious and dangerous and sometimes desperate harmony, but always a harmony of some kind which, even when the environment destroys them, is some kind of harmony. I'm looking for some way to *relate* to things again and this is the reason I dislike so much these poets of alienation who feel humiliated by everything and who are endlessly examining their own motives" (*Night Hurdling* [Columbia and Bloomfield Hills: Bruccoli Clark, 1983]: 251).

See also: Gordon Van Ness, "Living Beyond Recall" and Ron McFarland, "An Interview with James Dickey" in *The Voiced Connections of James Dickey*, ed. Ronald Baughman [Columbia, South Carolina: University of South Carolina Press, 1989]: 253 and 184–85.
6. In addition to Oates, Spears, Pair, and Dickey, others have mentioned briefly that the stewardess in "Falling" is some kind of goddess. Richard Calhoun and Robert Hill perceptively say that her function is "to serve the American agricultural heartland as a new-found fertility goddess" (*James Dickey* [Boston: Twayne, 1983]: 84). Neal Bowers claims that "Falling" is "the myth of the stewardess turned goddess in free-fall over Kansas" (*James Dickey / The*

Poet as Pitchman [Columbia, Missouri: University of Missouri Press, 1985]: 49). Ronald Baughman uses Dickey's own term to call her a " 'goddess' " as well "as a sexual and religious symbol of renewal" (*Understanding James Dickey* [Columbia, South Carolina: University of South Carolina Press, 1985]: 93). Marion Hodge rightly notes that she is "the earth-goddess, mother earth" who "transforms those who come near her body" ("James Dickey's Natural Heaven," *South Atlantic Review* 56:4 [November 1991]: 66). Laurence Lieberman accurately sees the positive power of the stewardess when he asks, "Who would have guessed that a woman's falling to her death from a plane could be converted by Dickey's imagination into a symbol of fantastic affirmation of life?" ("James Dickey": The Deepening of Being" in Harold Bloom, ed. *Modern Critical Views / James Dickey* [New York: Chelsea House, 1987]: 9).

    7.   Robert Kirschten, *James Dickey and the Gentle Ecstasy of Earth / A Reading of the Poems* (Baton Rouge: LSU Press, 1988), 119.

    8.   An earlier, shorter version of this article was presented at a SAMLA Special Session on James Dickey entitled "Measuring the Motion" on 15 November 1991 in Atlanta. The version presented at SAMLA appears in the *James Dickey Newsletter* 9 (Fall 1992).

    9.   James Dickey, *Poems, 1957–1967* (Middletown: Wesleyan University Press, 1967), Poems. 293; hereafter cited in the text as *Poems*.

    10.   The gaps in the run-in text follow Dickey's own spacing in the poem.

    11.   Dickey, *The Eagle's Mile* (Hanover: University Press of New England, 1990), 3; hereafter cited in the text as *Eagle's Mile*.

    12.   Erich Neumann, *The Great Mother*, translated by Ralph Manheim (Princeton: Princeton University Press, 1963), 145–46; hereafter cited in the text as *Great Mother*.

    13.   Neumann, *The Origins and History of Consciousness*, translated by R. F. C. Hull (Princeton: Princeton University Press, 1954), 76.

    14.   Heinrich Zimmer, "The Indian World Mother" in *The Mystic Vision* (Princeton: Princeton University Press, 1968), 84; hereafter cited in the text as *Mystic Vision*.

    15.   Carol Christ, *The Laughter of Aphrodite* (San Francisco: Harper & Row, 1987), 168; hereafter cited in the text as *Laughter of Aphrodite*.

    16.   Joseph Campbell, *Historical Atlas of World Mythology*, Volume 2, "The Way of the Seeded Earth," Part 2, "Mythologies of the Primitive Planters: The Northern Americas" (New York: Harper & Row, 1989), 143–46; hereafter cited in the text as *World Mythology 2*.

    17.   Charles H. Long, *Alpha: The Myths of Creation* (New York: George Braziller, 1963), 125–26.

    18.   D. H. Lawrence, *Etruscan Places* (New York: Viking, 1963), 49.

    19.   James Dickey in "The Energized Man," eds. Bruce Weigl and T. R. Hummer, *The Imagination as Glory: The Poetry of James Dickey* (Urbana: University of Illinois Press, 1984), 164; hereafter cited in the text as *Imagination as Glory*.

    20.   Jane Harrison, *Epilegomena to the Study of Greek Religion* and *Themis, A Study of the Social Origins of Greek Religion* (Hyde Park, New York: University Books, 1962), 68.

    21.   Marija Gimbutas, *The Goddesses and Gods of Old Europe* (Los Angeles: University of California Press, 1982), 152.

    22.   Friedrich Nietzsche, *The Birth of Tragedy*, trans. World Mythology. A. Haussmann (Edinburgh: T. N. Foulis, 1909), 21; hereafter cited in the text as *Birth of Tragedy*.

    23.   Nietzsche, *Twilight of the Idols* in *The Portable Nietzsche*, trans. Walter Kaufmann (New York: Viking Press, 1954), 518; hereafter cited in the text as *Twilight of Idols*.

    24.   Herbert Marcuse, *Eros and Civilization* (Boston: Beacon Press, 1955), 166.

    25.   Theodore Roethke in Neal Bowers, *Theodore Roethke / The Journey from I to Otherwise* (Columbia, Missouri: University of Missouri Press, 1982), 8–10.

    26.   James Dickey, *Babel to Byzantium* (New York: Grosset & Dunlap, 1968), 148.

    27.   Joseph Campbell, *Historical Atlas of World Mythology*, Volume 2, "The Way of the Seeded Earth," Part 1, "The Sacrifice" (New York, Harper & Row, 1988), 36; hereafter cited in the text as *World Mythology 1*.

28. Campbell, *The Masks of God: Primitive Mythology* (New York: Penguin, 1959), 186; hereafter cited in the text as *Primitive Mythology*.

29. Campbell, *The Power of Myth* (New York: Doubleday, 1988), 109.

30. Kenneth Burke, "The Vegetal Radicalism of Theodore Roethke" in *Language as Symbolic Action* (Berkeley: University of California Press, 1966), 244.

31. Theodore Roethke, "Root Cellar" in *The Collected Poems of Theodore Roethke* (New York: Doubleday, 1961), 38.

32. Mary Ellmann, *Thinking about Women* (New York: Harcourt Brace, 1968), 29.

33. Equally wrong-headed are two sets of claims by Paul Ramsey and Ralph Mills against "Falling." Ramsey charges that the stewardess is a "stripteaser aiming at seducing all the farm boys and men in Kansas, on her way to death" ("James Dickey: Meter and Structure" in Richard J. Calhoun, ed. *James Dickey: The Expansive Imagination* [Deland, Florida: Everett / Edwards, Inc, 1973]: 192) To be sure, the stewardess' sexual power increases dramatically when she removes her clothes; however, her energy is not the provocation of a striptease but the Dionysian amplification and purification of natural sexual instinct which passes not only to "the farm boys and men in Kansas," but to the women as well and to the entire earth. Mills criticizes "Falling" for being "drawn out, repetitive, overwritten, blurred, and diffuse." The idea behind the poem, he charges, is "contrived" and "cannot be sustained even by Coleridge's 'willing suspension of disbelief'" ("The Poetry of James Dickey" in Bruce Weigl and T. R. Hummer, eds. *The Imagination as Glory* [Urbana: University of Illinois Press, 1984]: 41). Many of these issues center on the very conception of "form" herein discussed. "Falling" is not "drawn out" if it is in the shape of a ritual conversion which requires considerable dramatic length to effect emotionally the transformation at the heart of the poem. Neither is the poem "repetitive" or "overwritten," for the stages of its story are clearly demonstrable in terms of the series of changes the stewardess experiences, several of which shade off into each other but do not merely replicate the same aspect of development. If our reading of the form and genre of the poem are accurate, then the piece is not "blurred" but quite focused as to what happens and the kind of action that does happen. Perhaps Mills confuses one aspect of the stewardess' hallucinatory sight as she falls with the heart of the poem. What is "diffuse" is not the poem, but rather her energy which is "diffused" throughout the setting, animating everything it touches. Finally, the premise of "Falling" is "contrived" only if one assumes that the transformation of a stewardess into a goddess is somehow trivial or even, as Mills says, "boring."

34. Christine Froula, "When Eve Reads Milton" in *Canons*, ed. Robert von Hallberg (Chicago: University of Chicago Press, 1983), 160.

35. Alicia Ostriker, "Dancing at the Devil's Party: Some Notes on Politics and Poetry" in *Politics & Poetic Value*, ed. Robert von Hallberg (Chicago: University of Chicago Press, 1987), 221.

Dickey, Dante, and the Demonic: Reassessing *Deliverance*

PEGGY GOODMAN ENDEL

"I come from Minot, North Dakota," said the instructor, "land of the big beet. It is flat up there, and all the fields are running red, Cadet Quow, not with blood but with beet juice. My way out of it was down, not up. I went to Colorado School of Mines as a chemistry major. Underground is my territory."

—Alnilam

Bradley Asbill, the civilian instructor who lectures on the mysteries of heart-cut aviation fuel in *Alnilam*, is but one of several philosopher-metaphysicians who people James Dickey's large novel; as Asbill says, his "territory" is "underground," and, in his down to earth way, he is Dickey's Heraclitus, a classroom reminder to celestial navigators that the way up and the way down are the same. Dickey's work has elicited much fine commentary, and, not surprisingly, critics have been tempted into a bit of celestial navigation of their own: particularly in discussions of *Deliverance*, commentators have approached Dickey as a neo-Romantic, a poet and novelist in the tradition of the great romantics from Wordsworth and Coleridge to Whitman, Dylan Thomas, and Theodore Roethke.[1] As Dickey himself has observed, however, his work has always possessed a powerful, anti-Romantic concern with a moral evil that exists in tension with the Romantic sublime.[2] I wish to suggest that we have neglected the vision of unsublimated evil in *Deliverance* and that Dickey's pre-Romantic model for the anality of evil—"the way down" in this novel—is the *Inferno* of Dante.

Dickey's own remarks on the creation of *Deliverance* are suggestive. In a 1972 interview, David L. Arnett quotes Dickey as saying that the idea for *Deliverance* first occurred to him in 1962 when he was living in Positano, Italy; but, Dickey adds, any "literary or mythological precedent" for the novel came from a review by Stanley Edgar Hyman which he had read as a student more than a dozen years earlier. What struck him, he says, was Hyman's description of Van Gennep's pattern of separation-initiation-return in the "monomyth" of Joseph Campbell: "'a separation from the world, a penetration to some

Peggy Goodman Endel, "Dickey, Dante, and the Demonic: Reassessing *Deliverance*." *American Literature*, 60: 4, pp. 611–624. Copyright Duke University Press, 1988. Reprinted with permission of the publisher.

source of power, and a life-enhancing return.'" The action sequences on the river in *Deliverance*, he says in the same interview, were suggested by the voyage of Satan through Chaos in Milton's *Paradise Lost*.[3] It is to the point that Dickey's tale of a "gut-survival situation" in north Georgia was conceived in Italy in mythic, epic, and infernal terms.

Near the end of *Deliverance*, Ed Gentry is joking with the young doctor who has been working on his injured side. Ed says, "You mean you don't have any moonshine in this here hospital? And you way off in the country like this? What the hell is north Georgia coming to?"[4] It is the mark of this finely wrought novel that even such apparently pointless banter should constitute an element of design. Ed's first two questions—"You mean you don't have any moonshine in this here hospital? And you way off in the country like this?"—reflect his intoxicating moon-vision of the river. His last question—"What the hell is north Georgia coming to?"—recalls that moonshine's sober context: north Georgia is "the Country of Nine-Fingered People and Prepare to Meet Thy God," and it is a land which is about to be both dammed and damned.

As a born-again narrator in the Augustinian mode, Ed Gentry is part of a postlapsarian, antediluvian order where cemeteries move, graves open, and the nameless dead arise in green coffins to presage apocalypse (p. 226). The profanities in the novel bear on a genuine eschatology. When two mountain men step out of the woods and demand, "What the *hail* you think you're doing?", "Do you know what the *hail* you're talkin' about?", "What the *hail*"; when Bobby Trippe wails, "I want to get the hell and gone out of this goddamned place," "Let's get the hell out of here," "We've got two guys who don't even know where in the hell they are. . . . We haven't got a goddamned chance"; when Lewis Medlock insists, "there's a lot of resentment in these hill counties about the dam. There are going to have to be cemeteries moved like in the old TVA days. . . . I'm goddamned if I want to come back up here"; when Ed says, "one of Drew's feet flew up and we were free and in hell," "we've come an awful goddamned long way," "We've been through a goddamned bad time," Dickey is pointing to a serious consideration of last things.

In his visionary moment of insight, Ed will have briefly "*beheld*" the sinuous river as an amoral, icy pit of brightness (p. 146); but deep within the coiling river, which runs through him at last "as though immortally," lie the bodies of two men—one good, and one evil ("I had a friend there who in a way had died for me, and my enemy was there" [p. 234]). The antithetical moral bodies submerged deep within the Romantic moon-pit are human bodies, and they inhabit that part of a pre-Romantic, Dantean cosmology in which evil is figured as part of the human body—unsublimated, unrefined.

In Dante's cosmology, at the center of the earth, the nadir of the Inferno's inverse cone, stands the body of Satan, a monstrous giant frozen waist-high in the cosmic cesspool into which drain the foul rivers of Hell. The exact center of the earth and the void is Satan's anus, an abyss whose negative status Dante conveys with a narrative gap.⁵ Somehow—the poet deliberately does not say how—the area around Satan's haunches becomes the liberating cleft in a rock through which the pilgrim is both excreted and reborn, as though from a primitive cloaca:

> At [Virgil's] bidding I clasped him round the neck; and he watched his chance of time and place and, when the wings were wide open, caught hold of the shaggy flanks, then descended from tuft to tuft between the matted hair and the frozen crusts. When we were where the thigh turns, just on the swelling of the haunch, the Leader with labour and strain brought round his head where his legs had been and grappled on the hair like one climbing, so that I thought that we were returning into Hell again.
> "Hold fast," said the Master, panting like one spent, "for by such stairs must we go forth from so much evil."
> And he passed out through the cleft of a rock and put me on the edge to sit, then reached toward me his cautious step. I raised my eyes and thought to see Lucifer as I had left him, and I saw his legs held upward; and if I became perplexed then let the dull crowd judge who do not see what is the point that I had passed. (*Inf.* XXXIV)⁶

Through this mysterious gap, at the end of a spiralling descent, Dante and his guide find deliverance from Hell. The infernal journey that begins with the pilgrim's realization that he is lost in the middle of a dark wood ends with his return into the bright world to the sound of a winding stream. With the advantage of hindsight—quite literally—Dante's reader can finally perceive the nine concentric zones of the *Inferno* as the bowels of hell, great loops of intestine in the world's body.

The mountain man in *Deliverance* who rapes that "incompetent asshole," Bobby Trippe (or "Tripe"), is the scruffy heir of the King of Hell. Dickey's whorl-faced, drop-gutted mountain man reigns in a cesspool, a "sump" deep in the woods of North Georgia where the ground is "mulchy like shit" and where the shallow trench that receives his body is hollowed out with a latrine shovel. Ed describes this place in the labyrinthine, dark wood where he and his party have become willfully lost:

> Around us the woods were so thick that there would have been trouble putting an arm into it in places. . . . After the first few turns I had no idea where we were, and in a curious way I enjoyed being *that* lost. If you were in something as deep as we were in it, it was better to go all the way. When I quit hearing the creek I knew I was lost, wandering foolishly in the wood holding a corpse by the sleeve.
> Lewis lifted his hand again, and we let the body down on the ground. We were by a sump of some kind, a blue-black seepage of rotten water that had either crawled in from some other place or came up from the ground where it

was. The earth around it was soft and squelchy, and I kept backing off from it, even though I had been walking in the creek with the others. (Pp. 115–16)

The sump "at the soft center of the earth" in *Deliverance* has its correlate in the Dantean abyss: As Lewis aims at the sump with the arrow that he has used to kill Bobby's rapist, Ed notices, "There was nothing there but the black water, but he was aiming at a definite part of it: a single drop, maybe, as it moved and would have to stop, sooner or later, for an instant." Then, he concludes, "It went. . . . There was no sense of the arrow's being stopped by anything under the water—log or rock. It was gone, and could have been traveling down through muck to the soft center of the earth."

The *Inferno* is the *locus classicus* of mid-life crisis, the malaise which afflicts Ed and his middle-aged, middle-class companions—"the kind of thing that gets hold of middle-class householders every once in a while," Bobby says. The first sentence of *Inferno* I, is the touchstone of beginning again *in medias res*: "In the middle of the journey of our life I came to myself within a dark wood where the straight way was lost." Early in *Deliverance*, surveying the rows of "gray affable men" he has hired to promote Shadow Row Shell Homes and Kitt'n Britches, Ed thinks, "They are in some way my captives." And then, with a shock of recognition, he adds, "I was not really thinking about their being my prisoners, but of being my own." The familiar paradox is that one must lose oneself to find oneself: to echo Ed, in a curious way one can enjoy being *that* lost.

The narrative stance in *Deliverance*, as in the Augustinian prototype, is that of the new man describing the old, dead man. The process of the old man dying to the new in *Deliverance* is a gradual one: "I was either awake or dead, and I always came back slowly" (p. 27); "I was dead, and riding, which is a special kind of sleep not like any other" (p. 38); "I rolled, I tried to crawl along the flying bottom. Nothing worked. I was dead" (p. 124); "I lay there on my side . . . as though I were in a sideways grave. . . . I simply lay in nature" (p. 145); "I got ready to die again" (p. 188). Rebirth, too, occurs gradually: "A shower would have made me a completely new person, but I was half-new anyway, and half-new was very good; it is better to come back easily" (p. 214).

The stance presupposes change, and, even in a secular theodicy, such change presupposes the advent of grace. ("He has changed, too," Ed concludes of Lewis.) The agent of grace or its equivalent in *Deliverance* is the river: "I looked back down at the river. It was beautiful, and I was sure I would feel all my life the particular pull of it at different places, the weight and depth and speed of it; they had been given to me" (p. 195). There is a *before* and there is an *after* in this scheme; in it, deliverance consists of the new man's deliverance from the old.

Dickey divides *Deliverance* into five sections: "Before"; "September 14th";

"September 15th"; "September 16th"; "After." The three-day descent into the Country of Nine-Fingered People takes place in the middle of September—that is, at a midpoint early in the fall—and the fall, like the dam, is a pun made flesh. *Deliverance* is, among other things, about the Fall that binds man to his proper humanity, the earned knowledge of his own insufficiency: "*Il existe à base de la vie humaine un principe d'insuffisance,*" the first epigraph reads. The *Inferno*'s pilgrim limps because he is *homo claudus*, fallen and divided man; his descent into hell is the means by which that breach in his nature becomes reconciled with a principle of unity. When in *Deliverance*, Ed falls from a tree onto his own arrow, he says, "Walking was odd and one-sided but not impossible." The correspondent object in nature is the half-dead, yellow tree stripped by lightning which Ed embraces as the emblem of his experience: "It was about half-dead, with the bark scaled off one side in a jagged pattern. It must have been struck by lightning at one time; the fire had ripped it deep. That was the kind of image I wanted in my mind: like that, the whole tree" (p. 192). At the novel's end, Ed includes Lewis in the fraternity of lamed men made whole by the knowledge that they have fallen: "Lewis limps over from his cabin now and then, and we look at each other with intelligence, feeling the true weight and purpose of all water."

Insofar as the hellscape of *Deliverance* is internal, its nadir is a psychological nadir; its muck is human muck; its pit of filth which is "mulchy like shit" is a pit of moral filth. Deliverance from the pit may occur only when one immerses oneself in a dreadful but fortunate fall. In his description of the burial at the sump in the middle of the woods, Ed says, "Lewis fell." He continues,

> He started to dig with the collapsible GI shovel we had brought for digging latrines. The ground came up easily, or what was on the ground. There was no earth; it was all leaves and rotten stuff. It had the smell of generations of mold. They might as well let the water in on it, I thought; this stuff is no good to anybody.
>
> Drew and I got down and helped with our hands. Bobby stood looking off into the trees. Drew dug in, losing himself in a practical job, figuring the best way to do it. The sweat stood in the holes of his blocky, pitted face, and his black hair, solid with thickness and hair lotion, shone sideways, hanging over one ear. (P. 117)

Drew's pitted face is the visible sign of his engagement with the pit. Ed will eulogize Drew as "the only decent one; the only sane one." Only Drew—the decent one, the sane one—devotes himself fully to the burial in the sump just as he devotes himself fully to its analogue, his diabolically disfigured son with the mark of Cain on his brow. Ed first says of Drew, "He was devoted to his family, particularly to his little boy Pope, who had some kind of risen hornlike blood blister on his forehead that his eyebrow grew out of and around in a way to make you realize the true horrors of biology." One must acknowledge and embrace the demonic as a part of one's own gargoyle flesh, the novel enjoins; like Drew's counterpart, the albino boy Lonnie, we all have one sane, rational eye and one insane, irrational eye. Descent into the black water of the sump as well as immersion in the river enables one to die. "By such stairs," Virgil tells Dante, "must we go forth from so much evil."

On the first page of *Deliverance*, Dickey literally maps out his characters' itinerary as an oblique descent—"downstream, northeast to southwest"—and each stage of that descent contracts into a sphere of anality more deadly and more diabolic than the one which precedes it. Because Dickey adjusts the pre-Romantic vision of the anality of evil to the Romantic vision of fruitful intercourse between Mind and Nature, the violation or collapse of the bond between Mind and Nature takes the primary form of anal rape.

The first episode of anal rape in the novel is figurative—the exploitation of the model in the Kitt'n Britches ad. (The word that recurs in this connection is 'use': Ed says, "and now we were going to use her"; Ed's partner says that he does not believe that the girl is "good enough to use again.") The "incredible countrified jerk" who manages sales for Kitt'n Britches wants the model's buttocks bared like those of the little girl in the Coppertone Ad: in his session with the model Ed rapes her privacy just as effectively as would the "countrified jerk" he deplores. As he recalls this brutalizing session, Ed says,

> It reminded me of prisons and interrogations. . . . That was one side of it, all right, and the other was pornography. I thought of those films that you see at fraternity parties and in officers' clubs where you realize with terror that when the girl drops the towel the camera is not going to drop with it discreetly, as in old Hollywood films, following the bare feet until they hide behind a screen, but is going to stay and when the towel falls, move in; that it is going to destroy someone's womanhood by *raping her secrecy*; that there is going to be nothing left." (P. 21; emphasis added)

The Country of Nine-Fingered People is about to be eternally dammed, but even in that "goddamned" place sodomy, Lewis says, is still a capital offense (p. 104). Ed's unreal city is already damned to a living death, and there the unnatural act of raping someone's womanhood is simply bound up with capital and is a normal by-product of the marketplace. Insofar as the city is Ed's creation, circumscribed by his own tunnel vision, its damnation consists of its damming up. Himself cut off from natural process, Ed defines it with images of containment—prisons, cubicles, boxes, halls within halls, and corridors within corridors.

The description of the living dead from the section entitled "Before" clearly echoes the haunting passage from *Inferno* III which T. S. Eliot appropriates for *The Waste Land*. As Dante's journey is about to begin, Virgil brings the pilgrim to a group of wretched souls at the portal of Hell who have lived "without disgrace and without praise," who "never were alive" and who "have no hope of death." These are the Neutrals, faceless and numberless: "And I looked and saw a whirling banner . . . and behind it came so long a train of people that I should never have believed that death had undone so many." As his journey is about to begin, Ed is looking for a "decent ass" in a crowd of "horned" women, and he is shocked to find that he must include himself among the faceless, numberless legions of the living dead in this urban equivalent of the portal of Hell. He observes,

> The women were almost all secretaries and file clerks, young and semi-young and middle-aged, and their hair styles, piled and shellacked and swirled and horned, and almost every one stiff, filled me with desolation. I kept looking for a decent ass and spotted one in a beige skirt, but when the girl turned her barren gum-chewing face toward me, it was all over. I suddenly felt like George Holley, my old Braque man, must have felt when he worked for us, saying to himself in any way he could, day after day, "I am with you but not of you." But I knew better. I was of them, sure enough, as they stretched out of sight before me up the hill and into the building. (Pp. 16–17)

Ed looks for "decent ass" at the portal of hell; he merely commands decent ass in its suburbs. Ed and Martha's intercourse is an even more desolate version of anality than the version that has preceded it because the potential for communion is so much greater: "The blood in me fell and began to rise in the dark, moving with her hands and the slight crackling of the lubricant. Martha put a pillow in the middle of the bed, threw back the covers with a windy motion and turned facedown on the pillow. I knelt and entered her, and her buttocks rose and fell. 'Oh,' she said, 'Oh yes'" (p. 29). Martha's back labors; it heaves and it works, Ed says. Neither joy nor pain accompanies such lovemaking, although the promise of deliverance exists in the form of "another life."

To effect the transition from suburbia to the "red-neck South" Dickey returns to *Inferno* III for Dante's transition from the portal of Hell to the First Circle. Here Charon, who may ferry only the dead across Acheron, challenges Dante, "thou there that art a living soul, take thyself apart from these that are dead"; and Virgil replies that the source of will and power has willed that Dante shall cross the river of death even though he lives: "Charon, do not torment thyself. It is so willed where will and power are one, and ask no more." Canto III ends with Dante's falling "like one that is seized with sleep"; Canto IV begins with his waking from the "deep sleep in my head," having somehow been transported into the First Circle.

In Dickey's transition, Ed begins his river journey at Will's Ferry Road together with Lewis, whom he describes as "the only man I knew determined to get something out of life who had both the means and the will to do it"

(p. 10). (Lewis directs Bobby and Drew, "Ed and I'll meet you'all early Friday, around six-thirty, where Will's Ferry Road runs into the four-lane, at the big new Will's Plaza Shopping Center.") Lewis Medlock, the man of will, stands to Ed Gentry as Virgil, the man of circumscribed knowledge, stands to Dante: the great guide who is initially the Poet's "Master" and "Leader" ultimately becomes an aspect of himself to be mastered and transcended. Just as, paradoxically, one must lose oneself to find oneself, in *Deliverance* one must transcend the will by an effort of will. The journey to the river begins as an experiment in the will, an effort to "rise above time" by finding "the thing that must be there, and that must be subject to the will"; it ends with the acquired knowledge that "dying is better than immortality." That the human will is subject to a primal will and power will be the lesson of the "goddamned river."

As Ed and his party drive out of the suburbs and into "the red-neck South," the descent continues from one sphere of anality to the next. Ed describes this stage of their journey as a radical falling off:

> The change was not gradual; you could have stopped the car and got out at the exact point where suburbia ended and the red-neck South began. I would like to have done that, to see what the sense of it would be. There was a motel, then a weed field, and then on both sides Clabber Girl came out of hiding, leaping onto the sides of barns, 666 and Black Draught began to swirl, and Jesus began to save. We hummed along, borne with the inverted canoe on a long tide of patent medicines and religious billboards. From such a trip you would think that the South did nothing but dose itself and sing gospel songs; *you would think that the bowels of the Southerner were forever clamped shut; that he could not open and let natural process flow through him, but needed one purgative after another in order to make it to church.* (Pp. 37–38; emphasis added)

Here on the billboards for patent purgation—for Black Draught and 666—Dickey inscribes his directive in inverted or parodic form: open and let natural process flow through you. This directive is the final lesson of the undammed river, spelled out backwards on billboards as on the banners of Hell.

The descent continues: Ed has observed, "There was something about me that usually kept me from dreaming. . . . every night I went down deep, and if I had any sensation during sleep, it was of going deeper and deeper, trying to reach a point, a line or border." Lying in his tent in the dark woods, as Ed begins to lose consciousness, his memory of Martha's "heaving and working" back dissolves into a nightmare in which the buttocks of the model in the Kitt'n Britches Ad are racked by "a little orange concretion of pure horror."[7] The clawing cat stands to the model in the dream as both the dog to the child in the Coppertone Ad and, by implication, as Ed to Martha ("You're hairy as a goddamned dog, ain't you?" [p. 101], the tall man in the wood will ask Ed.) Recalling his dream, Ed says,

I saw Martha's back heaving and working and dissolving into the studio, where we had finally decided that the photographs we had taken were no good and had asked the model back. We had also gone ahead with the Kitts' sales manager's idea to make the ad like the Coppertone scene of the little girl and the dog. There was Wilma holding the cat and forcing its claws out of its pads and fastening them into the back of the girl's panties. There was Thad; there was I. The panties stretched, the cat pulled, trying to get its claws out of the artificial silk, and then all at once leapt and clawed the girl's buttocks. She screamed, the room erupted with panic, she slung the cat round and round, a little orange concretion of pure horror, still hanging by one paw from the girl's panties, pulling them down, clawing and spitting in the middle of the air, raking the girl's buttocks and legbacks. I was paralyzed. Nobody moved to do anything. The girl screamed and cavorted, reaching behind her. (P. 77)

The "countrified jerk" in the city who wants a girl's buttocks in his ad is a part of Ed himself, and his domain is deep in Ed's unconscious. Ed awakens to find that here in the Country of Nine-Fingered People, one knuckle of a deformed fist has punctured the canvas of his tent.

The cat that claws the girl's panties in Ed's dream and the owl that rips the canvas of Ed's tent anticipate the bestial man who commands Bobby to "drop them panties" in the next circle of anality, the clearing in the wood where Bobby is encircled and sodomized. The opposite of a sexual act, Bobby's anal rape is an emasculation, a prelude to the lean man's threat to Ed, "You ever had your balls cut off, you fuckin' ape?" (p. 98). As the whorl-faced man penetrates Bobby, Bobby's screams become higher: "A scream hit me and I would have thought it was mine except for the lack of breath. It was sound of pain and outrage, and was followed by one of simple and wordless pain. Again it came out of him, higher and more carrying." The effect of the rape is to violate Bobby's manhood: Ed observes, "He stood up and backed away, still naked from the middle down, his sexual organs wasted with pain." The opposite of a sexual act, Bobby's anal rape is also the opposite of natural process: The white-bearded man directs Bobby, "Now let's you just drop them pants"; Ed's visceral response is, "My rectum and intestines contracted. Lord God."

Bobby is, Ed says, an "incompetent asshole" (p. 171), "a useless ass" (p. 183). But the men who sodomize him and try to sodomize Ed embody evil in a quintessential way. They are foul. They are at one with the sloppy woods. Like the Griner brothers, they are cloven or double. Moreover, they also have doubles. When Ed examines the body of the man whom he has shot he says, "he was dressed like the toothless man in the clearing, whether exactly like him I truthfully couldn't say, but very much like. He was about the same size, and he was thin and repulsive-looking" (p. 170). Confronting these men, Ed confronts the void: "I shook my head in a complete void," he says. Then, "I shook my head, trying to get my breath in a gray void full of leaves." And, finally, "I was blank."

The demonic is a condition of the spirit, however, and the demon lover that sodomizes Ed Gentry is a part of his own being. As Ed stands, elated, over the body of the man whom he has "center-shot," he is encircled and possessed by this "ultimate horror":

> you can do what you want to; nothing is too terrible. I can cut off the genitals he was going to use on me. Or I can cut off his head, looking straight into his open eyes. Or I can eat him. I can do anything I have a wish to do, and I waited carefully for some wish to come; I would do what it said.
>
> It did not come, but the ultimate horror circled me and played over the knife. I began to sing. It was a current popular favorite, a folk-rock tune. I finished, and *I was withdrawn from. I straightened as well as I could.* (P. 170; emphasis added)

Finally, the river, too, enters Ed and possesses him, and rape modulates into something "complicated" which, like the demon of a medieval exorcism, threads up his rectum and out his mouth: "There was green and blue, in some kind of essential relation, and then the river went into my right ear like an ice pick. I yelled, a tremendous, walled-in yell, and then I felt the current thread through me, first through my head from one ear and out the other and then complicatedly through my body, up my rectum and out my mouth and also in at the side where I was hurt" (p. 177). The gloss on this critical scene occurs back at the juncture of the suburbs and the red-neck South, where Ed surveys the billboards for purgatives and Jesus.

Ed's "tremendous, walled-in yell" is succeeded by a birth cry. The imagery of tunnels and of funnels pervades the last third of the novel, and as Ed's canoe is finally funnelled into what he calls "the hole" (p. 189) of the river's last rapids, he meets "some supernatural force of primal energy" with a primal scream: "'Hold on, baby,' I hollered. 'We're going home.' . . . I closed my eyes and screamed with Lewis, mixing my voice with his bestial scream, blasting my lungs out where we hung six feet over the river for an instant and then began to fall. . . . Now, in calm water, I began to collect everything we needed to make a future with."

The river has become a birth canal, but somewhere the black water of a sump merges with the bright coiling pit still. Ed and his party first put their boat in the water at Oree, "a little nothing town." They take it out at Aintry. Just as the river threads through Ed, up his rectum and through his mouth, Ed threads through the river, down its mouth (or orifice) at Oree, and through its rectum (or anus) at Aintry, the cloacal "hole" in the rapids through which he finds deliverance.

And yet the whorl-faced man who rapes Bobby in a gray void of leaves insists, "This-here river don't go nowhere near Aintry." When he is asked

"Where does it go?" he hesitates, "It goes . . . it goes," and the thin, repulsive man who "is missing his teeth and not caring" says, "It goes to Circle Gap" (p. 96). In the context of the novel, Circle Gap is the ultimate symbol and the ultimate mystery, taking its shape from the body, which is primary, but not limited to the body. Like the primitive cloaca, Circle Gap—the hole in the rapids through which Ed is made whole—is both the uncreating void and the fruitful womb.

That the opposites of the natural world interpenetrate is the final lesson of the river, and it is this rich principle of natural design which Dickey's narrator embraces at last as a principle of artistic design. Just as the river has pulsed with Ed's whole being (p. 146), so his whole being finally pulses with the river: "In me it still is, and will be until I die" (p. 234). And, having "*beheld*" the river pulsing with itself, the eye beholds "something primally graceful" in the very body of evil—the diabolic, whorl-faced man seen, significantly, from the back: "There was something relaxed and enjoying in his body position . . . I had never seen a more beautiful or convincing element of design" (p. 161).

As Ed and his companions speed onto the four-lane highway that will lead ultimately to Bobby's rape in the wood, Ed notes, "As we went past, I gave the others the Churchill V-sign, and Bobby replied with the classic single-finger" (p. 36). Safe at last in a boarding house near Aintry, he says, "I turned back to Bobby and held up a circle of fingers" (p. 211). Ed's circle of fingers is a version of Circle Gap, a bodily sign for perfection encompassing in context both the Primum Mobile and the Pit. The victorious V-sign, the phallic single-finger, and a circle of fingers stand for the central issues of the novel, and they are the homely hieroglyphics of the body.

Notes

1.   See, for example, Arthur Gregor, "James Dickey, American Romantic: An Apprecia-tion," in Richard J. Calhoun, ed., *James Dickey: The Expansive Imagination* (Deland, Fla.: Everett / Edwards, 1973), pp. 77–89; Calhoun and Robert W. Hill, *James Dickey* (Boston: Twayne, 1983); Bruce Weigl and R. T. Hummer, eds., *The Imagination as Glory: The Poetry of James Dickey* (Urbana: Univ. of Illinois Press, 1984); Barnett Guttenberg, "The Pattern of Redemption in Dickey's *Deliverance*," *Critique*, 18, No. 3 (1977), 83–91; and George Lensing, "The Neo-Romanticism of James Dickey," *South Carolina Review*, 10 (1978), 20–32.

2.   See Carolyn Kizer and James Boatwright, "A Conversation with James Dickey," *Shenandoah*, 18, No. 1 (1966), 3–28; rpt. in Calhoun, pp. 1–33.

3.   "An interview with James Dickey," *Contemporary Literature*, 16 (1975), 286–300. For Hyman's essay, see his "Myth, Ritual, and Nonsense," *Kenyon Review*, 11 (1949), 455–75.

4.   *Deliverance* (New York: Dell, 1970), p. 201. All further references to this work appear in the text.

5.   See Robert M. Durling, "Deceit and Digestion in the Belly of Hell," in *Allegory and Representation*, ed. Stephen S. Greenblatt (Baltimore: Johns Hopkins Univ. Press, 1981), pp. 61–93; Durling, " 'Io son venuto': Seneca, Plato and the Microcosm," *Dante Studies*, 93 (1975),

95–129; John Freccero, "Satan's Fall and the 'Quaestio de Aqua et Terra,'" *Italica*, 38 (1961), 99–115; and Freccero, "The Sign of Satan," *MLN*, 53 (1961), 11–16; rpt. in *Dante: The Poetics of Conversion*, ed. Rachel Jacoff (Cambridge: Harvard Univ. Press, 1986), pp. 167–79. Norman O. Brown ventured a popularized version of this reading of *Inferno XXXIV* in *Life Against Death* (New York: Vintage-Random House, 1959), p. 207.

6. Dante Alighieri, *Inferno*, Vol. 1 of *The Divine Comedy*, ed. and trans. John D. Sinclair (New York: Galaxy-Oxford Univ. Press, 1961), p. 425.

7. Describing associational thought, Dickey says that artists and intellectuals "have thought, when younger, that the excited, deep, associational kind of mind would bring them to the earthly paradise. But it is not so; the place is hell. Believe me, it is better to the stupid and ordinary." See *Sorties: Journal and New Essays* (Garden City, N.Y.: Doubleday, 1971), p. 7.

James Dickey's *The Zodiac*: A Self-Translation?

Romy Heylen

In his foreword to *The Zodiac* (1976), James Dickey refers to the poem of the same title written by his Dutch fellow-poet Hendrik Marsman. Furthermore, he states that his poem is in no sense a translation of Marsman's poem but that he has taken certain liberties with the original. Having read some biographical information on Dickey as well as a few of his works, I could not find any indication of his acquaintance with Dutch literature or the Dutch language, nor of any translating activity which some of his contemporaries consider a very important part of their craft. Finally, Dickey himself explained in a personal letter that his literary contact with Marsman was mediated through an English translation by Adriaan J. Barnouw.[1] When Dickey states that he was "inspired" by the original poem he means Barnouw's text (a confusion between translated and original work often encountered in practice). This translation of Marsman's "De Dierenriem" (1940) first appeared in the *Sewanee Review* and was reprinted a year later in Barnouw's anthology *Coming After: An Anthology from the Low Countries* (1948).[2]

The title of any text functions as an important hint which prepares the reader to interpret the text within a certain framework of connotations and associations. Needless to say, the reader has to be aware of its referent(s) for the allusion(s) to be effective. Although Dickey mentions in his preface that he borrowed the title of his volume from Marsman's poem, this reminder will be worthless for the American reader unfamiliar with Marsman's "De Dierenriem." By the same token, Dickey himself has been excused in advance because he does not know Dutch. Since he does not know the language he is not responsible for the interpretation and the rewriting of Marsman's Dutch text. But nearly 30 years after the publication of Barnouw's anthologized translation, Marsman's "De Dierenriem" generated another poem: *The Zodiac* by James Dickey. This literary contact is, to my knowledge, determined not so much by receptive conditions in American literature as by the receptive attitude of a single poet, his personality and poetics. However, certain artistic conditions needed to be fulfilled to make a creative reception possible. It is

Originally printed in the *James Dickey Newsletter* 6.2 (Spring, 1990): 2–17. Reprinted by permission.

clear from the preface to *The Zodiac* that Dickey does not consider his poem to be a (second) translation (to escape allegations similar to those triggered by Robert Lowell's *Imitations?*) but rather that his text aspires to be a poem in its own right. Nevertheless in coming to terms with Barnouw's translation Dickey unveils many experiences shared by translators.[3] Hence, the main thrust of this essay is to demonstrate the extent to which Dickey's *The Zodiac* is a poem about interpreting and writing, and thus also about translating. What is more, *The Zodiac* is a self-translation by and of a poet who cannot escape his self and who delivers a pastiche of his own poetics.

How did Dickey appropriate Barnouw's *The Zodiac*? Not unlike any other creative poet-translator. Whereas Barnouw presents the reader with a finished product, a polished, translated poem, Dickey confronts us with what we could call a workshop poem, a poem in the making. In each section of *The Zodiac* Dickey seems to try out different drafts of his poem. He thereby demonstrates how much writing and re-writing (or translating, for that matter) is a live performance, and not a prescriptive exercise. Dickey is stage-managing the act of reading and rewriting Barnouw's translation using lyricism within the framework of his narrative epic poem. He has a sense of the spine of the story and of the imagery used in Barnouw's text. He simply retells the story in many ways and many times. Once he has learned, almost memorized, the development of the poem, he can go off in his own direction. All he needs then is the inner imagery, the imagination at work, the basic structures set in place, and a certain number of his own poetic formulae. Dickey uses *leitmotifs* (such as the struggle with Time and the creation of a new constellation, a Lobster) which create patterns and sinews which run throughout, intertwine and in the process tighten the whole work. These *leitmotifs*, which reinforce certain themes, are not unlike the song accompanying epic story telling.

As Ben Belitt sees it, translation is "a kind of jungle gym for the exercise of all the faculties and muscles required for the practice of poetry." Translation, according to Belitt "serves the calisthenic function of bringing to bear upon what is translated one's total resources and cunning as a poet."[4] In *The Zodiac* Dickey does indeed practice his own poetic "calisthenics." The poet-protagonist repeatedly demonstrates the physical aspects of writing poetry, how demanding and sweaty the act of poetry writing is, how much labor and energy are involved. Dickey's tone is up front aggressive compared to that of the more cerebral, ponderous and portentous Barnouw translation. His voice is more Dionysiac and less recherché. Barnouw's text becomes much more alive, its imagery less Biblical and more base and vital in Dickey's rewriting of *The Zodiac*. However, unlike most translators, Dickey's practice does not take him far beyond the genre of his own recognizable style and idiosyncracies as a poet. In this sense, Dickey's *The Zodiac* is basically a self-translation. Barnouw's translation of Marsman's "De Dierenriem" neither compelled nor seduced Dickey into writing poetry other than his own. Dickey "scored" Barnouw's text in a way that (cor)responds to his own manner of hearing. He put a pulse under Barnouw's rather neutral English and rewrote the translation in the sense that he tried to project qualities, identities, skills, predilections, textures—his own, such as they are, and perhaps Marsman's such as he imagines them to be. His version is more subjective than imitation and more visceral than paraphrase (Belitt, 58). In his transformation and transvaluation of Barnouw's translation Dickey shows how inadequate poetry in its literal state can be. He makes the point that poetry is not information and that the poet's task has only begun when all the facts of syntax and substance have been reliably extrapolated. His point is to isolate something else—something absent or missing—by maximizing the vacuum where all has been suspended in the search for meanings and is now in danger of disappearing entirely from the transaction: the power of imagination (Belitt, 59). By emphasizing the theme of imagination and creativity throughout *The Zodiac*, Dickey renders a critical reading of Barnouw's translation and complements or compensates for what is missing in the latter's text.

Belitt further remarks that as a translator "one must move with equal plausibility through hot and cold, through what is congenial and what's remote, roll with the punches on some least common denominator of continuing energy" (Belitt, 67). Obviously this strategy does not apply to Dickey's working method. Although his style in *The Zodiac* is characterized by the repetition of certain words and expressions, the sum of the number of words used in Barnouw's translation, compared to that in Dickey's work will nevertheless give us some idea of the extent to which Dickey elaborated on Barnouw's text: Barnouw only used 2,595 words, Dickey 6,880.[5] The first section, which makes up one third of Dickey's volume, contains many interpolations and is five times as long as Barnouw's. Here Dickey seems to demonstrate how all works of imagination are improvisation at some stage, certainly at the beginning, and how valuable this sheer invention is in the making of a poem. Long poems are, however, very difficult to sustain in translation—or in Dickey's case rewriting. Starting with the fourth section of Dickey's *The Zodiac*, far less new material is introduced and from the eighth section onwards the number of interpolations is reduced to a few lines. Either Dickey's energy flagged or he experienced the later sections as less congenial and more remote from his own interests. These later sections do indeed tie in more with Marsman's personal experiences and often, as in the very last section, become less mundane and more metaphysical.

Where provisionality abounds in Barnouw's translation, Dickey often lets the determinations remain suspended or vague. Dickey is merely faithfull: as faithful as he can be under the circumstances. His operative credo is faith, not as with Barnouw, fidelity. Barnouw may have sensed the desire of Marsman to express something that never got expressed, or possibly exceeded the poet. Dickey went ahead and rewrote the translation as a work-in-progress perhaps in order to find what Marsman and / or Barnouw left out. As Belitt would put it, Dickey wears his conscience where it belongs: at the tip of his pen (Belitt, 69). Whereas Barnouw adheres to the principle of responsibility, Dickey uses the strategy of volatility. With Barnouw we have the certainty that all the elements have been subjected to atomic scrutiny—all the words as they pass from the original into the ink of the translation, with no leaps of convenience or deletions such as we find in Dickey's *The Zodiac*. Here we can weigh the disadvantages of expressive rewriting as a personal mode against the translator as nobody in particular. As Belitt points out, both are "ploys, impersonations, heuristic deceptions" in reading and rewriting poetry (Belitt, 70). As opposed to the "midwifery" of Barnouw who is endlessly self-effacing and diligent as an intermediary between Marsman and the American reader, Dickey reveals a sensuous, histrionic projection of his visceral and intellectual fascinations and his own pleasure in appropriating Marsman's poem second hand. Throughout *The Zodiac* he has opted more flamboyantly for one continuous voice, indelibly and conspicuously his own, while he is rewriting as he pleases from Barnouw's translation of Marsman. In other words, Dickey uses Barnouw's text as a trampoline or a "jungle gym" to arrive at his self-translation. His motive is self-preservation, survival rather than charity. "Betrayal" of an original can, in Dickey's case, be understood as part of a creative undertaking—"creative" in the aberrant sense and as the transfiguring of invention. In Barnouw's text "the enlightened disclosure of admiration is primary—a kind of substantive embodiment of *praise*." Ultimately it is a question of bravura. Dickey interlopes on Marsman's poem and "his readers admire the performance because they have come to hear or read *his* performance and not because they are calculating fidelity" to Marsman or Barnouw at every stage of the poem (Belitt, 72).

Dickey is not an over-awed literalist at work on someone else's poetry. He follows a powerful lead of his own: to put his poem together from beginning to end, to find a gusto that guarantees a continuum *for him* as well as for Marsman (Barnouw). Dickey brought Marsman's persona back to life and his prosody forces the reader to pay attention and follow through. Imagination is not a phenomenon that can be limited to the poem "in its original state." Dickey understands this. Belitt pointedly argues that as a translator, "it is legitimate, it is imperative, to work imaginatively, joyfully, energetically, ingeniously, patiently, inventively, yourself." Dickey exploits these qualities, since imagination cannot be present in the original alone, and absent from a translation or version based on that translation. *The Zodiac*'s poet-protagonist knows, however, that imagination is "the most risky and most daring, the most desired and mistrusted faculty: the most dangerous" (Belitt, 74). In the first section Dickey's poet fulminates against Pythagoras who created a mechanical model of the Cosmos. He suspects that Pythagoras had the same intentions as he has: to take over God's task. God created the Zodiac. The poet considers himself God's equal, capable of creating a new constellation. To boost his courage and imagination he drinks whiskey. He works with constellations and bargains with God: What new creation does He want in His Heaven? He warns God that He is dealing with a poet who does not want to be taken lightly. Besides, his father was an amateur-astronomer who argued that the whole sky was *invented*. Now it is his turn to *invent*. Since the Zodiac already has a crab, he invents a Lobster. He wishes everyone to see his Lobster. It is no Cancer, no crab and no cancer, but an auspicious sign. People will worship his Lobster which will have a beneficial influence on Earth. The poet wants to bridge the distance between Earth and Heaven. But as soon as the Lobster starts moving (in section II), it starts waving its feelers:

> Imagination and dissipation both fire at me
> Point-blank O God, no NO I was playing I didn't mean it
> I'll never write it, I swear CLAWS claws CLAWS
> He's going to kill me (II, 36).[6]

Invention is a dangerous game. The poet is frightened, claims that he was only playing and promises not to write, not to create a new constellation. These passages, first occurring in section I and repeated in section II, remind us of the story of Babel.

The tribe of the Shems decided to raise a tower to reach all the way to the heavens and to make a name for themselves. Similarly, Dickey invents a Lobster not only to relate himself to the Universe but to make a name for himself as a poet. On the basis of their sublime edification the Shems wanted to impose their tongue on the entire Universe. Dickey creates a Lobster. Incidentally, the word "lob" suggests "lip" to Dutch speakers and "ster" means star in Dutch. With his imagination, Dickey thus imposes his "lip" / tongue on the entire universe for everybody to worship. Had the Shems' enterprise succeeded, the Universal tongue would have been a particular language imposed by force, by violent hegemony over the rest of the world. But God—i.e., that God who is capable of resentment, jealousy, and anger— became beside himself in the face of this incredible effrontery and proclaimed his name loudly: Babel.[7] This conflict between two proper names (Shem and God / Babel) is re-enacted in Dickey's poetry (Lobster and God) with the same consequences. Dickey's persona experiences the dangerous aspects of imagination and will have to learn to live with confusion, the confusion of tongues and, we could add, texts.

Although *The Zodiac* enacts the poet's confusion, it tries nevertheless to find a workable dissemination of the Universe's avowedly irrecoverable myster- ies as well as Marsman's original. Marsman's poem demands curiosity and survival. Dickey does not know for a fact what the poet knew, but he believes he can imagine how his text might sound in his own language. In so far as Marsman's text itself has been touched by the imagination, it can never be definitive. Dickey is all too aware of this. He enacts what he expressly claims for his own poetry: its experimental nature and, hence, its fallibility. He does not hope for terminal completions; readers and critics alike are already construing the experience differently. Dickey's persona construes poetry as a provisional art. He continually confronts his work in terms of what else it might be. Like a true gambler he conceives of his version as ludic, and not ethical—the most serious play imaginable: playing with language (itself provisional). As Belitt would put it, he plays the game "for risk and pleasure," for "the good of chastening misgiving" (Belitt, 78).

In Greek thought the term *hermeneia* signified not so much the return, by way of exegesis, to a kernel of hidden meaning within a shell, but more the act of extroversion by the voice, the natural instrument of the soul. It signifies an active and prophetic productivity. For the Greeks as well as for Dickey's persona, the poetic performance of rhapsodes is a "hermeneutic" performance (reading, interpreting and rewriting Barnouw's translation). Thanks to the *energeia* of speech (i.e., a word's capacity to make the image of a thing present to the mind), language can act on man's will and induce him to act. The wavering speech of Dickey's protagonist propels him to see various creatures in the Zodiac and to launch a creature of his own in the heavens: a Lobster (I, 23; II, 35–36). This blasphemous action fails and makes the poet feel even more angry and frustrated. But *energeia* can also incite man to translate anger (*ira*) into a libidinal form (*concupiscentia*). Indeed, Dickey's poet, in holding the stars in his "balls" (II, 34), perceives erotic features in the constellations (e.g., with Venus, IV, 43) and has a female apparition visit his room (X). This positive appetite transports man towards woman in *hymene*, allowing for a translation of semen, thanks to which the forms of life succeed each other. Thanatos becomes Eros. The creative thought process of the poet-protagonist in *The Zodiac* is—with the exception of a few lapses— predominantly physical, sexual, or erotic. Through his libidinal translation, Nature—the Universe or Cosmos—manifests itself, over time, in its totality. To refuse this translation is to refuse life. Dickey's persona reflects the very principle of mutability and transformation, two powers that also embody the glory of humankind. Through translation one actual experience is translated into another. Yet this translation is not redundant, nor is it simple repetition. It is a gateway to the future; it is the principle of abundance and not of redundancy. Dickey's discourse reveals that figural capacity which allows humankind to express the diversity of its nature, as well as that of surrounding Nature, and even to inaugurate mutations in its being.[8] Like the Renaissance poets, Dickey is not only a translator of a poetic legacy from the past (Marsman and other poet-predecessors), but also a translator whose poetic performance is prophetic in the sense that it inaugurates a future—in this case, a future for a generation born in "a space-faring, postliterate age"[9]:

> So long as the hand can hold its island
> Of blazing paper, and bleed for its images:

Make what it can of what is:
So long as the spirit hurls on space
The star-beasts of intellect and madness (XII, 62).

If we focus on Dickey's protagonist we can read his poem on two levels. There is *The Zodiac* as a workshop-poem in which a wordsmith is hammering away at and sweating over a poem-in-the-*making*. This manual laborer even *made* his own universe, a mobile whose axis is spinning through the Zodiac and which he considers godlike (I, 16). Moreover, in his audacious hallucinations he wants to take over God's task and *make* his own zodiacal sign. In this reading *The Zodiac* is a physical, *self-made artifact*, where inspiration is linked with hard, sweaty, physical work. Dickey's protagonist, however, also tends to become symbolic and mystical in his reflections. Thus, there is also *The Zodiac* of a medieval monk trying to decipher "the book of creatures" in his cell. The idea that the universe is a broken text is a variation of the idea of nature as a book. This time-honored metaphor identifies "the material product of cosmic creativity as a decipherable text—the so-called book of nature" (Hernadi, 754). It was a popular image in the Middle Ages and through the Renaissance and was taken up by the Romantics and the Symbolists.[10] Baudelaire ("Le Voyage"), and after him Rimbaud ("Le Bateau ivre" ["The drunken Boat"]), stated that poetry is essentially analogy. The idea of universal correspondence comes from the idea that language is a microcosm, a double of the Universe. Between the language of the Universe and the Universe of language, there is a bridge, a link: poetry. The poet, says Baudelaire, is the translator, the universal translator and the translator of the universe. According to Rimbaud, who considered Baudelaire too classical, too poetic and artistic, no poet ever got to the bottom of things and explored the depths of the human soul where the essence of our intelligence lies. Dickey's persona is partly a follower of Rimbaud. Rimbaud insists on the method by which one can exploit one's gifts and become clairvoyant ("voyant"). He espouses the will to know oneself by a systematic process of reasoning; paradoxically he follows the rules to create systematic disorder. To that purpose he takes in experiences with alcohol, drugs and sex: the will to change himself in order to know himself. This knowledge of self would destroy all the old ways of thinking and would free his self so its creative faculties can express themselves. It liberates the subconscious in terms of automatic writing without control, form, or rules, under the influence of alcohol and dictated by inspiration. Dickey's poet likewise idolizes "la Dive Bouteille" (the divine bottle) and finds truth in drink (*in vino veritas*) at the end of a long journey. In a drunken state the poet tries to relate himself to the larger cosmos whose coded message he tries to interpret. He has become the interpreter of divine truth, using alcohol as an aid to transport himself to a dream-like state of communion between "the other" and reality. His trance-like state reveals Dionysiac tongues (fury) and truth on the prompting of a spirit. Here, poetry is *inspiration* and form is adapted to whatever inspiration dictates. The poet sees himself as the Creator of a new order, a Prometheus who stole God's fire (Dickey's aquavit) to animate his own creation. He wants to recreate humanity and to bring back joy, to point people to a new light so they can spiritually advance and develop. The poet who creates a healing Lobster is a driving force behind humanity's progress. With his Lobster he invents his own, new language which becomes a universal language. This language comes from the soul, for the soul, and communication becomes a sort of communion—a communion with God to create truth for humankind. In *Le Bateau ivre* Rimbaud becomes the Boat, in *The Zodiac* (in which Rimbaud's poem reverberates) Dickey becomes the Zodiac:

> Oh my own soul, put me in a solar boat.
>
> . . . .
> And give this home-come man . . . .
>
> . . . .
> The instrument the tuning-fork -
>
> . . . .
> Which at a touch reveals the form
> Of the time-loaded European music
> That poetry has never really found.
> Undecipherable as God's bad, Heavenly sketches
> Involving fortress and flower, vine and wine and bone,
> And shall vibrate through the western world.
>
> . . . .
> So long as the spirit hurls on space
> The star-beasts of intellect and madness (XII, 61–62).

Throughout *The Zodiac* Dickey's poet reanimates an "absent text," the one he is helped to conceive of by the existence of the text before him: Barnouw's translation of Marsman's poem "De Dierenriem." Not only is he interpreting and rewriting Barnouw's text but he is also decoding and relating himself to the Zodiac or the universe as a text. Dickey's poet very slowly begins to understand Barnouw's (Marsman's) and the Universe's text, the sacred relationships between the letters or signs and the plotting in them of mystic truths. The voice in this poem is that of a mystic seer and a drunk poet helped by the intermediaries of a translation (Barnouw's) and drink (aquavit, whiskey, gin). Both media transport him to *inspiration, faith* and *prophesy*.

One of the simplest and most creative ways of considering the act of interpretation (translation) is to regard it as a minimal, perhaps vestigial, but still exemplary encounter with the "other." Barnouw, the translator who tries to imitate, is getting to know "the other." But Dickey, who rewrites Barnouw's translation, is largely ignoring "the other" because he is reducing that text to his own interests and pre-established terms. In this sense, Dickey's poem could be called a "self-translation."

Dickey's own poetic voice and alter ego resonate throughout *The Zodiac*. The reader comparing Barnouw's and Dickey's texts is immediately struck by the interpretation or re-creation of the protagonist in Dickey's poem. In Barnouw's text, the protagonist is an intellectual poet, the prototype of a highbrow, Apollonian personality. Dickey's character could qualify as an intellectual too, but one addicted to drinking and suffering from delirium tremens. His surroundings, a cell, clash with his personality, except that he appeals to another current idea of the poet, namely the poet as a marginal figure, a Dionysian personality. He has hallucinations, speaks drunkenly, rages and swears (like a Dutch sailor?). As he is dying, his physical decay is emphasized time and again. Moreover, he has a morbid interest in diseases like cancer, tetanus and jaundice, is obsessed with the idea of reincarnation, and hopes to immortalize himself by creating a new sign in the zodiac. In other words, whereas Barnouw's poem is stilted and poised, Dickey's voice is impatient, irritable and aggressive. Dickey's poem incorporates yet another notion of the poet-translator, namely that of the translator as actor. He took something of somebody else's and put it over as if it were his own. In addition to this technical feat, there is the psychological and physical workout which re-writing involves: something like being on stage. Dickey not only took on a persona, as an actor does, but in the process changed it dramatically.

In the original and in Barnouw's text a certain distance prevails between narrator and protagonist; in Dickey's text this distance disappears, most markedly so in the first three sections: narrator and protagonist quite simply merge. Here the protagonist can be considered a persona of the narrator. Moreover, reality and experience blur in the presentation of the protagonist's hallucinations, which extend and reorient the empirical world of sensory impressions toward an expressionist frame of inner associations. Dickey's sailor-poet is a quiet "monster" of inwardness, and his creator understands him all too well. His poetry has a quality of demented lyricism, a tendency to lose itself in mystery, hidden meanings, intimations that someone is encoding our experience in ways we are not meant to decipher. His home turf is a realm of indeterminacy, quasi-apprehension, a nightmarish sense of being connected to the cosmos which is either showing us the way things really are or is simply a shimmering mirage, just another deceptively suggestive metaphor. Moreover, Dickey's writing in *The Zodiac* is strangely eroticized as prisoner's poetry. The protagonist weaving through these pages seems the product of a consciousness drifting toward the ecstatic, inducing visions as a form of self-stimulation: the solitary play of the confined, of sailors and Dionysiac poets. Dickey's poet experiences this kind of consciousness: he is aroused by playing with constellations and flirts with the one he creates himself, the Lobster which claws back at him. The hero of *The Zodiac* is totally self-absorbed, a man much like Dickey himself, a man sitting in a room, thinking and waiting, dreaming of the convergence of his vivid private world and the hazy, unfathomable cosmos outside. The other characters (his father, his mother, a female and a male friend) are not developed, nor are they unpredictable enough to rescue his work from becoming self-absorption or self-translation. The protagonist is constantly and restlessly searching for a cosmic system with which to explain and enlarge himself.

Dickey's *The Zodiac* is perhaps not unlike Herbert Mason's *Gilgamesh*, which became "an inner tale that made sense of the confusion caused by loss, the metaphysical worry, the pain, in the face of these experiences."[11] Section VIII of *The Zodiac*, for instance, contains an additional line with a specific number: "Death is twenty-eight years old / Today" (VIII, 49), which one is tempted to explain in biographical terms.[12] If we subtract the date of the publication of Barnouw's anthology (1948) from that of the publication of Dickey's *The Zodiac* (1976) we obtain the result 28. Dickey married Maxine Syerson in 1948; she died in 1976 and he married Deborah Dodson. Apart from the traumatic event of his wife's death is the possibility that Dickey conceived *The Zodiac* in 1968, 28 years after Marsman's death, an explanation which appears more plausible for this specific number of years. In his Foreword, Dickey does, indeed, mention the year of Marsman's death (1940) and he pays homage to his brother-poet within his own poem as well. Moreover, from a *New York Quarterly* interview we can gather that Dickey works many years on a single poem and that he writes several versions of it: "If I have one principle, rule of thumb, I guess you could say, as a writer, it's to work on something a long, long time. And try it all different ways."[13]

As Mason points out, translators need to live with a work for a long time before actually beginning to do something about it. They get different ideas as to what is most effective in the rewriting.[14] In Dickey's case he created a completely different protagonist, another tone and voice which serve to expand and to reevaluate the imagery and Barnouw's poetics of translation. Barnouw's *The Zodiac* became more of a personal story, combined with an increasing desire to understand and to transform the text. Dickey had to come to terms with Barnouw's text through repeatedly reading and re-writing it, a process reflected throughout *The Zodiac*. Over the years he concentrated his own thought on the themes of loss, the confrontation with one's own mortality, and the quest for immortality. Dickey feels that he has a sense of the "original" text, but this comes about by way of identifying his own intuition and his own self with the translation of that text.

Dickey's persona, that of the brooding writer who is trying to make all the right connections, to find the pattern in the chaos of crude facts and the divine order, is in a constant struggle against the seduction of solitude: the temptation to wipe out the mess of traumatic experience (e.g., "his bandless wedding-finger" [62]) by pure exercise of the intellect and of imagination, to abstract everything in a grand and perfect metaphor (e.g., the Lobster), something that can be held in the mind, isolated and complete. His investigation—itself a metaphor for the translator's project—takes him through despair, solipsism, poetic reverie, sorrowful anger at his own limitations, euphoria: his method is a kind of creative drift, an unfocused receptivity.

Dickey must have appreciated the timeless and original quality of Marsman's epic poem. Moreover, his own writing is stimulated by narrative and dramatic situation and character. Some things must have converged that made him surrender to the text of the story or plot and its uncovered form dictated a language, Dickey's language. The substance of Barnouw's text began to overtake Dickey; then he made another evocation of the subject of this text. Dickey tried to find out exactly what his own voice was in this material; he wanted to write *his Zodiac* because he identified personally with its protagonist. So he wrote another dramatic narrative. He wanted most of all to dramatize the poet-protagonist's inner life and bring him out as a real person to himself and to others—using some of Barnouw's translated lines in his language, and his sense of structure of a narrative poem.

The translating or rewriting of a poem is very much based on the literary style of the poet-translator. In *The Zodiac* the poet-protagonist examines his own writing. Not only does he comment upon his own style (and imagination) but also that of the text which he is re-writing. In the fifth section, for instance, the poet communicates in his nightmares with the man and the cosmos. He thinks that the faster he sleeps, the faster the Universe sleeps; the deeper he breathes, the higher the night can climb and the higher the singing will be: "Bird, maybe? *Nightingale?* Ridiculous" (V, 43). The romantic, Keatsian image which he finds in Barnouw's text is ridiculed. Furthermore, in opposition to Barnouw's translation, the narrator often takes an ironic view of his hero and his wavering thoughts: "—'*listen*' to me—how can he '*rise*' / When he's '*digging*'? Digging through the smoke / Of distance, throwing columns around to find" (III, 40). Dickey wanted, however, to make his readers believe in the authenticity of a voice, even if it is somewhat strange. And in order to make Marsman's / Barnouw's often strange and clashing metaphors more plausible he invented a drunken, half-crazed sailor-poet who can elaborate even further on those images. He thus embeds some of the words and lines of Barnouw's text—those which he finds agreeable. Most often, however, he expands and changes Barnouw's lines and metaphors to make them conform to his own poetic style and imagination. He transfers some of Barnouw's words; then he writes a few lines, completely his own but generated by the translation, and continues by closing off and again picking up again Barnouw's translation.

Marsman has a keen historical sense; his persona is overwhelmed by a sense of history, a quality which makes him a "European" poet, a literary spokesman for his hemisphere. He is suffering from the burden of tradition, its authority is hanging over him, like a heavy threat. Sometimes its presence becomes too insistent, the motifs it inspires too predictable. Marsman, however, also presents an ironic view of tradition, which he establishes by a "deflation," by an abrupt contrast between expected formality and down-to-earth colloquialism or a "prosaic" tone. Dickey's poem completely erases the concern for the decay of civilization and the appeal for the redemption of a culture. Although he transposes some of the images and metaphors which in Marsman's poem (and Barnouw's translation) function within the frame of a reflection on culture, this reflection is missing in Dickey's poem.[15] The problems with which Marsman's persona is concerned are partly personal: his feelings of loneliness, his questioning of the meaning of existence, and his cosmic searching; however it is especially culture—and more specifically European culture—which preoccupies him. Dickey's persona cares little or not at all about Marsman's issues, but is looking for his place in the cosmos whose meaning he tries to discover and recover. To that purpose he uses cultural elements in a pragmatic, selfish way.

Why did Dickey feel the need to write original work based on another poem? According to Harold Bloom the origin of Dickey's quest as a poet can be located in guilt. This guilt has been the feeling of "being a substitute or replacement for a brother dead before one was born"[16]: "I am alone: / I am my brother:" (I, 15–16). Other critics have pointed out the guilt of being a war-survivor (Marsman did not survive World War II), and we can now perhaps add the guilt of having survived his wife: "The instrument the tuning-fork— / He'll flick it with his bandless wedding-finger—" (XII, 62). Furthermore, Bloom indicates Dickey's literary heroes as being "the unlikely combination of Keats, Malcolm Lowry, and James Agee, presumably associated because of their early or relatively early deaths, and because of their shared intensity of belief in what could be called the salvation history of literary art" (Bloom, 2). Hendrik Marsman (1899-1940) fits the description of this triad: not only did he die young but he also believed in the redemption of culture through the writing of poetry.[17] Affinities between Marsman and Dickey can be found both in their poetic career and in their personalities. Such a comparison, however, would lead us toward a traditional influence study.

The elements Dickey borrowed from Barnouw's translation did not really affect his own poetics. On the one hand he took the narrative of Marsman's poem as a structure onto which he could graft his own problems and interests; on the other hand the images of Barnouw's translation are modelled in a way that is essentially different. Hence, the migration of items is mainly restricted to the modulated plot and to the imagery. One of the artistic conditions we can postulate for Dickey wanting to write his own version is his fascination with Marsman's biography, that of a poet who died young and wrote an epic poem which contains stimulating metaphors. Secondly, there is Dickey's own interest in poems with a narrative basis and a protagonist. And, thirdly, we may perhaps venture the supposition of a crisis in Dickey's personal life as well as in his poetic imagination. Dickey's "creative treason" vis-à-vis Barnouw, and indirectly vis-à-vis Marsman, has, however, generated a completely different verse form. In rewriting Barnouw's text, Dickey was forced to lay bare his own poetic techniques and strategies and thus to render a pastiche of his own poetics. Whereas both Barnouw's and Marsman's texts could be labelled "reflection poetry," primarily concerned with the expression of ideas, Dickey's text is a participation poem or performance poem that quite simply must be experienced. For this experience to take place, Dickey's writing is guided by such elements as the narrative thread, the character's stream of consciousness, the split line, *melopoeia*, "presentational immediacy" and subjective imagery. However, without Barnouw's intermediate text Dickey's *The Zodiac* would probably not have been written. Barnouw's translation made available and explained Marsman's poem to Dickey, who in his turn modelled his own poetics on Barnouw's translation. Most of all, though, in rewriting Barnouw's translation, Dickey has been translating himself.

Notes

1. In a letter which dates from May 15, 1979 and which is addressed to Joris Duytschaever, director of my licentiate thesis, Dickey writes that he read Adriaan J. Barnouw's translation of Marsman's poem "De Dierenriem;" "The Zodiac" in *Coming After: An Anthology of Poetry from the Low Countries* (New Brunswick: Rutgers University Press, 1948). What little information he obtained about Marsman he found in the *Columbia Dictionary of Modern European Literature* (1971) in which the lexicon entry for Marsman is again written by Barnouw.

2. An in-depth study comparing Marsman's poem, Barnouw's translation and Dickey's poem appeared in *Dierenriem Triptiek: Vergelijkende Studie van Hendrik Marsman: "De Dierenriem," vertaald door Adriaan J. Barnouw en James Dickey: "The Zodiac."* (Universitaire Instelling Antwerpen, 1981). An English article based on my licentiate thesis was published in *Dispositio*, Vol. VII, No. 19–20 (1982), 85–93.

3. Although translators rarely comment on their art, Edwin Honig managed to engage some leading translators in thought-provoking conversations. Many reflections in this paper are based on Honig's spontaneous interviews. See Edwin Honig, ed. *The Poet's Other Voice: Conversations on Literary Translation* (Amherst: University of Massachusetts Press, 1985).

4. Ben Belitt, in *The Poet's Other Voice: Conversations on Literary Translation*, ed. Edwin Honig (Amherst: University of Massachusetts Press, 1985) 55–78; 57; hereafter cited in text.

5. Chart comparing the number of words used in Barnouw's and in Dickey's *The Zodiac* according to the sections distinguished in their texts:

	Barnouw	Dickey	X times longer
I.	551	2,767	more than 5 times longer
II.	199	816	more than 4 times longer
III.	137	607	more than 4 times longer
IV.	112	279	more than twice as long
V.	110	262	more than twice as long
VI.	98	152	
VII.	140	320	more than twice as long
VIII.	108	194	
IX.	503	680	
X.	171	189	
XI.	225	247	
XII.	241	367	
	2,595	6,880	more than twice as long

6. James Dickey, *The Zodiac* (New York: Doubleday, 1976). All further citations are from this edition; both section and page numbers are noted parenthetically in the text.

7. I owe this interpretation of the Babel story to Jacques Derrida's close reading in his

essay "Des Tours de Babel", in *Difference in Translation*, ed. and trans. Joseph Graham (Ithaca, New York: Cornell University Press, 1985), 165–207, and his discussion on translation in *The Ear of the Other: Otobiography, Transference, Translation*, ed. Christie V. McDonald, trans. Peggy Kamuf (New York: Schocken Books, 1985), 100–102.

8.   These reflections are based on Eugene Vance's discussion of hermeneutics in the "classical" or "traditional" sense of the term in a "Roundtable on Translation" with Derrida, in *The Ear of the Other*, 135–138.

9.   Paul Hernadi, "Doing, Making, Meaning: Toward a Theory of Verbal Practice," *PMLA*, 103.5 (1988): 749–758; 756; hereafter cited in text.

10.   Several writers and critics such as Octavio Paz (Honig, 157), Paul Hernadi (754) and Ernst Robert Curtius in his book *European Literature and the Latin Middle Ages* (Princeton: Bollinger-Princeton University Press, 1973), 302–47, refer to the topos of "the Book of Nature" in their discussions.

11.   Herbert Mason, in *The Poet's Other Voice: Conversations on Literary Translation*, ed. Edwin Honig (Amherst: University of Massachusetts Press, 1985) 43–53; 45.

12.   Another line which we can interpret biographically occurs in the eleventh section where the poet-protagonist visits a friend. In his friend's room where the heater is on, "he shakes free of *two* years of wandering / Like melting-off European snows" (58). (Barnouw's text faithfully renders Marsman's lines as: "He shakes off *three* years of travel / Like a layer of Europe's snow (286)") (emphasis mine in both instances). We know that Dickey did, indeed, visit Europe twice, the first time around 1954 and the second time in 1962. In an interview with Franklin Ashley we find a reference to Dickey's second trip to Europe: "The Guggenheim people wrote to me and asked me if I would like to stand for a fellowship and to send in whatever I had to offer . . . , they gave me some money—several thousand dollars . . . I swore I was going to go back to Europe before I was forty. I made it at the age of thirty-nine [i.e., in 1962]." See Franklin Ashley, "James Dickey. The Art of Poetry XX," *The Paris Review*, XVII (Spring 1976): 53–88; 59.

13.   See William Packard, ed., "Craft Interview with James Dickey," in *The Craft of Poetry: Interviews from "The New York Quarterly"* (New York: Doubleday, 1974), 133–151; 149.

14.   Herbert Mason, in *The Poet's Other Voice: Conversations on Literary Translation*, 45–46.

15.   Dickey does not miss the chance, however, to make a stereotypical reference to Dutch tulips, which appears neither in the original nor in the translation. In an interview with Franklin Ashley, Dickey talks enthusiastically about the sights in Europe. The tulip fields in Holland must have made quite an impression: "When an American goes to Europe, he doesn't go there to get just another version of America. He wants *difference*. You see fields of tulips in Holland. You never saw anything like that in your life" (Ashley, 59). Hence, the image: "he'd ambled grumbling like a ghost / In tulip shadow," (IX, 52).

16.   Harold Bloom, ed. and introd., *James Dickey* (New York: Chelsea, 1987), 1; hereafter cited in text.

17.   Arthur Rimbaud (1854–1891) whose "Le Bateau ivre" resonates in the last section of *The Zodiac*, fits Bloom's description as well.

James Dickey and the Macho Persona

DOUGLAS KEESEY

On the back cover of his most famous book of poetry, *Poems 1957–1967*, James Dickey is described as "a former star college athlete, night fighter pilot with more than 100 missions in World War II and the Korean conflict, hunter and woodsman, and an advertising executive in New York City and Atlanta."[1] As critics like Neal Bowers have suggested, Dickey's "macho" male persona has helped him sell poetry to the average Joe who might otherwise associate it with elitism, bookishness, or effeminacy.[2] But what may have worked with the common man has alienated him from academia. Though few academics have actually gone on record to protest Dickey's macho stance, anecdotal evidence abounds to show that many university faculty deplore him.[3] Dropped from reading lists, unavailable in college bookstores, and unmentioned in oral histories of American poetry, Dickey's work seems increasingly unwelcome and, to many students, unknown. One has only to carry the latest volume of Dickey's poetry, *The Eagle's Mile*, to an academic conference and note the number of puzzled and disapproving looks to realize how unpopular Dickey is these days among the university crowd.

Many of Dickey's detractors seem to have carried on in the tradition of Robert Bly's famous 1967 attack on "The Firebombing," a poem which Bly regards as "teaching us that our way of dealing with death is right: do it, later talk about it, and take two teaspoonsful of remorse every seventh year. . . . If we read this poem right, we can go on living with napalm."[4] Even more than "The Firebombing," *Deliverance* has served as a lightning rod for academic critics, particularly feminists and Marxists, who blast Dickey for the belligerence, authoritarianism, and homophobia they associate with Dickey's macho stance. Thus Fredric Jameson argues that the "advantage of an adventure story like Dickey's [*Deliverance*] lies in the way it permits the exercise of a kind of ideological double standard: on the individual level it allows you vicariously to experience and to satisfy this 'ineradicable' instinct for violence, which is then the object of your critique on a social and political level, where it causes you to posit the need for Leviathan, or the authoritarian state, to hold the disorder and anarchy of individual violence and of human nature in general in check."[5] Carolyn Heilbrun describes the novel's protagonist, Ed Gentry, as

This essay was written specifically for this volume and is published here for the first time.

201

having "fled with his buddies into the world of the American movie fantasy where it's 'either him or us,' where the need to kill is conveniently unavoidable, where murder and violence and the homosexual rape he calls 'a kind of love' are all that can be mustered up in opposition to the 'long declining routine of our lives.' " Heilbrun ends with a statement that perfectly summarizes the position of the anti-Dickey camp: "How long must we wait before American novelists and critics, with their true gift of vision, will look clearly at this terrible masculine ideal from which our lives so surely need deliverance?"[6]

I have no quarrel with these critics' attacks on machismo and its unfortunate political and sexual ramifications. What I take issue with is their easy equation of Dickey with machismo. To make such a simplistic identification is to ignore the extent to which Dickey's work already constitutes a powerful critique from within of machismo. To read Dickey as Bly, Jameson, and Heilbrun do is to misrecognize the complex attitude displayed by Dickey's work toward machismo. An appreciation of this complexity is certainly a prerequisite to any real understanding of what machismo is and of how to deal with it. Critics have long been aware that machismo is a central theme in Dickey's work, but they have been strangely resistant to seeing the complexities of this theme, as if fuller comprehension necessarily brings with it complicity. It would seem to me that the opposite is true: Dickey's critics are never more belligerently macho than in their uncomprehending attacks on his work. If it would be absurd to claim that Dickey is not, in many ways, a macho writer, it should be equally ridiculous to claim that that is all he is.

In response to critics who have misunderstood his work, Dickey has given frequent interviews and written numerous essays explaining his intent. Indeed, there are now so many of these nonfiction pieces running parallel to Dickey's poetry and fiction as to make up an entire oeuvre of self-interpretation, vital to an understanding of Dickey's meaning, but seldom read or discussed. If my essay draws most of its examples from Dickey's nonfiction, it is because I am trying to listen to what Dickey himself has been trying to tell us about what he means.

In a 1990 interview, Dickey calls his macho stance an "assumed personality: big, strong, hard drinking, hard fighting," and he makes it clear that "[n]othing could be less characteristic of the true James Dickey, who is a timid, cowardly person." When the interviewer expresses some skepticism ("I don't think that many people would agree with you there"), Dickey says, "Well, maybe not, but you can't fool yourself, so you spend your life fooling yourself. The self that you fool yourself into is the one that functions. Isn't that so?"[7] Earlier in the interview Dickey discusses T. E. Lawrence and Ernest Hemingway as men who had "great invented selves, people who wished to become other than they really were and who wrote and acted out of the assumed personality." Dickey's description of Lawrence is especially detailed and relevant to Dickey's own macho persona: "Lawrence . . . was a timid fellow who became a superman in warfare because he willed the personality that he wished to be. Instead of being a little, weak guy he became a military genius and a wonderful writer. But the self he was writing out of was not his real personality. . . . I'm essentially a coward, so therefore I flew with the night fighters in the Pacific, or in football I hit the guy especially hard because essentially I was afraid of him. I think you must turn these things to your favor" (Suarez, 131).

Dickey's admiration for Lawrence has numerous fictional and poetic analogues in the Dickey oeuvre: Ed's emulation of Lewis Medlock in *Deliverance*, Frank Cahill's fascination with Joel in *Alnilam*, and the thrilling identification of human speaker with animals in many of the poems. The dysfunctional male who assumes a macho persona in order to perform successfully and to survive in a harsh world is the Dickey character par excellence, the perennial focus of his life's work. Precisely because he has attended so long and so closely to this kind of character, Dickey's exploration of machismo is complex and finely nuanced—not the blunt stereotype that critics have accused him of presenting.

We can begin to get a sense of this complexity from Dickey's comments in the interview above. Not only is the macho persona an "assumed personality," but the split between true character and invented self is always there, even when the self has donned its macho cover: "you can't fool yourself, so you spend your life fooling yourself." The macho persona is thus a mask that has to be put on again and again because the true self always sees through its own self-deception. We may hear a certain desperation in Dickey's admission that every attempt at a functioning macho persona is ultimately doomed to fail, creating the need for repeated attempts for the rest of his life. On the other hand, we may also detect a note of self-congratulation over the self's continued striving to reach a worthy goal (a fully assumed and effective macho personality). Most interesting of all, though, is the hint that there may well be a certain value in facing the truth, in the self's continual confession of a gap between true character and macho persona. Why is Dickey so insistent on identifying his "true" self as a "timid, cowardly person"? Granted, such an identification might be seen as a sign of modesty or as lending a sense of grandeur to his struggle to achieve a macho persona (how much harder it is for a timid man to be macho). But the statement should also make us wonder whether admission and acceptance of one's true self does not have its own kind of value for Dickey, and whether maintaining some distance from macho self-deception might not have a corollary interest for him.

In *Sorties*, Dickey writes that "The body is the one thing you cannot fake. It is what it is, and it does what it does. It also fails to do what it cannot do. It would seem to me that people would realize this, especially men."[8] Dickey has Lewis speak this same line in *Deliverance* ("The body is the one thing you can't fake")[9]; Lewis is the character who embodies Dickey's macho persona: "I am Lewis; every word is true" (*Sorties*, 75). Both Dickey and Lewis are dysfunctional males who attempt to transform a hatred of internal weakness into an identification with invincible strength: "I think that we all yearn to be something other than what we are. I'm really very dissatisfied with what I am. This is the whole secret of Lewis, because he despises himself. Lewis is no more or less than an intellectual and physical counterpart of Charles Atlas, who was once a skinny, ninety-seven-pound weakling, but now can be proud of himself, because he's put all this time in on his body."[10]

It might seem that Dickey has made a fully admiring identification with his macho persona, but as Dickey's description of Lewis continues we can see him beginning to critique this hypermasculine personality from within. Lewis, Dickey says, is "a victim of a crushing inferiority complex, so that he spends enormous amounts of time on himself, making himself impressive intellectually—physically first, and then hopefully intellectually—with all his theories and mystiques, so that he can make other people feel inferior. And Ed is sort of taken in" (Baughman, 74–75). The man who tries to live the macho ideal remains driven and troubled by the disparity between his true weakness and the superman persona he aspires to but can never quite achieve. Thus the constant need to prove other men inferior, the paranoid violence which is really directed at his own inalienable insecurity. The strong man's body is supposed to serve as incontrovertible proof of all kinds of invincibility, but not only is man more than a body and therefore intellectually and spiritually vulnerable, the body itself is also vulnerable. As Dickey explains, the "trouble with Lewis, which I did mean to show, is that he is almost totally without humor. He's so serious about these things and about this self-image of his. But at the end that breaks down some, and he becomes more fully human, as when he's lying on the bottom of the canoe with his leg broken" and must depend on Ed for help (Baughman, 75).

No body is invincible. The rugged male individualist must depend on the bodies, minds, and spirit of others and on his own heart and soul to survive when his body fails—as all bodies do. Humor, defined as the ability to recognize the difference between true self and self-image, between male weakness and macho persona, is crucial to man's survival. The macho male, with delusions of grandeur born of an inferiority complex—paranoid, belligerent, refusing to admit his vulnerability or to accept help—is doomed to an early death.

Ultimately closer in spirit to Ed than to Lewis, Dickey "likes [Lewis], he's fascinated by him, but he's not taken in more than, say, about halfway by Lewis" (Baughman, 75). To be taken in by Lewis (Lewis before he becomes humanized) would be to believe in the body's strength as evidence of invulnerability and in the philosophy of "might makes right." Dickey has always insisted on the dangerous connection between the macho mystique of the body and fascism. As one interviewer put it, "With his intrepid war service [Dickey] nevertheless speaks of a persistent admiration for Quakerism and the pacifist ideal. He admits to being able to understand the Fascist reverence for force and the superman, yet he has liberal convictions, a tenderness for all living things, and a love for the expression of this tenderness in art."[11] The male characters in *Deliverance* are attracted to Lewis's powerful physique as if it itself constituted a form of—or substitute for—morality. As Dickey explains, "Lewis doesn't claim to be able to do anything that he can't do. And this, coupled with the fact that I gave him a tremendously impressive middle-aged body, would—I thought then, and I still do—would be so impressive to these guys that they would take his advice on anything, including questions of morality. Whether or not to bury the guy that Lewis has shot, for example, or to make a clean breast of it and stay within the law" (Baughman, 73).

The implication is that the men should not have taken Lewis's advice. But elsewhere we read that Dickey approves of their following Lewis: "Lewis is right, you know. I would have felt exactly as Ed does."[12] It's clear that Dickey does indeed "understand the Fascist reverence for force and the superman," but we should not be too ready to conclude that he is comfortable with the collapse of moral questions into matters of physical force. True, Dickey does often seem to long for a world without the complexities of the one in which we actually live, a simpler world where macho men can prove their great strength through violent physical acts. In one breath Dickey will deny that *Deliverance* "tries to show how man's essential malehood depends on his going out and killing somebody," while in the next breath he adds a large qualifier:

Nevertheless, American life is so structured that a lot of areas of one's existence—or one's potentiality, maybe, for either good or evil never get a chance to surface. And sometimes these *are* repressed feelings of violence. That doesn't mean one must go out perpetrating violent acts. This wasn't the case in *Deliverance*, where the violent acts by Ed Gentry were forced upon him. It was self-defense. Knowing this, he can take even more of a kind of secret pride in what he's done because he's a peace-loving person. He's never had any record of any criminal activity, much less murder. It was forced upon him and he brought it off. He got away with it, and this is a kind of index of secret powers he never suspected he had. Now he knows what he's capable of doing.
(Baughman, 127)

This is the kind of passage that sickens certain Dickey critics. They find in it no remorse over the murder Ed has committed, but only a triumphant exultation at the macho man's violent proof of his ability to survive. Dickey has often said that he "write[s] mainly from the standpoint of a survivor" of the war (Baughman, 12), and being a survivor is a complicated matter. Throughout his life Dickey has been torn between a revulsion at the horrors of war in which he participated and a nostalgia for the feeling of power and importance that being on the "winning" side gave him. Thus, in his war letters, Dickey can say "If I ever get through this I'll never take another chance as long as I live," but then add that war "has a horrible fascination. It makes everything else seem trivial."[13] Here a heightened sense of personal vulnerability alternates with an opposite and equally potent assumption of power, of being taken out of individual weakness and into something invincibly larger than oneself. As Dickey puts it, "You can never do anything in your life that will give you such a feeling of consequence and of performing a dangerous and essential part in a great cause as fighting in a world war. . . . You feel a nostalgia for war because all the intensities of life, youth, danger and the heroic dimension, as nearly as you will ever know them in your own personal existence, were in those days."[14]

I would argue that, in *Deliverance* and other works, Dickey has attempted to re-create the life-and-death situation that was the war, to find in a trivial, postwar society, arenas for warlike combat in which a man can assume his macho persona and prove he has the power to survive. But Dickey is at least as interested in the physical danger to others and the peril to one's own soul created by such macho combativeness as he is in celebrating any superman's victory. Ed Gentry may discover he has secret powers when he kills a hillbilly in self-defense, but Ed's assumption of the macho persona is itself a danger, the very ability that enabled him to survive becoming something against which he must defend himself. By taking on the ferociousness of his opponent in order to defeat him, Ed risks becoming the very thing he hates. As Dickey explains, "There are men in those remote parts that'd just as soon kill you as look at you. And you could turn into a counter-monster yourself, doing whatever you felt compelled to do to survive."[15] After Ed has killed the hillbilly, he picks up the dead man's rifle and points it at Bobby, one of Ed's friends. Possessed by a spirit of paranoid aggression, Ed comes close to shooting his friend, as if he must prove through killing again and again that he is superior to other men, that he does not share their weakness: "I ought to take this rifle and shoot the hell out of you, Bobby, you incompetent asshole, you soft city country-club man. . . . I walked back and picked up the gun, and my craziness increased when I touched it. I sighted down the barrel and put the bead right in the middle of Bobby's chest. Do it, the dead man said" (*Deliverance*, 201–2).

As much a cause of as an antidote to violence, the macho persona may be necessary to counter monsters, but it also creates crazy counter-monsters made in the macho image of the evil they fought to destroy. This is the paradox of machismo to which Dickey calls attention in work after work. If a man is most a man when aggressively defending himself and his friends against outside attack, how ironic that this should be the very moment when he comes closest to losing himself and turning on his friends in a homicidal-suicidal rage. In taking on the macho persona, a man risks being taken over by it.

A similar, even exacerbated ambivalence toward the macho persona can be found in *Alnilam* and in the notes for its sequel, *Crux*. Like Lewis Medlock, the charismatic Joel Cahill may be the focus for other men's admiration and emulation, but Dickey, enthralled as he clearly is by some of Joel's attributes, insists on maintaining an ironic distance from this potentially dangerous leader. At first Joel may seem to be the embodiment of Dickey's hopes for the younger generation of men, particularly his son, Chris, on whom he modeled the character (*Sorties*, 148). As a "real adolescent seer" and not just "another Jerry Rubin-like student revolutionary in uniform," Joel is truly willing and able to fight for his ideals (*Sorties*, 136). The most aggressive of good men, a militant pacifist, Joel believes in subverting the U.S. military establishment itself rather than helping it make war (*Sorties*, 125). In this Joel resembles the narrators of certain Dickey poems, like the pilot in "Two Poems of Flight-Sleep" who, during military training, finds himself "dreaming of letting go letting go / The cold the war the Cadet Program."[16] As Joel himself phrases it, "I don't like machines. If I were going to have any attachment to flying at all, it would be to soaring, which has no military purpose, is slow, and has some aesthetic value" (*Sorties*, 128). No wonder Dickey calls Joel "the Rimbaud of the air" and insists, "I don't mean R-A-M-B-O, I mean R-I-M-B-A-U-D."[17]

Yet what makes Dickey so interesting is that he will elsewhere disturb this Rimbaud / Rambo distinction, casting doubt on men's understanding of Joel and on their willingness to follow his leadership—and perhaps, by implication, making us question Joel's own—or any man's—understanding of himself. Joel's militantly pacifist "scheme of subverting the entire American Armed Forces" is modeled on the "plan of attack" outlined in T. E. Lawrence's *Seven Pillars* (*Sorties*, 133), and Lawrence, we recall, is Dickey's own model of a "timid fellow" who, by assuming a macho persona, "became a military genius and a wonderful writer" (Suarez, 131). Thus, when Dickey begins to cast doubt on Joel and his macho persona, we should understand him as launching an implicit critique of his own idol, Lawrence, and of his own fascination with machismo. A closer look at Dickey's work reveals him to be truly concerned about the possibility that his Rimbaudian masculine ideal may in fact be a Rambo. Assuming the macho persona may not lead to peace but only to increasing war.

Joel's aggressivity may have been adopted in the service of a good cause (pacificism), but once he has felt the thrill of wielding power against those who have abused it, will he still recall the importance of peace? Dickey speculates that there are two ways Joel might go after his successful "take-over" of the military: the "first would be toward some kind of brotherhood, and the second would be toward the acquisition of some sort of power by himself, or by an elite headed by himself" (*Sorties*, 133). Has Joel "taken on" a macho persona in order to combat belligerence in the name of brotherhood, or has he assumed this persona because he wants to wrest power for himself? (Has Ed killed the homicidal hillbilly and laid to rest any doubts he may have had about his own virility, or will the insanely aggressive spirit of the dead man live on in Ed, causing him to seek out other life-and-death situations where he can give murderous proof of his secret powers?)

Although we do not have the finished version of *Crux* to check our hypothesis, it appears that in the end Dickey critiques the macho persona as powerfully as he admires it. After enthralling us, he wants us to understand and repudiate the superman ideal to which we were drawn. One of Joel's former followers, Harbelis, will come to realize that Joel's "youthful fanatical approach to life" must be replaced by a "broader humanitarianism": "Fanaticism, with all its allure, glamor, sense of consequentiality, must, in the end, go. It is terribly sad to be humdrum; efficient, honest, loving, and human. But we imply that these are the necessary conditions, despite the attractions of the other."[18]

The macho persona thrills with its feeling of power and self-importance, but it is driven by fear of weakness in others and in the self and it results in the death of others and moral suicide. Sometimes Dickey forgets these facts and writes with a kind of triumph, desperation, and regret about the necessity of assuming a macho persona. This is the Dickey who can say, "I have self-dramatized myself out of myself, into something else. What was that other thing I have left? I don't know, but this is better; it can do something" (*Sorties*, 74). More often, though, Dickey remembers what that "other thing" is, and his writing moves beyond a fascination with a macho persona to a critique of and alternative to it. This is the other Dickey, the one who, like Harbelis at the end of *Crux*, will write "the word that is lacking from the whole language of conquest and mystery and power: the word for sorrow and pity" ("Notes," 17). This other Dickey is a success as a man and as a writer despite, not because of, his macho persona. The true self that writes the word for sorrow and pity is not weak. It too can do something.

Notes

1. James Dickey, *Poems 1957–1967* (New York: Collier, 1968), back cover.
2. Neal Bowers, *James Dickey: The Poet as Pitchman* (Columbia: University of Missouri Press, 1985), 4.
3. Given the strength of the prevailing negative attitude toward Dickey and his supporters, it would not be professionally prudent for me to mention the names of the many Dickey detractors in academia with whom I am personally acquainted.
4. Robert Bly, "The Collapse of James Dickey," *Sixties* 9 (Spring 1967): 75. [Reprinted in part in this volume.]
5. Fredric Jameson, "The Great American Hunter, or, Ideological Content in the Novel," *College English* 34 (1972): 182. [Reprinted in part in this volume.]
6. Carolyn Heilbrun, *Saturday Review*, January 29, 1972, p. 44. [Reprinted in part in this volume.]
7. Ernest Suarez, "An Interview with James Dickey," *Contemporary Literature* 31.2 (Summer 1990): 132; hereafter cited in text.
8. James Dickey, *Sorties* (Garden City, NY: Doubleday, 1971), 4; hereafter cited in text as *Sorties*.
9. James Dickey, *Deliverance* (Boston: Houghton Mifflin, 1970), 42; hereafter cited in text as *Deliverance*.
10. Ronald Baughman, ed., *The Voiced Connections of James Dickey: Interviews and Conversations* (Columbia: University of South Carolina Press, 1989), 74; hereafter cited in text.
11. Paul Binding, *Separate Country: A Literary Journey through the American South* (Jackson: University Press of Mississippi, 1988), 151.

12. James Dickey, *Night Hurdling* (Columbia, SC: Bruccoli Clark, 1983), 294.

13. Gordon Van Ness, " 'When memory stands without sleep': James Dickey's War Years," *James Dickey Newsletter* 4.1 (Fall 1987): 9.

14. James Dickey, *Self-Interviews* (Garden City, NY: Doubleday, 1970), 137–38.

15. Walter Clemons, "James Dickey, Novelist," *New York Times Book Review*, March 22, 1970, p. 22.

16. James Dickey, *The Central Motion: Poems, 1968–1979* (Middletown, CT: Wesleyan University Press, 1983), 111.

17. Charles Trueheart, "James Dickey's Celestial Navigations," *Washington Post*, May 24, 1987, p. F6.

18. James Dickey, "Notes for Works in Progress," *Pages* 1 (Detroit: Gale Research, 1976), 10, 12; hereafter cited in text as "Notes."

"Breeding Lilacs Out of the Dead Land": James Dickey's *Alnilam* and *Deliverance*

JOHN BLAIR

> At last I opened my eyes
> In the sun, and saw nothing there.
> That night I parted my lids
> Once more, and saw dark burn
> Greater than sunlight or moonlight
> For it burned from deep within me.
> —"The Owl King"

Frank Cahill's blindness and the access to insight that results from it, are the focal images of James Dickey's second novel, *Alnilam*. From "The Owl King" through "The Eye-Beaters" to *Alnilam*, Dickey's fascination with blindness parallels his fascination with rivers or the air: it provides the possibility for experience; it places one in another world, where the old accomodations no longer function—it also gives *vision* by changing the focus of one's attention from oneself to the world. As Gary Kerley has pointed out, Dickey's description of Orion in "For the Nightly Ascent of the Hunter Orion" as one who "Grows blind, and then sees everything" nicely describes Frank Cahill as well.[1]

That identification seems rather familiar. Another author wrote in the notes to his most famous poem, "What Tiresias *sees*, in fact, is the substance of the poem";[2] as *seer*, Cahill's character functions in a way that is strikingly similar to blind Tiresias in T. S. Eliot's *The Waste Land*. Though Dickey's approach uses the myth of Orion instead of that of the Fisher King, like Eliot he is lamenting the secularization and lack of vision of modern civilization. Dickey, however, is not an Anglican (or, as in Eliot's case, an Anglican-to-be); he is at once a quasi-Christian mystic and an advocate of self-determination, and his characters spend the breadth of the novel exploring possibilities for redemption of the secular self through connection with community and with the universal.

Dickey has used *The Waste Land* as inspiration before, in his poem "The Vegetable King"; even so, collecting allusions is not an especially helpful method for understanding a writer's work. In the case of Dickey's second

This essay was written specifically for this volume and is published here for the first time.

novel, though, seeing it through the lens of Eliot's poem can help us understand not only *Alnilam*, but also Dickey's first novel, *Deliverance*.

The incidental intersections between Eliot's poem and Dickey's novel are many and cumulative, and probably not especially important in themselves. There is the omnipresence of winter in the novel, from the harsh winds at its beginning, when Cahill says, "I'd just as soon be cold. It seems like it's that kind of a time," to the "Winter took it" at the end. The incantation taken from Joel Cahill's totem poet, James Thomson—"As I came through the desert: Meteors ran / And crossed their javelins on the black sky span"—identifies Frank Cahill, like Tiresias, as a traveler in the desert (the "javelins" are the golden streaks he sees across his blinded eyes). There are details dropped casually, the palmist's shop among the few businesses of the town where Cahill stays, the occasional mentions of Cahill's developing foresight: "the window frost seemed to him somehow visible, an opening into the world, and in which there might actually be visions, reality a truth you could see."[3]

But more importantly, both works explore spiritual "wastelands" in the midst of a world war—a landscape symbolized in *Alnilam* by the blasted field of ashes into which Joel Cahill, Dickey's version of Christ, disappears:

> Through Cahill's window came the smell of the frozen afterburn, a smell of dead smoke, dirt, and rusty nails. But as they moved deeper, McCaig could tell that the river bank had held only the outlying part of the fire, and that they were passing from what had been only a scrappy blackening into a sort of all-out desolation that McCaig felt imposed upon to have to accept. Like the beginning of nausea an involuntary shudder came into his stomach, and he realized with surprise and confusion that he was not sick, and that it was fear that had reached him. . . .
> . . . the scene was filled with a strange horror of the air itself that stood above the fields, of things that were once solid now rendered weightless, and the sense of a vast floating of dead things around them. (250–254)

This "vast floating of dead things" in Dickey's blasted landscape is an image reminiscent of the "death in life" Cleanth Brooks observed as the central concern of *The Waste Land*, an image at once of animation and dissolution. Northrop Frye, too, writes of this, observing, "The misery of war-torn Europe is in the background of *The Waste Land*, but all we hear are voices asking querulously, Are you alive, or not? We have to see in such incidents as the seduction of the typist, who lets her body be used like a public urinal because she is bored and tired, the full horror of the denial of humanity."[4] This, I believe, is the essential message of *Anilam* as well, and reviewing Eliot's exploration of it can help make clear the meaning and intent of Dickey's novel. Against a background of young men at preparation for another war in Europe, Dickey's protagonist is brought to ask himself and those around him the same question—Are you alive?—and the answer entails the same imperatives Eliot gives in *The Waste Land* as buttress against the civilized world's "denial of humanity": Give, Sympathize, Control.

As diabetes-induced retinopathy destroys his eyesight, Cahill's doctor reassures him: "What people want in their lives, and almost never have, is meaning. That, the blind have, and it's with them every second. Everything means." And the doctor is right; as Cahill grows blind, observation and interpretation become his preoccupation. Like Eliot's Tiresias, Frank Cahill moves in the clarity of his blindness as witness to a postlapsarian world: ". . . he was invisible, and could enjoy the unstoppable and doomed parts of the world, the savage and foolish frenzy outside, wherever it might be, however far or near" (98). But Cahill himself, before the time frame of the novel, is a doomed wanderer of this wasteland, a man without purpose or meaning. His blindness becomes a point of exit, then, and he begins to discover the emptiness of his life through his discovery of his world and of his son. Dickey describes Cahill, as the character is developed in *Sorties*, as a man distanced from the realities of involvement:

> One of the points here is that Cahill is a relatively ordinary man, and has had nothing whatever to do with political thought, revolutions, or anything of that sort. He just wants to run his swimming pool and skating rink, and go along with the rest; the society does pretty well by him, and he is grateful enough, in his way. Now that his own son is revealed to him . . . he is not so sure where he stands. The point here is to show the slow awakening of a complacent and seriously maimed ordinary man toward political and social realities, and to the fire, or at least the flicker, of genius.[5]

Cahill, like everyone around him, is content in a life which is essentially purposeless; his blindness gives him vision, but he must also learn, from observation, from coming to know his son, the imperative of community. He must learn, above all else, to *participate*. As Northrop Frye observes of *The Waste Land*, "The inhabitants [of Eliot's unreal city] live the buried life (a phrase from Portrait of a Lady) of seeds in winter: they wait the spring rains resentfully, for real life would be their death. Human beings who live like seeds, egocentrically, cannot form a community but only an aggregate, where each man fixed his eyes before his feet, inprisoned in a spiritual solitude . . ." (64). Through most of the novel, as he is learning, Frank Cahill declares often in different ways, "I don't need nobody but myself." Like the "trimmers" of Eliot's inferno, who "lived without blame and without praise," Cahill must commit himself to others and thus to life in order to be redeemed. Commenting on the commands to Give, Sympathize, and Control in the fifth section of *The Waste Land*, Phillip Headings explains, "What Tiresias sees, the substance of the poem according to Eliot's often-misinterpreted note, is . . . the necessity of pure concern for one's fellow-humans without the sins of lust that violate the proper natural order and make individuals incapable of genuine love."[6]

But in Eliot's poem—and in Dickey's novels—lust isn't simply physical desire (though it is that, too); it is as well the antitheses of the three commands: self-centeredness, lack of compassion, and lack of self-control. And "pure concern for one's fellow humans" is precisely the antidote for these sins. In his egocentricity and excesses, from his voyueristic exploitation of the women who unknowingly change before his one-way mirror to his alienation from his own son, Cahill has been guilty; through his blindness and the witnessing it entails, he begins to learn the need for settling his debt.

This process of learning begins in his search for a son he has never known. Its culmination is the acknowledgment of the human in himself. Robert Kirschten has noted something of this same movement in Dickey's poetry: "Although The Owl King is a fantasy, its therapeutic end, like that of Hunting Civil War Relics at Nimblewill Creek, returns us to the human subject, and thus brings us into the literary camp of those writers whom Dickey calls, when speaking of his favorite poet Theodore Roethke, 'the great Empathizers,' like Rilke and D. H. Lawrence.[7] As *Alnilam* comes to a close, Cahill is invited in from the cold of his hermetic isolation: "Come on in with the rest of us. Other people ain't so bad, when you get used to 'em" (540). And Cahill responds. As the novel begins, Cahill's only companion is his dog; toward the end, his dog is dead, and he answers the suggestion that he get a new dog with, "No; I don't think so; no more dogs. I think maybe I'll go with people. . . ." (676). For the first time in many years he speaks to his wife, and discovers "He could not hang up, and he did not know what he wanted to say, or if he could say anything. All at once, in a change of thought like a swerve in wind, he was no longer glad that he would never have to talk this way again, but was afraid he would not get a chance to" (556). This is reentry, simple enough. It is the "pure concern" that is suggested to the reader of *The Waste Land*, and through it he finds the answer to that all-important question: yes, he is alive. Unlike Lucille, the woman who sleeps with Colonel Hoccleve and possibly Joel Cahill among the "dead sheeps," and who is so much like the secretary in Eliot's poem who "lets her body be used like a public urinal"; and unlike the by-the-book officers such as Lieutenant Purcell Foy, who lives very much a "buried life," he has broken free from his spiritual solitude and entered into the salvation of community, of participation and compassion.

For Dickey as for Eliot, the wasteland is as much a loss of paradise as it is a loss of values. The woods, which have always been Dickey's sanctum, the reliquary of romantic possibility, are victim to the wasting fire in *Alnilam*. In *Deliverance* it is flood which threatens devastation, turning "our" paradise, Dickey's paradise, into, as Lewis Metcalf describes it, "one of their paradises," the paradise created by developers for the undifferentiated masses that inevitably metastasize from the urban wasteland of our own "unreal cities." And as both Dickey and Eliot conceive it, the city is the clear antithesis of Eden, a place marked by indifference and inconsequence.

* * *

It is this inconsequence which drives Ed Gentry into trying himself against the wilderness. Northrop Frye notes of Eliot's use of Dante in his creation of his version of London, "This scene is closely associated in Eliot's mind with the vision of modern life in Baudelaire's *Les Fleurs du mal* . . . modern life in the 'fourmillante cité' is characterized by boredom or ennui" (51). Dickey's Atlanta is certainly worthy of Baudelaire, filled with faceless secretaries, "their hair styles, piled and shellacked," and workaday "captives" of the nine-to-five world—"I was of them, sure enough," Ed declares in his despair. The mark of his desolation is the same as that of Frank Cahill, the rejection of the community of man: "I couldn't have cared less about anything or anybody," he tells his wife.[8]

Ed Gentry is, simply enough, one of the "trimmers" of Eliot's (and Dante's) wasteland, one who refuses to commit himself to involvement, positive or otherwise: "I am a get-through-the-day-man. I don't think I was ever anything else. I am not a great art director. I am not a great archer. I am mainly interested in sliding. . . . sliding is living antifriction. Or, no, sliding is living *by* antifriction. It is finding a modest thing you can do, and then greasing that thing. On both sides. It is grooving with comfort" (41). Like the inhabitants of Eliot's London, Ed lives a life of inconsequence and disconnection, as much dead as alive, filled with "a sense of being someone else, some poor fool who lives as unobserved and impotent as a ghost, going through the only motions it has" (18). It took blindness to knock Frank Cahill from his groove; a river provides the same service for Ed Gentry.

Lewis, in *Deliverance*, calls it "breaking the pattern"; Joel Cahill's disciples talk of "turning out of the pattern": " 'It's all different . . . All. Everything. When you make that one turn out, that one turn that sets you completely free, and then you look out . . . you just look, and see what you've got" (69). Both advocate rebellion against the status quo, against normalcy and mediocrity. "Here we go," Lewis tells Ed, "out of the sleep of mild people, into the wild rippling water." Out of Emerson's "lives of quiet desperation" into the uncertain elements, or, rather, into the element of uncertainty, leaving behind the script of their prescribed lives.

And, again, what Ed gains through his separation from his "sleep," is vision. As he ascends the cliff-face that will take him above the river to his rendezvous with the man he is to kill, his sight changes: "The river was blank and mindless with beauty. It was the most glorious thing I have ever seen. But it was not seeing, really. For once it was not just seeing. It was beholding. I *beheld* the river in its icy pit of brightness . . ." (171). And what he looks for in the river with his new vision is connection: "Fear and a kind of enormous moon-blazing sexuality lifted me, millimeter by millimeter. And yet I held madly to the human. I looked for a slice of gold like the model's in the river: some kind of freckle, something lovable, in the huge serpent-shape of light" (176).

The "slice of gold" which has been the token of Ed's dissatisfaction and ennui changes meaning here; it no longer suggests deliverance from boredom but deliverance from self-absorption. Ed moves from egocentricity to what I would characterize as *geocentricity*. Through this trial, his scope becomes more encompassing—the world revolved around Ed Gentry the adman, the universe around the Ed who has aquired *vision*: "Above me the darks changed, and in one of them was a star. On both sides of that small light the rocks went on up, black and solid as ever, but their power was broken. The high, deadly part of the cliff I was on bent and rocked steady over toward life, and toward the hole with the star in it, where, as I went, more stars were added until a constellation like a crown began to form"[9] (176). The same process, of course, takes place in Frank Cahill as Alnilam, the center of Orion and of the novel's universe.

Ed does what he has to do and returns to the world, broken but not defeated, alive to the possibility of community: "I crawled onto the stretcher and turned on my back. It was hard to do; I didn't want to turn loose the driver. He not only felt good to me, but he felt like a good person, and I needed one bad; just that contact was what I needed most. I didn't need myself anymore; I had had too much of that for too long" (234). Like Cahill, he has begun to enter into life, thereby obviating the possibility that he might return to the death-in-life he had lived before. Richard Calhoun and Robert Hill have noted this transaction before: "It [the river] has led Ed to realize that he needs a second deliverance; he must return to the human. It is his wife, his family, and his friend George Holley who must now save him."[10] He grows closer to his wife, admitting he has "undervalued" her. And George Holley, the "old Braque enthusiast" Ed had fired because his single-minded dedication to his art made Ed's own lack of center more apparent, becomes his best friend, "next to Lewis," who "has changed, too, but not in obvious ways. He can die now; he knows that dying is better than immortality. He is a human being, and a good one" (277).

Both Ed Gentry and Frank Cahill have seen themselves as limited men and both have transcended their limitations. But both have needed a catalyst to do so. In Ed's case, it was the enthusiasms of Lewis Metcalf; for Frank Cahill, it was Joel, his son. Both Joel and Lewis act, then, as *saviors* of a sort, nearly supernatural beings in their ability to suffuse others with their own wills and visions (though Lewis does return to humanity, abdicating his immortality and becoming, as Ed notes, human). Both are Christ-like, in a sense. In Joel's case, the parallels are direct and pretty heavy-handed, from his initials (JC), to the relics (the tooth and goggles) that Frank Cahill collects, to the Turin-like bloodied shroud in which he was wrapped, to the obvious echo of John 3:16 in one of the phrases he gave as scripture to the Alnilam sect, "He who believes in me. . . ." Having gathered around him a select group of disciples, Joel Cahill proceeded to spread his own version of the gospel of salvation, complete with the promise of a psuedo-heaven to which the chosen would in time be translated.

It is not immediately apparent just why Dickey chose to invest the novel with this depth of religious allegory and suggestion. But again, *The Waste Land* can help provide a little insight. There is considerable Christian religious imagery in Part V of the poem, but little suggestion that Eliot is proselytizing. Rather, he seems to have intended to imply two things: that in mystical experience the opportunity of escape from death-in-life is to be found, and that in christian values—not necessarily in Christianity itself—is to be found the possibility of rehabilitation. I believe Dickey intends to suggest the same possibilities.

Late in the novel, Captain Whitehall explains the bombadier Faulstick's apocryphal story about the German ME-109 that seemed to have fired on him personally: "It's a war story, Mr. Cahill. . . . A lot of them are deliberate mysteries, because people want to have something to set against the realities they're in" (646). This, Major Iannone explains to Cahill later, is what his son and Julius Caesar and any other leader who has inspired blind loyalty has created: "They give people the notion that they can make life different in some way, and that the people who help them, who join in with them, will be different, will be made different, will exist in a new way. . . ." (655). "All these folks are cranks, if you ask me," Iannone declares, "Jesus Christ included. Some of them have come to plenty, though. Plenty of good, and plenty of bad." Joel, Christ, Caesar (and Lewis, as well), are all of a kind in this conception, men who offer, in Dickey's terms, deliverance. But it is a qualified deliverance. The writer intimates that in any belief system—and especially in those involving anything akin to a messiah—dogmatism and moral confusion can accompany the vision; one must always beware of confusing *form* with *essence*. The wise man, the man who has learned to *see*, gleans what is valuable from whatever is offered to him, regardless of moral categorizations. He understands the means of his awakening from death-in-life, but he also kens its limitations. Iannone is a wise man; Cahill and Ed aquire wisdom, and through it, grace.

Thus, perhaps, the equivocation we find in the novel about Joel and his father; both are often described in demonic rather than angelic terms, Joel as a hopping red devil, Frank as a man in black accompanied by his own Cerebus-wolf. *Faith* seems less important in Dickey's conception than *balance*, a term that appears in the book more than two dozen times. Zealotry of any sort is unproductive in the personal sphere; Cahill and Ed learn to be self-determining, balancing their lives with the divine and the mundane, the morally good and the personally good.

Writing about *The Waste Land*, A. J. Wilks explains that in Eliot's poem we are "shown how self-examination in the light of religious truths can give self-knowledge that makes the despair endurable."[11] That is, through internalization of certain imperatives—give, sympathize, control—we can,

Eliot suggests, overcome the angst inherent in our own existences, through coming to know the possibilities for positive action within ourselves. Wilks writes, "The poetry [of section V of *The Waste Land*] is moving towards that of the second voice—towards prescribing action, or a use for suffering . . ." (78). Eliot's "second voice" is the voice of the poet's address to the reader, and, as Wilks notes, Eliot caps his poem with an injunction to *do*.

Dickey, too, leans heavily on that verb, both in *Alnilam* and in *Deliverance*. Lewis tells Ed in answer to Ed's refuge in his "greased groove," "But when that river is under you, all that is going to change. There's nothing you do as vice-president of Emerson-Gentry that's going to make any difference at all, when the water starts to foam up. Then, it's not going to be what your title says you do, but what you end up doing. You know: *doing*" (41). That same formula is repeated in *Alnilam* several times, but is best put by the character of McLendon, the man who has taken Cahill in and given him comfort, as his understanding of the bravery of Whitehall and Faulstick, the war veterans: "That you don't try to back off, that you don't try to get out of doin'. You just try to do, as best you can. Especially when you've got other people. And sometimes you get lucky. But if you're not already in there tryin' to do, then the luck won't mean anything" (219). The onus, then, is to take responsibility for action, for participation. Then the luck comes, is granted. Deliverance is given. But it is, as McLendon points out, an especial imperative "when you've got other people." *Doing* is the medium of Eliot's three commands, the means for salvation.

Deliverance and *Alnilam*, like *The Waste Land*, are quest narratives, and the grail for all three is *meaning*, the answer not only to the question "Am I alive?" but, as Ed Gentry asks himself, "Why on God's earth am I here?" Through connection with the human comes redemption and purpose, but it is "God's earth," and participation in the universal is equally as important. Eliot's three truths are handed down from on high, and though as in *Alnilam*, the christian God is not explicitly identified, the values expressed are those which are classically attributed to Christ's mandate for brotherhood. Dickey, too, declines to name the "universal" which centers his characters in their world. Whitehall, the navigator, acting as minister (in the sense that he gives direction not only to airplanes but in part to Cahill's life) asserts "That's what we've got to work with. Everything and nothing. A design. . . . What matters is complicity, the connection: your complicity between you and the big thing, the biggest of all. When you have that, you can do anything you like" (56). But Dickey's "design" participates too much in christian iconography for his godlike "universal" not to be—at least in part—the christian, New Testament conception of God, despite Dickey's disavowal of formal religion. Commingled with the classical rendering of christian belief, though, is a large dose of something altogether different, something along the lines of Captain Whitehall's "deliberate mysteries," wherein a vague, inclusive, *intuitive* apprehension of the spiritual augments and to an extent replaces the mystical possibility of a traditionally conceived christian God. No dogma is involved, only a celebration of a considered (even self-conscious) mystery, a somewhat gnostic sense of something larger, of a community of men—of mystics—conceived in partially christian terms.

"Salvation" is, of course, an intensely personal business. For James Dickey the personal is a matter of memory and place; because he is a southerner, immersed in a culture centered in christian values, part of salvation is the classical injunction to be Christ-like, though Dickey himself might well deny the possibility of a historical, incarnate Christ through which the unquestioningly faithful might be "saved" in the conventional sense of the word. Ed Gentry and Frank Cahill must trod the path themselves, must determine their own destinies within the pattern given them, but in the process they must undergo the baptism of blood and water which brings them to what amounts to—because these are the terms available to Dickey—christian fellowship and love.

In *Sorties*, Dickey declares, "There is a fundamental difference between what I am trying to do and what Pound and Eliot were trying to do. They were trying to interpret culture in one way or the other. I am not trying to interpret; I am trying to give to people" (94). At least in one poem, however, Eliot was trying to do the same thing, trying to "give" what Barnett Guttenberg identifies as "a pattern of redemption."[12] Philip Headings writes of *The Waste Land*, "It is easy to see why Eliot denied that his poem was intended to express the disillusionment of a generation. Its message, though universal, is intensely personal; and the waste land exists in no one time or generation, but in a wrong psychic focus equally possible to all generations—and escapable, as our art reminds us, by individuals in every generation" (69). Both writers, as prophets, offer up a formula for renewal—a formula which involves mystical experience but which is profoundly secular and human-centered rather than (or, in Eliot's case, perhaps in addition to) religious and God-centered. With this knowledge their characters and their readers can return to the mundane, to their art, their carpentry, even to "Fishing, with the arid plain behind me," aware of the wasteland but imbued with "the peace which passeth understanding."

Notes

1. Gary Kerley, "Understanding 'This Hunter Made Out of Stars': The Myth of Orion in James Dickey's *Alnilam*," *James Dickey Newsletter* 4.1 (Fall 1987): 15–27.

2. T. S. Eliot, *The Complete Poems and Plays, 1909–1950* (New York: Harcourt Brace Jovanovich, 1971), 52.

3. James Dickey, *Alnilam* (Garden City, New York: Doubleday & Co., 1987), 94; hereafter cited in text.

4. Northrop Frye, *T. S. Eliot* (London: Oliver and Boyd, Ltd., 1963), 52; hereafter cited in text.

5. James Dickey, *Sorties* (Garden City, New York: Doubleday & Co., 1971), 135.

6. Philip K. Headings, *T. S. Eliot* (Boston: Twayne Publishers, 1964), 60; hereafter cited in text.

7. Robert Kirschten, *James Dickey and the Gentle Ecstasy of Earth* (Baton Rouge: Louisiana State University Press, 1988), 39.

8. James Dickey, *Deliverance* (Boston: Houghton Mifflin Co., 1970), 27; hereafter cited in text.

9. This "constellation like a crown" is probably the Corona Borealis, a constellation as central to the summer sky as Orion is to the winter sky (*Deliverance* is set in summer.)

10. Richard J. Calhoun and Robert W. Hill, *James Dickey* (Boston: Twayne Publishers, 1983), 118–119.

11. A. J. Wilks, *T. S. Eliot*: The Wasteland (Basingtoke and London: Macmillan Education Ltd., 1971), 91; hereafter cited in text.

12. Barnett Guttenberg, "The Pattern of Redemption in Dickey's *Deliverance*," *Critique* 18.3 (1977): 83–91.

To "Splinter Uncontrollably Whole": Circularity and the Philosophic Subtext in Dickey's *The Eagle's Mile*

GORDON VAN NESS

James Dickey's *The Eagle's Mile* presents two contrasting perspectives that dominate the overall work: the ideal, dispassionate, and inclusive gaze of the eagle in high flight and the restricted, anxious, and exclusive stare of a man walking closely on the ground. The speaker, both as he imaginatively rises with the bird in "Eagles," "receiving overlook,"[1] and as he stands on a beach in "Circuit," "foreseeing / Around a curve" (2–3), understands these points of view as essential to knowing "the circular truth / Of the void" ("Eagles," 2–3). Each poem in the volume captures a singular experience or stance, an emotional and physical complex addressing one of the perspectives that reveals a moment of acceptance, celebration, or even transcendence. Each captures a still point in time, Frost's "momentary stay against confusion," that increasingly links each poem to others by patterns of imagery. Taken together, these poems and images reveal the principled physical relevance of things and the vital and redemptive role of the imagination. Dickey's persona intuits life, the dynamic and mysterious process of creation, as well as the immobility and anonymity of death, an intuition that provides a double vision. The earthbound persona understands that the two perspectives, metaphorically rendered as the eagle's mile and the emmet's inch, encompass human truth and the artistic impulse as manifested in physical reality.

The book's poetic arrangement reflects this larger understanding of point of view and traces the speaker's own physical and spiritual journey through his understanding of what he sees or intuits. Yet, more importantly, the poems manifest Dickey's own struggle to reconcile Platonic and Aristotelian concepts of reality. Throughout his career Dickey has continually vacillated between the two philosophies. In early volumes such as *Into the Stone* (1960), *Drowning With Others* (1962), and *Helmets* (1964), where the speaker endeavors to lose himself in or identify with some idealized Other, Dickey depicts a conscious recognition of duality, a dialectical struggle continued in *Buckdancer's Choice*

This essay was written specifically for this volume and is published here for the first time.

220

(1965), *The Eye-Beaters* (1970), *The Zodiac* (1976), and *The Strength of Fields* (1979). In these later collections, the poems still seek to exchange states of being through the imagination's redemptive power, but the focus becomes more social and exhibits less assurance, even an acute sense of limitations. For example, from "Sleeping Out at Easter," in which the persona gleans a Platonic "source of all song at the root" (15), he asserts in "The Strength of Fields" that "My life belongs to the world" (49), an Aristotelian understanding of matter and form. In *Puella* (1982), Dickey began to achieve balance. For example, in "The Surround," the persona not only becomes an idealized Form but also admits of the sense of distinctions: "I am / The surround, and you are your own" (44–45). Finally in *The Eagle's Mile* Dickey has balanced the contrasting philosophies of reality to achieve, as he writes in "Expanses," "Joy like short grass" (19). The interaction between a Platonic realm, where Ideas or Forms reveal order and pattern, and an Aristotelian world, where constantly changing aspects dictate reality, provides the philosophic subtext of *The Eagle's Mile*. Dickey points to the synthesis in the title poem where the speaker admonishes the reader to "Splinter uncontrollably whole" (81) in a world whose circularity permits a constant state of Becoming.

Dickey's need for a philosophical dialectic that, on the one hand, recognizes distinctions before they lose their definite forms and, on the other, embraces ideals or absolutes, reflects his continued preoccupation with death. Stemming in part from his combat in the Second World War as a member of the 418th Night Fighter Squadron, where the brutality of the fighting caused both physical and psychological dislocation, his concern has been that of an intellectual suspended between the ideal and the real—what might be and what was. As his poetry has turned the cube of reality, to use William James's phrase, he seems to have confronted death, or the experience of death, as a means to address life. Of the 84 poems that comprise his first three volumes of poetry, for example, fully 79 percent, or 66 poems, contain the word "death" or some variant such as "dying." However, *The Eagle's Mile*, published 30 years after his first volume, presents death not explicitly but indirectly, philosophically, through images that reveal the need to rediscover placid, eternal principles in the midst of swarming, relative truths. By age 67, Dickey has begun to manifest the elemental human condition, the philosophical connundrum, and the beginning of the artistic process that validates the individual presence against the emptiness of death. He seeks a double vision, uniting Platonic idealism and the human need for transcendence with Aristotelian dualities which provide wonder and richness even as their finitude denotes death.

Critics have generally failed to examine the philosophic influences that underlie Dickey's poetry. In his critical study *James Dickey and the Gentle Ecstasy of Earth*, Robert Kirschten has detailed Dickey's "lyric universe," arguing that Plato's conception of rhythm reveals itself in the poet's "unifying Absolute of Motion that joins all things, past and present, in a perpetual process of universal rhythm."[2] Neal Bowers, on the other hand, suggests in his bio-critical study *James Dickey: The Poet as Pitchman*, that the poet's background in advertising gave Dickey a pragmatic view of the world, one that enables him "to sell the things he had to offer: himself, the poem, and (in his own view) God."[3] His poetry evidences an Aristotelian duality in its progressive movement from "the poem as an objective artifact, to the poem as a subjective expression of the poet's thoughts and emotions."[4] Such examinations, however, fail to convey the dialectic that Dickey's poetry manifests, particularly as the synthesis of Platonic and Aristotelian elements finds its most complete expression in *The Eagle's Mile*.

During Dickey's formal education at Vanderbilt University, he read extensively to recover the academic and intellectual ground lost while serving in World War II. Minoring in philosophy, he enrolled in such subjects as logic, social philosophy, the history of philosophy, and aesthetics, B. A. G. Fuller's *History of Greek Philosophy* was a course text, and Dickey additionally read Bertrand Russell's *A History of Western Philosophy*. Plato's *Republic, Phaedo*, and *Parmenides* and Aristotle's *Physics* and *Metaphysics*, which introduce the main philosophical elements unified in *The Eagle's Mile*, formed a basis of his philosophical study between 1946 and 1950. Dickey confronted these ideas again later in the 1950s when he read Kenneth Burke's *A Grammar of Motives* closely, making extensive notations in his early notebooks on those sections that discuss Plato and Aristotle and the principles of motion and inaction, actuality and potentiality, and form and end.

In *Self-Interviews* Dickey admits to searching during those years for a new weltanschauung centered in the beliefs of native tribespeople whom he had encountered during his service in the Pacific theatre of war; consequently, he read voraciously and eclectically in philosophy, history, psychology, and anthropology. He sought an understanding that reflected the "difference between the natives' outlook and the outlook of so-called 'primitive' people."[5] That native tribes viewed the physical world in intimate relation with the infinite reinforced his philosophic search. Anthropological books such as Sir Walter Baldwin Spencer's and Francis James Gillen's *The Native Tribes of Central Australia* and Jane Ellen Harrison's *Themis*, along with studies by W. H. R. Rivers, Bronislaw Malinowski, and Alfred Radcliffe-Brown, established Dickey's awareness that for primitive man finite reality interacted with the transcendent, rather than remaining a separate part of a dualistic universe. These years of study and poetry culminate in Dickey's effort in *The Eagle's Mile* to unify Platonic and Aristotelian philosophy by confronting a series of three opposing principles or contraries: first, Plato's belief in ideal Forms that constitute immutable archetypes of all temporal phenomena, and Aristotle's contention that form is immanent in matter and that both are concrete, individual realities; second, Plato's argument that life issues in and proceeds from death in a circular motion of continual Becoming, and Aristotle's assertion that material forms possess principles of motion and stillness; and, third,

Plato's view that art merely imitates what is already an imitation, and Aristotle's declaration that art may act as a final cause to complete what nature does not.

Plato's theory of knowledge derives from his belief that in this universe Ideas or Forms are real and immutable; by contrast, the physical world possesses only a relative reality that remains constantly in flux. Arguing in the *Republic* that only the ultimate truth, the knowledge of the Good, gives "their truth to the objects of knowledge and the power of knowing to the knower,"[6] Plato declares that a concrete reality partakes of a Form, which is the Ideal, but does not embody it. Dickey, on the other hand, has always reveled in the physical things of this world, declaring in his essay "The Wild Heart" "how much there *is*, there really *is*, upon earth: how wild, inexplicable, marvellous and endless creation is."[7] Though adopting early in his career the Platonic concept of Form, Dickey clearly qualified his desire for a union or exchange with some ideal Other by embracing material reality in all its manifestations, declaring that "God is so much *more* than God" (*Self-Interviews*, 78). In *The Eagle's Mile* he understands that the physical world intimately reveals God; things are not mere shadows of the Ideal but, as Aristotle states in his *Physics*, "everything which is generated is generated from a subject and a *form*."[8] Yet Dickey's acknowledgment of this Aristotelian attitude, the idea that form possesses no separate existence but remains immanent in nature, has not negated his desire for some transcendent Other. He has continued to search for an Ideal that provides some emotional or psychological guarantee of continuity, and poems such as "Eagles," "Two Women," "The One," "The Three," and "Weeds" reveal his struggle to resolve this dilemma through a dialectic involving both philosophies.

"Eagles" establishes the book's grounding premise by insisting upon the inability of the individual ever to escape the world fully enough to gain an ideal or Platonic understanding of it. While the effort remains doomed, the human need to strive above earthbound limitations is undeniable, necessary, and redemptive, as timeless as Icarus' failed attempt. The speaker imagines himself lifted by the feet of an eagle. The brief flight, which deposits him groveling on the ground among weeds, reveals a larger world, "the circular truth / Of the void" (1–2), one whose elements would satisfy any realm but the one where he lives and moves. Now, however, he only asks that the eagle leave "my unstretched weight" (42) and "remember me in your feet" (47). He understands that "The higher rock is / The more it lives" (48–49), a recognition of human limitation and the need to transcend those restrictions. Dickey's celebration of the ancient elements of earth, air, and water in the later three sections that comprise "Immortals" and of the atmospheric duality of heat and cold in "To the Butterflies" clearly confirms an Aristotelian belief in a physical reality. Yet, when the persona in "Earth" declares, "I cannot be anything / But alive, in a place as far / From the blank and stark as this" (8–10), he acknowledges the immanence of form in matter while fearing the void, or the nothingness of death, which qualifies the exhilaration felt within nature. Plato's eternal Forms, however, do not suffer from such impermanence, and because the persona's flight in "Eagles" has enabled him temporarily to become "One form with wings" (22), he desires such Ideality.

The psychological need to rise above the impermanence and enter an eternal realm often requires a conscious choice between the ideal and the real. In "Two Women," for example, the persona admonishes a mortal woman to restrain her "printed pursuit" (15) and "[u]nstemming impurity" (16), both characteristics of her finitude. He wishes, instead, for a figure whose ideality is manifested by her integration with her surroundings, a female principle "[b]orn infinite" (23) who possesses a "[s]andal without power / To mark sand" (18–19). This Platonic Ideal is desirable because she transcends death. His restricted vision, while offering him the world's rich variety, leaves him limited, anxious, and excluded from the infinite. What he requires is a double vision, acknowledging Platonic Ideals while simultaneously affirming the Aristotelian reality of physical things, whose concreteness is not merely undeniable but potentially redemptive. Such a perspective reveals itself metaphorically in "Weeds," when the narrator recognizes that

> Stars and grass
> Have between them a connection I'd like to make
> More of—find some way to bring them
> To one level any way I can. (1–4)

Integration of the multiplicity of phenomena requires first organizing them within philosophical principles; the consequent Platonic and Aristotelian systems remain separate dualities whose principles must then become unified themselves through a dialectic.

The distinction between Platonic Forms and Aristotelian duality becomes most apparent in "The One" and "The Three." Because the speaker has accepted his limited perspective while remaining accessible to the environment, he achieves in these poems an intuitive understanding of the significance held in an ear of corn and a flight of three birds, respectively. Dickey's insistence upon the primacy of the Ideal, the Form of a thing, appears in "The One" when the persona demands recognition of the lone stalk of corn "nearly transparent / With existence" (7–8). Artistically blocking out the nearby field, he insists on the transcendent relevancy of the single Form:

> One.
> Inside.
> Yellow.
> All others not.
> One.
> One. (16–21)

The concern here is with the imagined Ideal, the Form of the cornstalk as the poet perceives it and not the stalk he sees literally, as when Plato, referring to mathematicians, declares: "The very things which they mold and draw, which have shadows and images of themselves in water, these things they treat in their turn as only images, but what they really seek is to get sight of those realities which can be seen only by the mind" (*Republic* 510e). While the single ear of corn holds poetic possibilities, its visual form demands that Dickey conceive its ideal likeness, "The color one" (6), for it alone transcends its physical condition as "barometer" (1) of its existence. The ripe stalk, a forecast of time, will eventually give itself out and die.

The Platonic Ideal yields to Aristotelian duality in "The Three," when three birds distinguish themselves by flying higher than the remaining flock. Their elevation renders the birds a Platonic Ideal. Not only do they possess "the height to power-line all / Land" (24–25), but also their presence causes the lower birds to "give up part / Of your reality" (7–8). Grounded as he is, the narrator imagines them as "more than you would have / Be seen yourself" (10–11). His isolation from their ideal perspective repeatedly manifests itself; in four separate lines, Dickey describes him as "alone." In a moment reminscent of Emerson, however, the persona goes "oversouling for an instant / With them" (7–8), their Platonic transcendency existing in a sphere apart. Yet the images of the earthbound persona, the flock of low-flying birds, and then, at the highest point, a group of three birds, raise a dilemma with which Plato also struggled: the relation of Ideas to one another. To discover an ultimate principle of unity that resolves the One and the Many would yield the source of the world of Forms, which already transcends human predicates.

Dickey struggles with this issue but only after confronting the limitation of physical objects and the philosophic questions of motion and Becoming in a second group of poems, including "Gila Bend," "Circuit," "Sleepers," "Tomb Stone," and "To Be Done in Winter." These poems evoke the *Phaedo* where Plato argues for the continuity of living things, using the circle as symbol: "If there were not perpetual reciprocity in coming to be, between one set of things and another, revolving in a circle, as it were—if, instead, coming-to-be were a linear process from one thing into its opposite only, without any bending back in the other direction, or reversal, . . . all things would ultimately have the same form: the same fate would ultimately overtake them, and they would cease from coming to be."[9] He concludes: "if all things that partake of life were to die, but when they'd died, the dead remained in that form, and didn't come back to life, wouldn't it be quite inevitable that everything would be dead, and nothing could live? Because if the living things came to be from other things, but the living things were to die, what could possibly prevent everything from being completely spent in being dead?" (*Phaedo* 72d). While death remains, Plato's belief mitigates its finality, establishing the concept of circularity and suggesting that death constitutes one part of life, which exists in a continual state of Becoming.

"Gila Bend" and "Circuit" emphasize the limitations inherent in the physical world and anticipate the Platonic idea of perpetual reciprocity. In "Gila Bend," after 40 years the narrator revisits the place where he underwent aerial gunnery training and notices his solitude, his inability to leave footprints in the smashed rock: "you should brand, brand / The ground but you don't" (4–5). Feeling the intense heat of the place, he realizes no individual could rise; the sun burns one down, driving everything into the ground. The hard, physical realities of the human condition convince the persona that he is "a cadaver / On foot" (1–2), a weighted limitation who cannot reveal his individual presence and who will experience only the steady, remorseless drag of death into and off of the earth. "Circuit" then suggests the Platonic idea of perpetual reciprocity within nature, the circular motion of life that assures continuity. Standing on the shore at twilight, the persona observes the tendency of beaches to move toward completion:

> always slow-going headlong
> For the circle
> swerving from the water
> But not really, their minds on a perfect connection. (3–6)

From the scene he infers a human circularity, the principle that "no matter / How long it takes" (6–7), an individual will become what he was:

> You can't be
> On them without making the choice
> To meet yourself no matter
> How long. (7–10)

While Plato sees existence as a continuous movement, Aristotle believes both motion and its absence are natural prescripts, declaring "All things existing by nature appear to have in themselves a principle of motion and of standing still, whether with respect to place or increase or decrease or alteration" (*Physics* Book β, 192b 15). Aristotle considered nature not so much a transcendent principle, as a collective word for the natures of all living things working harmoniously together, and he attempted to disprove the idea of a void, a complete and empty stillness, either as a place separate from or occupied by bodies or as interstices in bodies. "Gila Bend" and "Circuit," in their dramatic situations, suggest the principles of stillness and motion, respectively, and raise the question of the nature of death. When Dickey declares in "Eagles" that "I used to know the circular truth / Of the void" (1–2), his use of "the void" is singularly important for it clearly underlines his concern with the stillness of death, the lack of all motion. While poems like "Daughter," "The Little More," "The Olympian," and "For a Time and Place" celebrate human life as it begins and progresses until the idea of family expands to include all South

Carolinians, the facticity of death constantly confronts the speaker. Motion characterizes these poems, from "Daughter" where the newborn's power is intimately associated with natural forces, to "The Little More" and the adolescent's "own gigantic / Continuous stride" (33–34), to "The Olympian" who "lumbered for gold" (148) in a footrace despite his "career of fat" (37), and finally to "For a Time and Place" where all South Carolinians possess a motion:

> our momentum
> In place, overcoming, coming over us
> And from us
> from now on out. (63–66)

For Dickey, motion connotes and denotes life, with its sense of growth and possibility; stillness, its opposite, suggests death.

Against the doctrine of the void Aristotle set the concept of matter's qualitative change of state, asserting "that there is a single matter for contraries, . . . that it is from potential being that actual being is generated, that matter is not separate though it is distinct in being, and that matter may be numerically one" (*Physics* Book Δ, 217a 20). Only in a special sense does Aristotle admit of a void, where when a heavy body falls or a light body rises, the matter of that body appears "void." Plato indirectly raises the issue of the void in the *Parmenides*. Though never specifically using the term "void," the discussion does involve the sense of nothingness. Asking what must follow if there is no thing but many things other than one, Parmenides paradoxically answers, "The others will not be one, but neither will they be many. For if they are to be many, there must be one among them, since, if none of them is one thing, they will all be no-thing, and so not many either. But there is no one among them, since, if none of them is one thing, they will all be no-thing, and so not many either. But there is no one among them; so the others are neither one nor many."[10] The dialogue shows through dialectical reasoning the relationship between and among things, implying that no-thing is composed of the many.

In "Sleepers," "Tomb Stone," and "Vessels," Dickey combines Plato's belief in contraries, that is to say, the "perpetual reciprocity" between living and dead things, which the image of the circle best conveys, with Aristotle's belief that actual matter becomes potential matter in death. Plato's continuous coming-to-be, apparent in "Sleepers," where Dickey links the two states of being through the image of the sound sleepers make, evidences itself in the dead, "that assault-force / Without a muscle, fighting for space" (8–9); the speaker knows that death-in-life and life-in-death are ontologically related even though sleepers may not yet recognize "where your tombs / Already lie" (21–22). Achieving the right sound enables them to "sail through / The lifted spaces, unburied" (22–23). Death, then, becomes only a qualitative state of being, not the absence of Self. Just as the living resemble the dead in sleep, so are they also dead when their presence fails to leave a footprint, fails as in "Gila Bend" to brand the ground. Both situations constitute forms of death just as death itself is a form of being.

Over the course of *The Eagle's Mile*, the persona gradually recognizes that death is not the void he previously conceived, that it not so much concerns emptiness or absence as it does state or perspective—potential rather than actual motion. Realizing in "Tomb Stone" that "deep enough / In death, the earth becomes / Absolute earth" (13–15), he comprehends that mortality involves a return to the elements; from "the rectangular solitude" (10) of life, man becomes in death no-thing and many. The poem, which remembers Dickey's first wife, Maxine, enables the speaker to comprehend where he stands, spatially and philosophically, to one lying horizontally. Rather than the absence of matter, death concerns space and potentiality, and because bodies change only quantitative states, no void exists. "Vessels" extends this Aristotelian idea by depicting Dickey's imaginative response to the death of his brother, Tom, a willed entrance into death to join "[m]y own blood" (7). The union, which sees

> the starry head that has hovered
> Above him all his life
> come down on his, like mine
> Exactly,
> or near enough (17–21)

blurs the ontological distinction between life and death to suggest their philosophic unity.

For Dickey, motion constitutes the Platonic Absolute, the principle of unity that resolves the One and the Many, but what becomes more important to human beings grounded in and on the sensible world is final cause, the innate principle which accepts the reality of the individual form by serving to complete its nature. Such completion, the mastery of a thing, lies with the artistic process, which reveals and justifies growth and the advancement of age. Plato dismissed most of the poets owing to metaphysical and moral considerations. Supremely interested in truth, he deprecated art, declaring that "mimetic art is far removed from truth" (*Republic* 598b), merely the imitation of an imitation. Aristotle, observing Plato's distinction between matter and form but also arguing that both are concrete realities, added that the former is related to the latter: "And since nature may be either matter or *form*, and it is the latter that may be an end while all the rest are for the sake of an end, it is *form* that would be a cause in the sense of a final cause" (*Physics* Book β, 199a 30). Aristotle uses the example of a plant which grows leaves in order to protect the fruit; a final cause exists, therefore, in things which occur or come into actual being in nature. If these things generated by nature, he declares, were also created by art, the method would be exactly the same, though in particular situations "art completes what nature cannot carry out to an end" (*Physics* Book β, 199a 15). For Aristotle, the artist inclines towards the ideal or universal element in things, not creating a mere copy but often making something better than it is in reality. The conflict between Plato's mimetic conception of art and Aristotle's view that the creative impulse fulfills the innate potentiality of a thing occurs in such poems as "The Six," "Meadow Bridge," "Moon Flock," "Night Bird," and "Daybreak," receiving its most thorough treatment in the title poem, "The Eagle's Mile." These poems center on the imagination's efforts to redeem the physical world by discerning or imparting meaning to temporal things, both individually and in groups.

Plato's accusation of art rests primarily on his charge that, though possessing its charms, it makes "only a dim adumbration in comparison to reality" (*Republic* 597b). Such a deficiency manifests itself in poems like "The Six," "Meadow Bridge," and "Moon Flock." "The Six" seemingly reflects Aristotle's argument that art completes nature. When the persona finds himself able to "think strong enough" (1), he imagines that six stones form the body of his lover and inexplicably hurtle toward and then through him. While the mind may stray dangerously from reality, the imagination may also paradoxically discern in the separation a hidden, undisclosed unity: "if you meet them head-on / You will know something nobody means / But her" (15–17). The persona, however, finally adopts a Platonic attitude that art distorts the truth, thinking,

> She is moving at the speed of light
> Some place else, and though she passes
> Through you like rock-salt, she is still six
> And not one. (17–20)

The imagination distorts truth, and material things remain finite.

The opening of "Meadow Bridge" explicitly acknowledges the philosophic subtext in *The Eagle's Mile*, the persona admitting: "There might be working some kind of throwaway / Meditation on Being" (1–2). As in "The Six," the imagination misrepresents the truth as it imitates reality. Standing before a steel bridge, he sees its shadow, a new bridge created when the sun "lined out, squaring off" (7) its reflection. He discovers himself wanting to complete the reflected bridge by adding suspension cables, "a vibration / Of threads" (15–16), and mist rising from the meadow, "gauze" (17) that keeps burning off. Facticity, however, thwarts the artistic impulse to extend a copy into something original, and he ends by asking, "Field, what hope?" (22). While the artistic impulse lies in the human instinct for expression, its imaginative symbolism fails to assert truth, though it might possess beauty and address the emotional in man.

"Moon Flock" is Dickey's attempt to convey the strength of that impulse and the subsequent frustration at its failure, using the analogy of the moon's effort to create life. While Aristotelian reality in the previous poem overcomes the artistic effort to create an idealized bridge, the imaginative ideal in this poem never begins to fulfill the world in which it finds itself. The speaker confesses: "nothing can be put / Up on a wind with no air" (10–11) and admonishes the reader not to inquire of his imaginative effort, for the moon remains merely "a wild white world" (7) whose emptiness reflects his own.

"Night Bird" and "Daybreak," on the other hand, reveal Aristotle's belief that the artist not only deals with types which resemble the univeral and ideal but also, and more importantly, that he acts as final cause to complete or extend a form. With the fall of evening in "Night Bird," the speaker, now deprived of eyesight, reacts intuitively to sound. From the blackness he hears the bunched beating of wings and senses that its up-and-down motion resembles "a curving grave" (4). Though concerned with death, his failure to see literally does not preclude his ability to perceive figuratively, and as he intuits the bird as "this gleam / Of air" (15–16), he also recognizes that "there is no limit / To what a man can get out of / His failure to see" (12–14). Aristotle's assertion that the artist depicts the universal becomes apparent when the persona imaginatively sees in the night bird "everything / There is of flight" (16–17). Dawn finds him contemplating the waves, and in "Daybreak" he tries to understand how sounds held by and conveyed through air now present themselves only as repetitive blanks. Walking into the water, he stares at "the cancelling gullies" (15) and "those crests / Dying hard" (11–12), concerned with the limitations of physical reality; however, he also observes the sky's reflection, finding his body no different from other images. Despite feelings of imperfection, he conceives the universal, seeing himself "purely somewhere, / Somewhere in all thought" (26–27). This Romantic statement of faith in himself reflects Aristotle's belief that the larger, imaginative forces extend creation. Yet the artistic process clearly has limitations that reveal the ephemeral quality of all matter and justify Plato's argument that artists are "imitators of images of excellence and of the other things that they 'create,' and do not lay hold on truth" (*Republic* 600e).

The series of opposite propositions or contraries become unified or reconciled in the volume's title poem. In "The Eagle's Mile," celebrating with Whitmanesque affirmation the godlike creative impulse, the speaker demands that William Douglas, who in life was blind in one eye, now "step out of grass-bed sleep" (39) and possess the world anew, "drawing life / From growth / from flow" (66–68). If he will "catch into this / With everything you have" (1–2), Douglas can enter again into the multiplicity of physical reality, the endless and marvelously varied creation, because potential form once again becomes actual. Here Dickey suggests the interrelationship of all things, all natural forces, all individualities merging in their motions to render an eternal Idea—"The whole thing is worth" (53). In a world of continuous Becoming, the individual can "[s]plinter uncontrollably whole" (81) because death constitutes part of life's headlong, unstoppable momentum, part of the very great hand of contraries dealt everyone. Dickey's imaginative re-creation of this motion both mirrors nature and extends it, enabling Douglas first to understand "the trout streaming with all its quick / In the strong curve" (2–3), then to reenter the living "as cautiously / As a spike-buck, head humming with the first male split / Of the brain-bone" (40–42), and finally after "possessing the trail" (64), to go "Side-faced, all-seeing with hunger, / And over this, steep and straight-up / In the eagle's mile" (73–75). Life's circularity will bring death, actuality will become potentiality, but the process, enhanced here by the artistic impulse, extends one into the many, which nevertheless always remain the One.

In a 1987 interview Dickey commented on the poet's role: "I think a poet is trying, whether he would say this or not, to validate the individual viewpoint. . . . The vision and the true reaction of people to things, the true and if possible imaginative reaction to things, are threatened more and more."[11] Dickey's attempt to establish the presence of the determining personality receives final treatment in "Expanses," the concluding poem, when the narrator becomes the eagle and now sees with the bird's sweeping gaze but without loss of his human perspective, a perspective that unites opposites. Grounding oneself only in and on the physical world limits the individual to an Aristotelian conception of reality that does not visualize the Ideal. As he views himself from the air walking on the beach, he experiences in his earthbound perceptions "[J]oy like short grass," an image alluding to the cemetery but which understands that life and death are both one and not one. The poem also returns the reader to the opening scene of the volume, thereby creating an additional sense of circularity. The human voice will fail, Dickey understands, will finally lose its heat and become cold, but for an instant will break like lightning against the emptiness of space. When he declares in "For a Time and Place" that we "begin with ourselves / Underfoot and rising" (1–2), he presents his philosophic awareness of the elemental human condition and the beginning of the imaginative process that validates and resurrects the individual presence, thus uniting, at the height of Dickey's own artistic career, elements of Platonic and Aristotelian philosophy.

Notes

1. James Dickey, "Eagles" in *The Eagle's Mile* (Hanover and London: Wesleyan and University Press of New England, 1990), line 5; hereafter poems in *The Eagle's Mile* referred to in text by line number.

2. Robert Kirschten, *James Dickey and the Gentle Ecstasy of Earth: A Reading of the Poems* (Baton Rouge: LSU Press, 1988), 28.

3. Neal Bowers, *The Poet as Pitchman* (Columbia: U of Missouri Press, 1985), 6.

4. Bowers, *The Poet as Pitchman*, 86.

5. James Dickey, *Self-Interviews*. (Garden City, NY: Doubleday, 1970), 36; hereafter cited internally.

6. Plato, *"Republic,"* in *Collected Dialogues*, eds. Edith Hamilton and Huntington Cairns. (1961. Princeton: Princeton U Press, 1985), 508e; hereafter cited internally.

7. James Dickey, "The Wild Heart," in *Night Hurdling* (Columbia and Bloomfield Hills: Bruccoli Clark, 1983), 215.

8. Aristotle, *Physics*, trans. by Hippocrates G. Apostle (Bloomington: Indiana U Press, 1969), Book A, 190b 20; hereafter cited internally.

9. Plato, *Phaedo*, trans. by David Gallop (Oxford: Clarendon Press, 1975), 72b; hereafter cited internally.

10. Plato, *"Parmenides,"* in *Collected Dialogues*, eds. Edith Hamilton and Huntington Cairns (1961. Princeton: Princeton U Press, 1985), 165e.

11. Cited in Gordon Van Ness, "Living Beyond Recall: An Interview with James Dickey" *James Dickey Newsletter*, 3 (Spring 1987), 23.

Lightnings or Visuals

JAMES DICKEY

When we think, we think in pictures, more than in any other way.[1] This is part of us, and it involves everything that makes us up, from the chemicals and laws of physics which are part of us, the genes and chromosomes down through—or up through—the biorhythms. In this interior theater something is always running—a film, a play, a documentary, a fantasy—or just appearing as a still life: appearing and disappearing and reappearing, changing, being supplanted, returning in another form. I have mine, you have yours.

Let me ask you: is your personal theater wide-screen? Color? Some individuals never attain to color, or to the big wrap-around screen: Panavision. They are limited by history: by the history of cinema up to 1935. *Too bad! My* wide screen, I am happy to report, is almost invariably in color, and if yours is not, I hope that your good works and improved character will eventually grant you both color and stereo. Now, about the images we have—we can assert some things concerning the image-making-and-recalling apparatus or magic that enables us to have this phenomenon as part of us. We can affirm that it is universal in all human creatures and probably some animals, that for human beings it is continuous, and that, above all, it is intensely personal, that the images are various beyond limit, and that they carry symbolic value that they not only make possible but impose.

These values: can they be reduced to scale and assigned degrees of priority? I think not, except in the very broadest sense. For example, there is an obvious difference in import between what Shakespeare makes available to us and what we get from the squire of Tarzana, California, Edgar Rice Burroughs: between *seeing* Lear on the heath in the thunderstorm and lightning and what came up, say, in Gore Vidal's mind when he read *Tarzan the Terrible* in his adolescence—Ah! but there is a battle on a cliff between Tarzan and a human-resembling creature with a prehensile tail . . . What epic conditions! But back to the subject! However you set your values, the main point is that both King Lear and Tarzan *appeared*, can appear, were what they were and meant what they meant, and have the power to keep on doing so, to whomever they come, in whatever circumstances. Vidal, a formidable imager, and one of my favorite essayists, says:

Originally published in the *South Atlantic Review* 57.1 (January 1992): 1–14. Reprinted with permission of South Atlantic Modern Language Association.

When I was growing up, I read all twenty-three Tarzan books, as well as the ten Mars books. My own inner story-telling mechanism was vivid. At any one time, I had at least three serials going as well as a number of tried and true reruns. I mined Burroughs largely for source material. When he went to the center of the earth à la Jules Verne (much too fancy a writer for one's taste), I immediately worked up a thirteen-part series, with myself as lead and various friends as guest stars. Sometimes I used the master's material, but more often I adapted it freely to suit myself. One's daydreams tended to be Tarzanish pre-puberty (physical strength and freedom) and Martian post-puberty (exotic worlds and subtle *combinazione* to be worked out). . . . My last serial ran into sponsor trouble when I was in the Second World War, and it was never renewed.

But then of course it was. Even though Tarzan might not have been featured in any of Vidal's adult scenarios, I am willing to bet that he made at least one guest appearance, or played a cameo part, in some of the later screenings! The theater, for Vidal as for everybody, is still open, the things that come up before the inner eye are always unpredictable, always changing, some controlled by the will and some not. And it is an incontrovertible fact that the self can be not only conditioned but actually altered by the images we have. John Keats's well-known theory of human existence as a "vale of soul-making," wherein each individual molds himself to an ideal he has of selfhood, is intimately bound to the image, in this case the self-image. T. E. Lawrence, of Arabian fame, is an extreme example of this connection. And, in keeping with this, the later, less fanatical Mary McCarthy, says that "you really must *make* the self. It's absolutely useless to look for it, you won't find it, but it is possible in some sense to make it. I don't mean in the sense of making a mask, a Yeatsian mask. But you finally begin in some sense to make and choose the self you want." I agree, and the self you want has first been projected on the interior screen; has come, has changed, but during the process has assumed certain characteristics that are fairly stable, and can serve. Again, one remembers the dilemma of the young William James, in his suicidal despair. He was delivered from his self-destructive pessimism by reading the French philosopher Charles Renouvier, who resolved for him the problem of free will. On 30 April 1870, James wrote in his diary, "I think yesterday was a crisis in my life. I finished the first part of Renouvier's *Second Essay* and saw no reason why his definition of free will—the sustaining of a thought *because I choose to* when I might have other thoughts—need be the definition of an illusion." What applies to the "sustaining of a thought" applies equally to the sustaining of an image, and it cannot be doubted that whatever thought James chose to sustain was pictorial: it was an image, though we will never know precisely what it was, that kept our greatest philosopher alive.

These are references to the process as one which can be controlled, but what I myself am most interested in are the unbidden, random and obsessional images that appear, having their own laws, or anti-laws, or beyond-laws: pictures, events, people, scenes, actions, objects, that occur not exactly out of

the blue—though some of them do that also—but those sparked by something—an incident, a memory, a wish-fulfillment (forever unfulfilled, except
here!), a report or statement in a newspaper ("Why Do the Heathen Rage?")—
but most of all, for me, those that are set in play by words, and especially
those of poetry, the most highly concentrated and evocative form of verbal
imaging, the most intense, the most meaningful and mysterious, necessary
and self-renewing. I am preoccupied with what C. Day Lewis calls, in his fine
phrase, "the visual word."

If someone asks me, as people are prone to ask writers, if such and such
a poem or incident in a novel or movie was "based on actual experience," I
never know what to answer. To those who have questions of this sort, "actual
experience" refers to occurrences in which the individual in question has been
either an onlooker or a participant—usually, they hope, a participant—and
they do not understand, or perhaps are not capable of understanding, that
"experience" is by no means limited to either onlooking or participating but
contains everything a mind, a human sensorium has ever had impinge on it:
not only "facts" but dreams, fantasies, anecdotes, movies, jokes, photographs,
fever visions, even whatever may come from racial memory, the collective
unconscious, the Anima Mundi, if Yeats is to be believed.

Experience does not have to be something that has "happened" to you,
something in which you have bodily participated. It can be an incident in
someone else's life, that came to your attention by whatever means. Years ago
when I lived in France, in 1954 and 1955, to be exact, I wanted to learn the
language, and this for obvious reasons, since I was living there. But unlike
many other tourists and / or expatriates, I wanted to learn it so that I could
read its literature, and most especially its poetry. I availed myself of several
anthologies and, with the help of a French-English dictionary, pored over
them. Little by little some things emerged, foggily, to be sure, but with certain
outlines: certain poems and their writers. One of the poets I struck slowly—
who struck *me* most definitely, and harder and harder the more I read—was
a man named Lucien Becker. At that time he had not written very much, and
I was able to get hold of all his slim volumes, his *plaquettes*. Over the years I
have read these many times and have found out everything about Becker I
could. In the early sixties a little book was devoted to him in Pierre Seghers's
excellent Poètes d'aujourd'hui series, edited and with a long biographical
introduction by a critic named Gaston Puel. I make a free—a *very* free—
translation of an incident which, quite literally, struck me like lightning, from
Puel's pages on Becker's early life:

> In mid-August of the year Becker was nine years old, he was in a field through
> which ran a river, gathering centauria, a medicinal plant. Not far from him a
> magnificent stallion, its mane shining with sun, raised its nonchalant silhouette.
> Suddenly there was a shattering explosion; the animal fell, lightning-struck.
> "In that instant of the lightning flash," Becker says, "I believe it was I who was

struck." He adds, "I went to the animal. Not at once, though: I waited ten minutes. Of any kind of storm there was only one simple cloud in the sky, completely surrounded by sun, and for this strange reason it seemed to hide from my eyes a kind of trap or trick, another lightning bolt intended for me, really *destined* for me, since I had been spared by the first one. I *saw* that immense horse laid out on his side, there, not a drop of blood on him, and I was, just simply, amazed. At the same time, language, my tongue, had been struck; words were forbidden me. I saw him, but I could not describe the animal, and since then I have often asked myself the question: was he really in the field before being struck? It was an event in its pure state: nothing, absolutely nothing preceding it could have foretold it, and then a whole continent of existence broke open. A few minutes later, though, I was gathering centauria again."

Puel comments: "The lightning-struck stallion was maybe not the revelation or the secret on which would depend the almost unequivocal voice of Lucien Becker; it was, however, the first image—not to say the fiery intrusion—of a major theme which would condition all his others, and that the poet was to end by treating as commonplace." He continues:

The event which, for the young Becker, froze his language on the riverbank gives us others a startling and, if I may say so, lightninglike glance into our own condition. The immanence and the permanence of menace can be deduced, one from the other. The horse, the lightning: nothing could have foretold what happened. It escapes, at the same time, causality and all appearances. It is not accompanied by any presage; it escapes time and space; it is the sword of Damocles in the scabbard of a sunbeam, the dagger hidden among flowers, the invisible ray: a single second of your life can bring it, unleash it. Death is identified with the event, and vice versa. "I thought it was I," Becker said, bringing into memory the image of the lightning-struck horse. It was he, certainly.

Lucien Becker became one of the best French poets of his generation, with several remarkable books and some almost equally incisive criticism, but he has not, as far as I know, been able to find the words for that riveting image in a field near a river, when he was nine years old. He is still searching for the words, as any real poet must do, and ever since I encountered his experience, I have been searching with him, too, in my own way. My own fascination with lightning has been augmented by his, and it was only with the greatest exercise of willpower that I was able to keep the figure of a horse out of my own poem "The Eagle's Mile." I was more or less astonished that in the poem lightning had formed not the image of a horse but that of a man: the original man, in fact: Adam—the instantaneous branching of his veins, his cardiovascular system, his blueprint—as he "splintered uncontrollably whole" over the North Georgia mountains. (Believe me, if you're a poet, you can *change* creation: you can have things as you will!) How the mind changes reality, and somehow comes to rest! But Lucien Becker's stallion is still waiting for its words; Becker and I are waiting for them in different languages. Becker thinks that the lightning was intended to hit him instead of the horse and that there is another bolt, being withheld, that will get him yet. Who is to say that these things are not true? As for myself, Becker's lightning has in a way hit me, also. And to shift emphasis, but connect things, too, I can also remember for us all that Randall Jarrell says that a poet is someone who makes a practice of standing out in thunderstorms all his life hoping to be struck by lightning: once, and he is remembered; half a dozen times and he is great. Ah! Let it fall! Or as one of Shakespeare's murderers says—"Let it come down!"

As a poet I am not only interested in how images arise in the individual mind out of words, and the ways in which these may be used, but how, conversely, images result in words, connect with them, call them into being, organize them into poems and other pieces of writing that have what we call the poetic quality. If I could choose a presiding spirit for these remarks, it would be Virginia Woolf. She is the one who comes the most quickly to mind as a vivid and incessant transformer of images into words. And not only into words, but into people, scenes, events, speculations, conclusions, denouements. It is Virginia Woolf rather than Proust I should like to have inform or haunt what I say, though certainly Proust placed more conscious emphasis on the process and brought forth from it a great many more words. Nevertheless, it is she who seems to me the more daring, the more truly poetic: the consciousness that relies more than most on the transformation process itself, beyond all theory, all philosophy, including that of Bergson. As she was coming to the end of writing *To the Lighthouse* and looked out of the window of her house at Rodmell over the marshes, she saw—or was aware of by some means—the image of a fin that rose and circled in a waste of water, and it was charged with significance and value beyond anything she had ever imagined. It seemed to her to be beyond words and yet to demand them; beginning with nothing but the image she wrote the first words of *The Waves*. Through draft after draft the vision of the fin developed into—who shall say how?—a story about six people. As John Lehmann comments, "Her aim, one can say, was to give a picture of the whole of life from the earliest dawning of sensation to the end; of its dreams, ambitions, aspirations, achievements and failures, to its final disillusionments, accompanied perhaps by acceptance or the joyous discovery of wisdom. More completely than ever before, it is the life of the soul she is giving us, stripping away everything that could encumber or obscure that vision. And, restless as ever to find new, more perfect ways of showing us *her* reality, she invents an entirely new technique. . . ."

How the vision of a fin in the midst of a waste of waters, seen through a window over a marsh, evolved into an experimental novel with six characters (three male and three female), nine episodes in which there are gardens, love

affairs, secret hiding places, formal dinners, and many other things, is one of
the miracles we have become accustomed to in the work of highly imaginative
writers such as Virginia Woolf. But all this from the image of a *fin*! Shades
of *Jaws*, indeed! But we believe Mrs. Woolf when later she writes, "I mean
that I have netted that fin in the waste of water which appeared to me over
the marshes out of my window at Rodmell, when I was coming to the end of
To the Lighthouse." This is fitting and convincing, though we shall never know
how it happened: how the fin was changed—or changed itself—by infinite
and buried stages into a reunion dinner at Hampton Court.

And these matters not only can't but *shouldn't* be known, any more than
God's purposes, His mysterious ways, can be known. Speculated about, yes.
But known and fully understood, never. Our only concern, really, is with the
work itself, and how it affects us: the images and insights it enables us to
have: enables, encourages, makes available not only to but *from* our own
minds. Even such an outstanding example of interpretive scholarship as John
Livingston Lowes's *The Road to Xanadu*, as thorough, resourceful, and thought-
provoking as it is, can only be a provisional sketch of what went on in
Coleridge's brain and body when he wrote his most memorable poems. The
real work, the alchemy of association, will always remain just that: alchemy,
magic, miracle.

A writer is inevitably pressed—mostly he presses himself—to offer his
own productions as evidence of whatever point he is trying to make, for it is
true enough that he believes—*believes* only, not knows—that he is sufficiently
acquainted with it to put forward such instances. I confess I am no exception,
and if I told you that the whole of my novel *Deliverance* came from an image
that appeared to me when I was half asleep in full sunlight after a picnic in
Italy, where I was living at the time, you could believe *that* much of it. The
image was that of a man standing at the top of a cliff: that, and no more. The
picture was powerful and urgent, but I had no clue as to any meaning, if there
was or could be one: one discovered, one assigned. Over the succeeding days
and weeks, the image stayed with me just as it had first come, but gradually
grew more and more enigmatic and necessary, surrounding itself with questions, and by means of these questions, began to fill in, to create an aura
around the image of the man and where he stood. Who was he? What was
he doing there? What was inland from him? What was at the foot of the cliff?
Had he come from inland, or—or—had he climbed up the cliff? If I told you
that speculations such as these eventually began to haze into a story which
had more and more definite outlines, created characters for it, literally turned
day into night, and worked itself into a final form on such a basis, you could
also believe me. But what I could not and cannot trace, whether for you or
for myself, is the history of all the small changes, the alterations, the shifts,
the colorings, the birth and death—and sometimes rebirth—of details, the
balancements of form that took place during the speculation about the story
and the writing of it. These are lost, and as I said, should be lost, for the aspect

of mystery, of the unknown and the unknowable, is a vital part of the creative process and should not be analyzed so much as relied upon.

My second novel, *Alnilam*, also evolved from an image, one I had heard about but never seen. I could imagine it, though, and still can. The novel is about the early days of World War II when the Air Force—in those days it was called the Army Air Corps—was desperately trying to prepare itself to fight a major war in the air. In fact, and probably because of these conditions, the air itself was full of myths and legends. One of these was that if you happen to look through a spinning propeller, on a flight line, say, and on the other side of it another propeller is turning and your look goes through both of them at the same time, the image of a man will be formed in the double-whirling metal, the blades. Whether true or not, that idea and that image appealed to me strongly; there was something about "the ghost in the machine" suggestion that sparked a part of my imagination I didn't until then know I had; there is always a feeling of excitement when something like that happens. As a result of the shadowy figure in the twin propellers, I began to feel that there might be some kind of spirit in the machines that men have made and that this might be both indifferent to them and superior to them, in short, not so much a ghost in the machine but a God. From this there stemmed a kind of religion and its inevitable prophet and martyr; out of it came the story of a blind man and the mysterious son he has never known: a whole sequence of events that lasts for almost a thousand pages, for better or worse.

Thus the given image, and its metamorphosis into words; the original image itself, always beyond words, presides over the words it makes possible, like some kind of Platonic archetype making demands for an interpretation, a perfection we cannot reach. I still see the man on the cliff and the ghost among the propellers; I can tell you, he has two legs and no arms. I would like to lay *that* one on Professor Freud!

Now, because we can, let us turn the whole thing around. Instead of moving the image toward the words, it might be interesting to see how the reverse may be done, *is* done. In John Malcolm Brinnin's harrowing and instructive memoir, *Dylan Thomas in America*, Brinnin attempts to pin Thomas down about some of his fundamental attitudes and techniques.

> We began to speak of working methods. I had noticed that on many of his manuscripts Dylan would add a single word or phrase, or a new punctuation, then recopy the whole poem in longhand. When another addition or revision was made, no matter how minor or major, he would then copy the whole poem again. When I asked him about this laborious repetition, he showed me his drafts of "Fern Hill." There were more than two hundred separate and distinct versions of the poem. It was, he explained, his way of "keeping the poem together," so that its process of growth was like that of an organism. He began almost every poem merely with some phrase he had carried about in his head. If this phrase was right, which is to say, if it were resonant or pregnant, it would suggest another phrase. In this way a poem would "accumulate." Once "given"

a word (sometimes the prime movers of poems were the words of other poems or mere words of the dictionary that called out to be "set") or a phrase or a line (or whatever it is that is "given" when there is yet a poem to "prove") he could often envision it or locate it within a pattern of other words or phrases or lines that, not given, had yet to be discovered: so that sometimes it would be possible to surmise accurately that the "given" unit would occur near the end of the poem or near the beginning or near the middle or somewhere between.

When I first read this account of Thomas's compositional methods I was not overly surprised; I was gratified to some extent, rather, to find that what I had expected from reading the poems was in fact the case. Compared to, say, Gerard Manley Hopkins, Thomas is not really an acute observer of the natural world, though to the less perceptive he may seem to be. If one reads intently, though, it is not difficult to sympathize with Thomas as he answers a gushing American admirer's enthusiasm over his various references to birds. Thomas replied, "Madam, I can recognize and identify at sight two species of birds: a seagull and a chicken." The connection Thomas makes with objects and creatures outside himself begins with words and radiates outward from there. Hopkins's emphasis on language, which is very nearly fanatical in quite another way, is wedded to the sharpness and originality of his observations, his vision of externals. Thomas's is not. This is not to render a value judgment at all. Thomas has his own way of going; his tremendous surge of natural rhythm has an incantatory power that depends on this approach. If this is a product of "giving the initiative to words," as Mallarmé suggested the poet do, it behooves us to investigate similar possibilities in our own practice. Speaking again for myself, I can say that my orientation is the other way: that is, from the image to the word. And yet, all is not exclusive in anyone's performance. I am much attracted to what I am tempted to call "word-radiance" and find myself very often both fascinated by single words and by a possible context in which and by which they might, to use Thomas's phrase, be "set." There are words that have this special aura for everyone, and I have two main ones which, for me, are so full of luminosity that I have never been able to conquer my fear of using them, lest it be misuse. These are a verb and a noun: "swerve" and "flock." These have, for at least one creature, spirit, soul, *Geist, mana.* Oddly enough, the image that arises from them when combined is not that of birds but of fish. Can there be a flock of fish? There can. Would it be able to swerve? It could. And that's as far as I've been able to get, so far. When one possesses words with such personal *mana* and one is a megalomaniac, as every true poet must be and is, expansion of effect is almost always a foregone conclusion: one wants to go the whole way, to encompass everything the words touch. But so far I have successfully resisted; I have decided that I don't really want every flock of fish in the sea to swerve; only the right ones. And so they wait until they generate their true setting, in a poem as well as in the sea.

One of the perennial pleasures in poetry—or any kind of writing that evokes images, but especially poetry, which evokes the most lasting ones— is the alteration of the mind-pictures by alteration of the words that call them up. Another related pleasure is found in encountering a distinctive word use in some total stranger's writing or conversation. I bring these two factors together for the sake of seventeen syllables—as you may have guessed, something in the *haiku* form—a classic form with no variations: five syllables followed by seven in the next line and, in the final line, again five. It is probably the most popular form that poetry has yet made available. Literally millions of *haiku* are written every year, and not just in Japan. I of course have not read all of these, or even the larger part of them, but I have read a good many in connection with my own writing, with teaching, and so on, but mainly because I like the form and can never have enough of it. And, again speaking very personally, it is an external justification of the human creative faculty that the best *haiku* I have ever come upon is not by Buson, by Issa, or even by the Zen Master Bashō, whose *haiku* on the old pond and the frog-jump-in-water sound is the most famous of all the millions of tries. It is not by one of the acknowledged masters of verse in English, either: not by Yeats, not by Hardy, not by Auden or Dylan Thomas, not by Shakespeare. The syllables were put down by an obscure American from Texas, Clement Hoyt, who died in 1970; I know nothing whatever of him except what is printed in the contributors' notes of the anthology in which I found him. The words are these: "In that lightning flash— / Through the night rain—I saw / Whatever it was."

That is startling, stark, unforgettable, though the poet and the reader— or beholder—doesn't even know what it was that was seen; no matter, it was *something.* And one guesses that if the lightning flashed again, the something would not be there. For me, the presentation is perfect, except for one thing: there are only sixteen syllables instead of seventeen. The first line is all right: five syllables. So is the last: "Whatever it was." But the middle line, which should by classic law have seven syllables, has only six. What to do? The easiest thing is just to say, what the hell, let it go; it's fine just as it is. But no real poet is going to be content to do this. The form calls for what it calls for: the form, the *law.* To the truly creative person that fact is going to assume the lineaments of a challenge rather than being viewed as a restriction. One has an additional syllable to provide—that is, one has the sanctioned privilege of providing it—and the search for the missing syllable is a microcosm, a paradigm of the poetic act itself; all poetry is in it.

The search—ah, the search! The quest, I would say, if I wanted to be *really* pretentious! No matter: the most eternally fascinating thing about the relationship of word to image is the way in which the image can be made to change, to acquire or drop characteristics by a change in word use. This is so obvious a fact that it is easy to forget that it happens, but when one reflects a moment the phenomenon becomes even more mysterious, and, to bring in my favorite word of the day—almost the theme song or the national anthem of these remarks—miraculous. When we look at the middle line of the *haiku* I have been talking about, which reads "Through the night rain—I saw" it becomes obvious that the best place for the one syllable needed to complete the classic pattern should probably—I say probably, because it is not the only possibility—be before "night," and this in turn makes it almost mandatory that it be an adjective. At the risk of sounding like Poe purporting to explain how he wrote "The Raven," I would then suggest that this as yet undetermined adjective should have some kind of kinaesthetic charge, some suggestion of violence. Perhaps, I'm thinking, the word should be "slant," which brings in wind as well: turbulence, violence. "Through the slant night rain—I saw . . . Whatever it was." Or maybe the word should not be "slant"; again, it is by no means the only possibility. But I like it pretty well, and I also like the three hard stresses—"slant night rain"—for the emphasis they give, and I suggest that Mr. Hoyt, now a member of the Dead Poets' Society, consider it; regardless, this little poem assures him, at least in my personal Parnassus, a high and permanent place. If we accept "slant," which provisionally we may do, the mental picture takes on a much different quality than it would have if the word had not come in. It is this change in what one sees in the mind as a result of a word that I would emphasize: this is a different rain: it has been made one; it has become one. For you, does the rain slant from left to right? From right to left? From forward to back, away from you, or from back to forward, coming—slanting—toward you?

My main emphasis is on the necessary and infinitely valuable personal nature of the image that is evoked, from whatever source, from words or from elsewhere. Words are my main lifetime concern, but in all the literary criticism I have ever read—fifty years of it, at least—I have never come on a single paragraph, a single sentence that focuses on the sense of personal *possession* that any image has for the individual in question. What each person sees in his head is the inevitable product of genes, chromosomes, heredity, environment, the past, the present, memory, fantasy, reality, dream, and many other factors which, when set in motion—or stillness—throw upon the screen the living picture. It is your *life* the picture lives with, your life and my life. Emerson asked about someone, "Is his eye creative?" For most of us, the inner eye is more creative than the outer, but both are involved; starting from words, for example, the inward-turned eyeball conjures up its own visions that are intimate parts of a unique sensibility—mind, spirit: what used to be called soul. The next vision of this kind that you have, look at it as closely as you can and retain it for as long as you can. It will take on dimensions and significance almost beyond belief.

A couple of technical points, if such a term may be used. I have always loved optical instruments of all kinds—magnifying glasses, eyeglasses, microscopes, telescopes, field glasses—and probably as a result, there is a *lensing* quality to everything I see inwardly. I even have problems of *focus*, but when the image comes clear—I have my own way of causing it to come clear—the detail and the clarity are beyond anything in the external world. What would be impossible to focus in outer reality is very clear in the mind. As an instance, one of the most beautiful similes I know occurs in two lines from Tennyson's notebooks: "As those that lie on happy shores and see / Thro' the near blossom slip the distant sail."

What would not be possible to focus—the near and far together, equally defined—by a telescope or field glasses is perfectly clear to the inner perspective. The flower is close to the face, each petal and vein distinct, and through it, miles away—and, for *me*, below as well as far off—passes the sail, white, curved, not urgent, moving, sharp in outline. It has a blue emblem, a blue logo on it; I think blue is a very pretty color on sails! And if your next mental image of a flower and a sail has a sail with a blue emblem on it, you will have gotten something from this lecture; I will have given you something. But not everything, for I haven't told you what the shape of the emblem is, and I'm not going to. It *is* blue, though; you have *that*!

If I could leave you with one impression, it would be to further in each of you the truth that there is no standardized way of reading poetry. People like I. A. Richards and Yvor Winters, in their foredoomed attempts to impose what they think are the standards of science or private sensibilities, to set up criteria for reactions—what *should* be felt, what *ought to be* the import of these words—lose sight of the fact that it is the very ability of the reader's mind to provide images from itself that is the main strength of poetry, which above all other uses of language is the one most empowered to give the reader—the overhearer—his own imagination through the words of the poet. The process is essentially one of calling forth, of calling up, as a magician calls up apparitions. In the theater where this happens, nothing is permanent: everything is flux, flow, replacement, return. But in the flow, certain images burn as with immortal light. These are ours, and ours alone. The most valuable thing a poet can give another person is this sense of personal *possession*, ownership. Nothing can interfere with it; everything is possible.

And so—my flock of fish is still waiting to swerve. When the words get here, over the celestial wireless or by some other means, the picture will fill in and realize itself. The image will be right, as right as it is capable of being, and it will be mine. If someone takes other fish, and other swervings, from my words, those fish and their movement will become exclusive possessions of that person, and this is as it should be. From fragments of this kind the true life is woven, a kind of moving tapestry of inner light. With death, of course, everything vanishes; the screen is shut down forever. But while consciousness lasts we have this miraculous situation, and it is *us*; and I promise that the flock of fish will swerve for us all. For all of us, surely, but most especially for *each*. Never doubt that the fish in that flock are waiting—waiting in the sea for their words, and waiting inside the mind, which contains the sea and all other things. The fish in their flock, with their swerve! They know who they are; they know how to do it.

Note

1. This was the 1991 South Atlantic Modern Language Association General Session Address, delivered on 14 November 1991 at the Hyatt Regency Hotel in Atlanta, Georgia.

Index

♦

DATE